YA 741.597 Gag
Gage, Christos.
Angel & Faith. Season 9, volume 4,
Death and consequences /

34028086420479
MM $17.99   ocn855200245
                          10/28/14

3 4028 08642 0479
HARRIS COUNTY PUBLIC LIBRARY

DISCARD

ANGEL &FAITH™

ILLUSTRATION BY REBEKAH ISAACS WITH DAN JACKSON

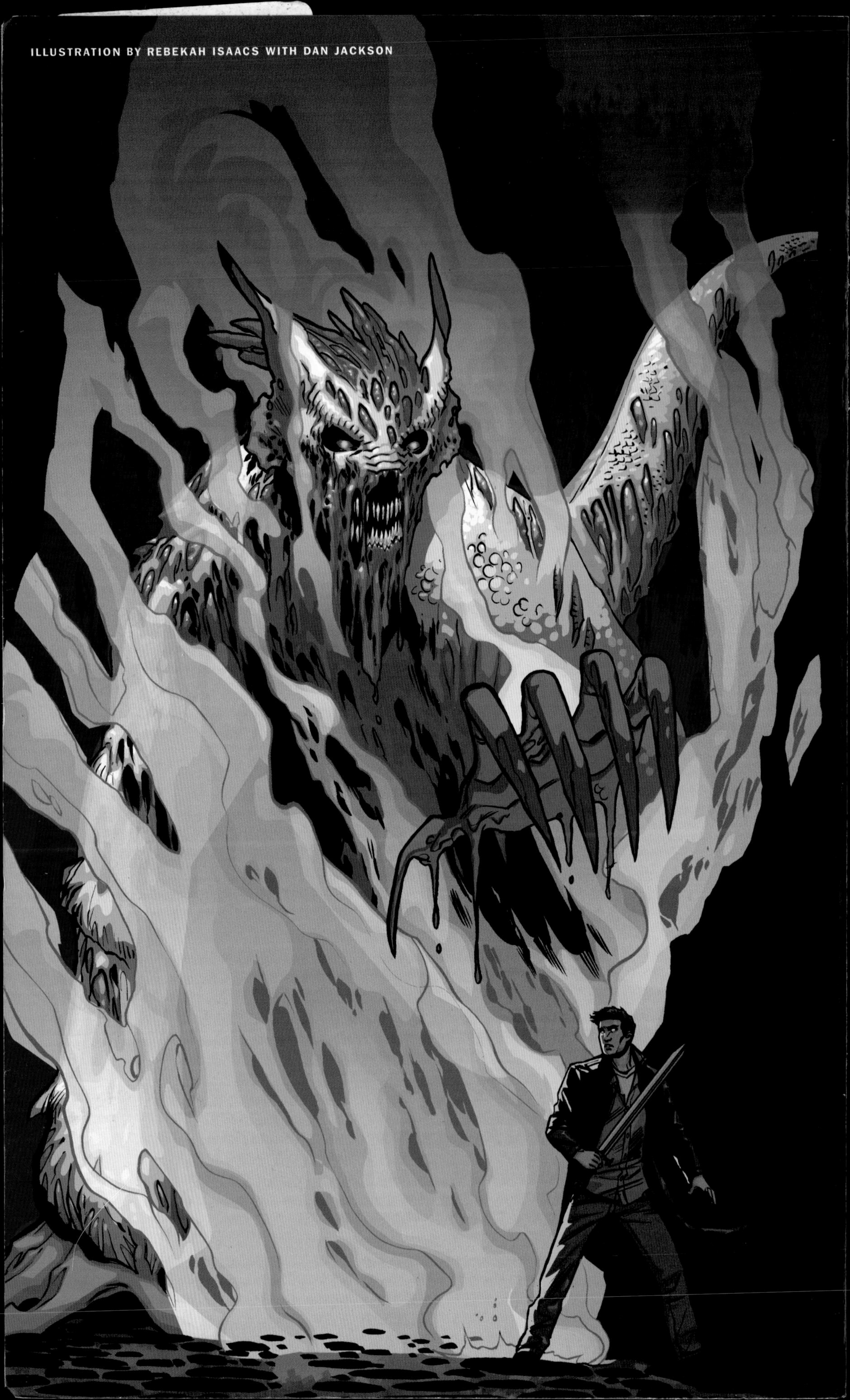

ANGEL & FAITH™

SEASON 9 · VOLUME 4

DEATH AND CONSEQUENCES

SCRIPT
CHRISTOS GAGE

ART
REBEKAH ISAACS

COLORS
DAN JACKSON

LETTERS
RICHARD STARKINGS *& Comicraft's*
JIMMY BETANCOURT

COVER ART
STEVE MORRIS

EXECUTIVE PRODUCER
JOSS WHEDON

DARK HORSE BOOKS

PRESIDENT & PUBLISHER
MIKE RICHARDSON

EDITORS
SCOTT ALLIE & SIERRA HAHN

ASSISTANT EDITOR
FREDDYE LINS

COLLECTION DESIGNER
JUSTIN COUCH

Published by Dark Horse Books
A division of Dark Horse Comics, Inc.
10956 SE Main Street
Milwaukie, OR 97222

DarkHorse.com
International Licensing: (503) 905-2377

To find a comics shop in your area, call the
Comic Shop Locator Service toll-free at
(888) 266-4226.

First edition: September 2013
ISBN 978-1-61655-165-0

10 9 8 7 6 5 4 3 2 1
Printed in China

This story takes place during *Buffy the Vampire Slayer* Season 9, created by Joss Whedon.

Special thanks to Lauren Winarski at Twentieth Century Fox, and Daniel Kaminsky.

NEIL HANKERSON Executive Vice President • TOM WEDDLE Chief Financial Officer • RANDY STRADLEY Vice President of Publishing • MICHAEL MARTENS Vice President of Book Trade Sales • ANITA NELSON Vice President of Business Affairs • SCOTT ALLIE Editor in Chief • MATT PARKINSON Vice President of Marketing • DAVID SCROGGY Vice President of Product Development • DALE LAFOUNTAIN Vice President of Information Technology • DARLENE VOGEL Senior Director of Print, Design, and Production • KEN LIZZI General Counsel • DAVEY ESTRADA Editorial Director • CHRIS WARNER Senior Books Editor • DIANA SCHUTZ Executive Editor • CARY GRAZZINI Director of Print and Development • LIA RIBACCHI Art Director • CARA NIECE Director of Scheduling • TIM WIESCH Director of International Licensing • MARK BERNARDI Director of Digital Publishing

ANGEL & FAITH™ VOLUME 4: DEATH AND CONSEQUENCES
Angel & Faith™ © 2012, 2013 Twentieth Century Fox Film Corporation. All rights reserved. Angel, Faith, and all other prominently featured characters are trademarks of Twentieth Century Fox Film Corporation. Dark Horse Books® and the Dark Horse logo are registered trademarks of Dark Horse Comics, Inc. All rights reserved. No portion of this publication may be reproduced or transmitted, in any form or by any means, without the express written permission of Dark Horse Comics, Inc. Names, characters, places, and incidents featured in this publication either are the product of the author's imagination or are used fictitiously. Any resemblance to actual persons (living or dead), events, institutions, or locales, without satiric intent, is coincidental.

This volume reprints the comic-book series *Angel & Faith* #16–#20 from Dark Horse Comics.

ANGEL
&FAITH™

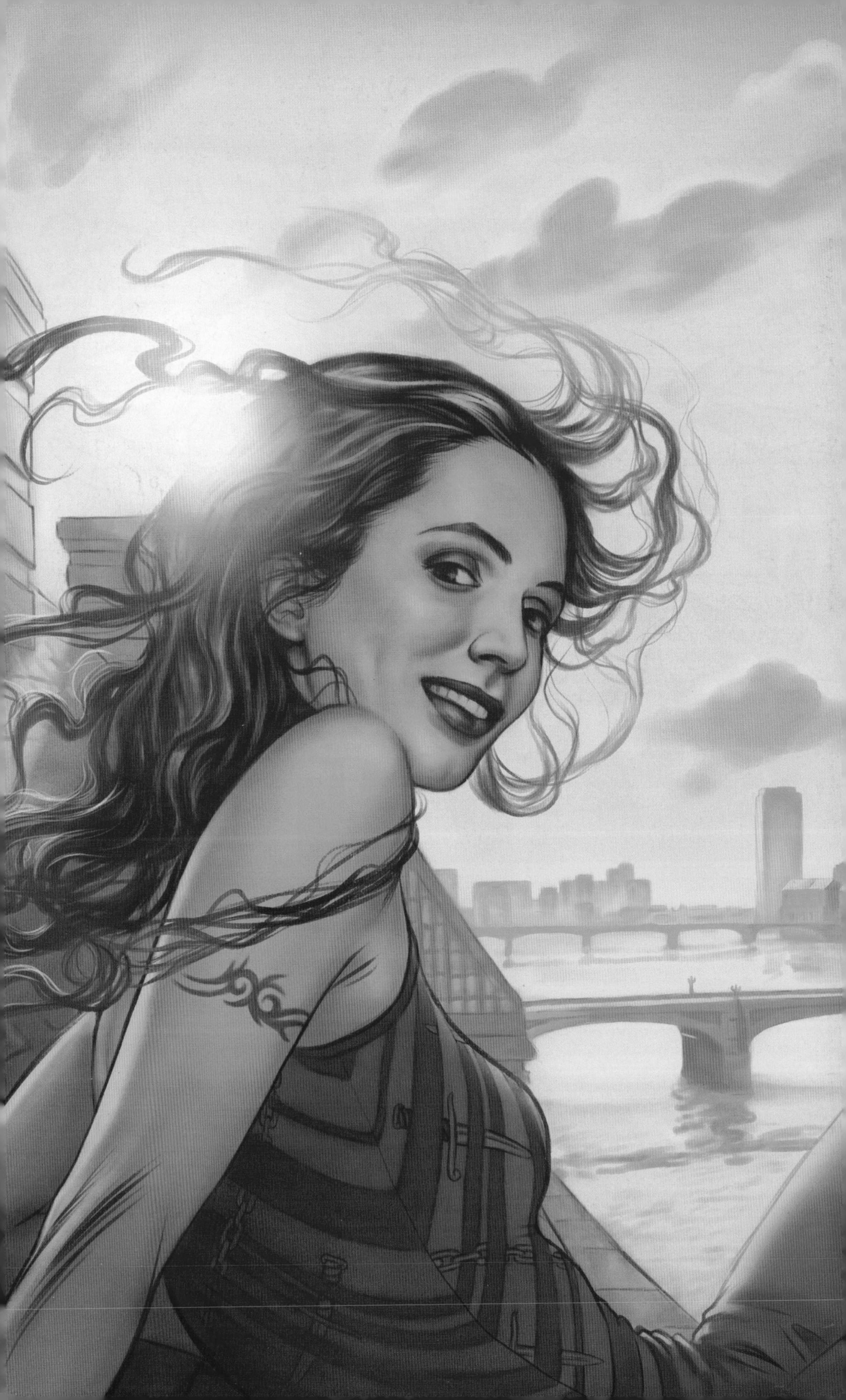

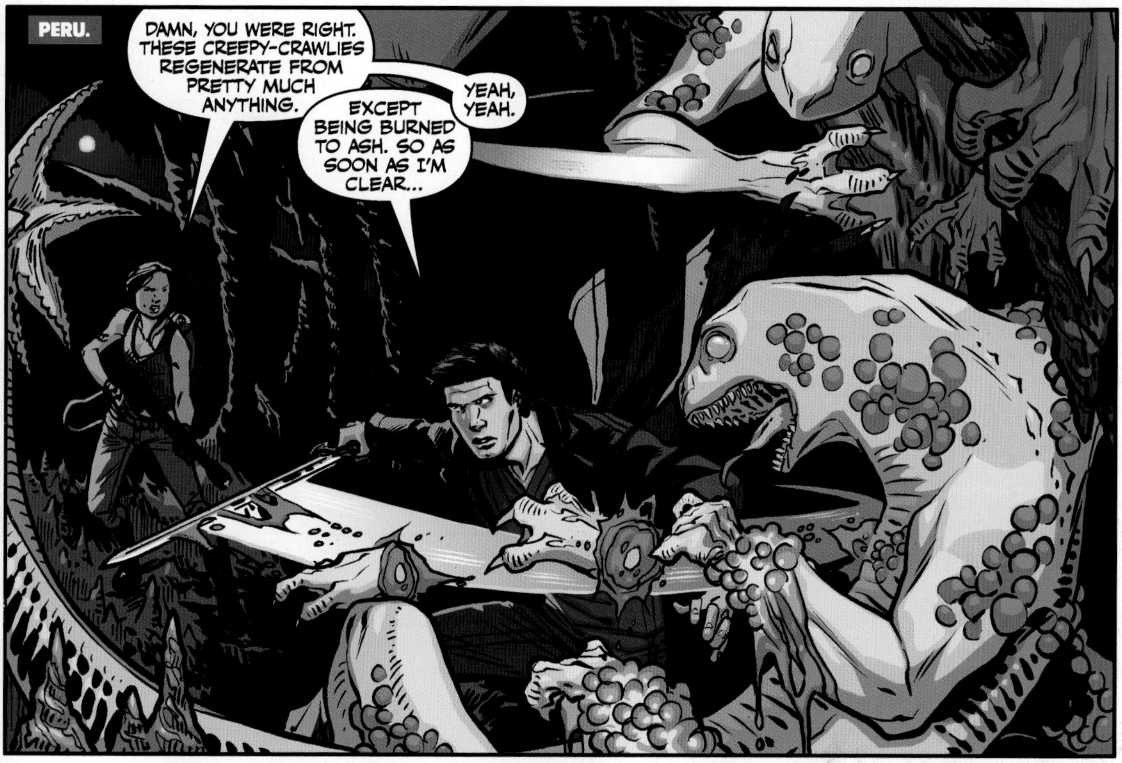
PERU.
DAMN, YOU WERE RIGHT. THESE CREEPY-CRAWLIES REGENERATE FROM PRETTY MUCH ANYTHING.
YEAH, YEAH.
EXCEPT BEING BURNED TO ASH. SO AS SOON AS I'M CLEAR...

DEATH AND CONSEQUENCES

PART 1 OF 4

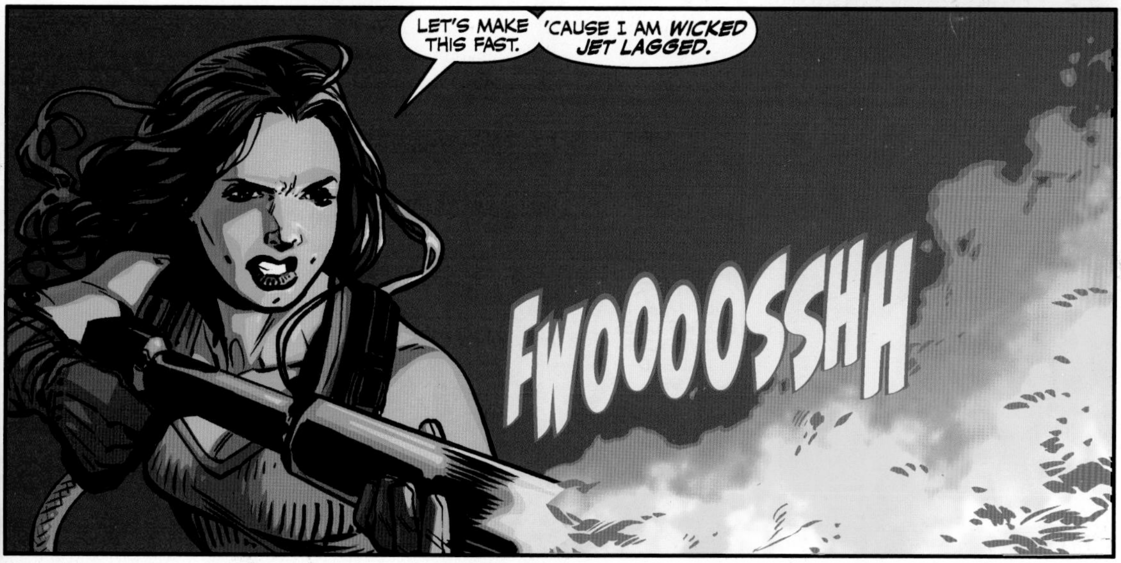
LET'S MAKE THIS FAST.
'CAUSE I AM *WICKED JET LAGGED.*
FWOOOOSSHH

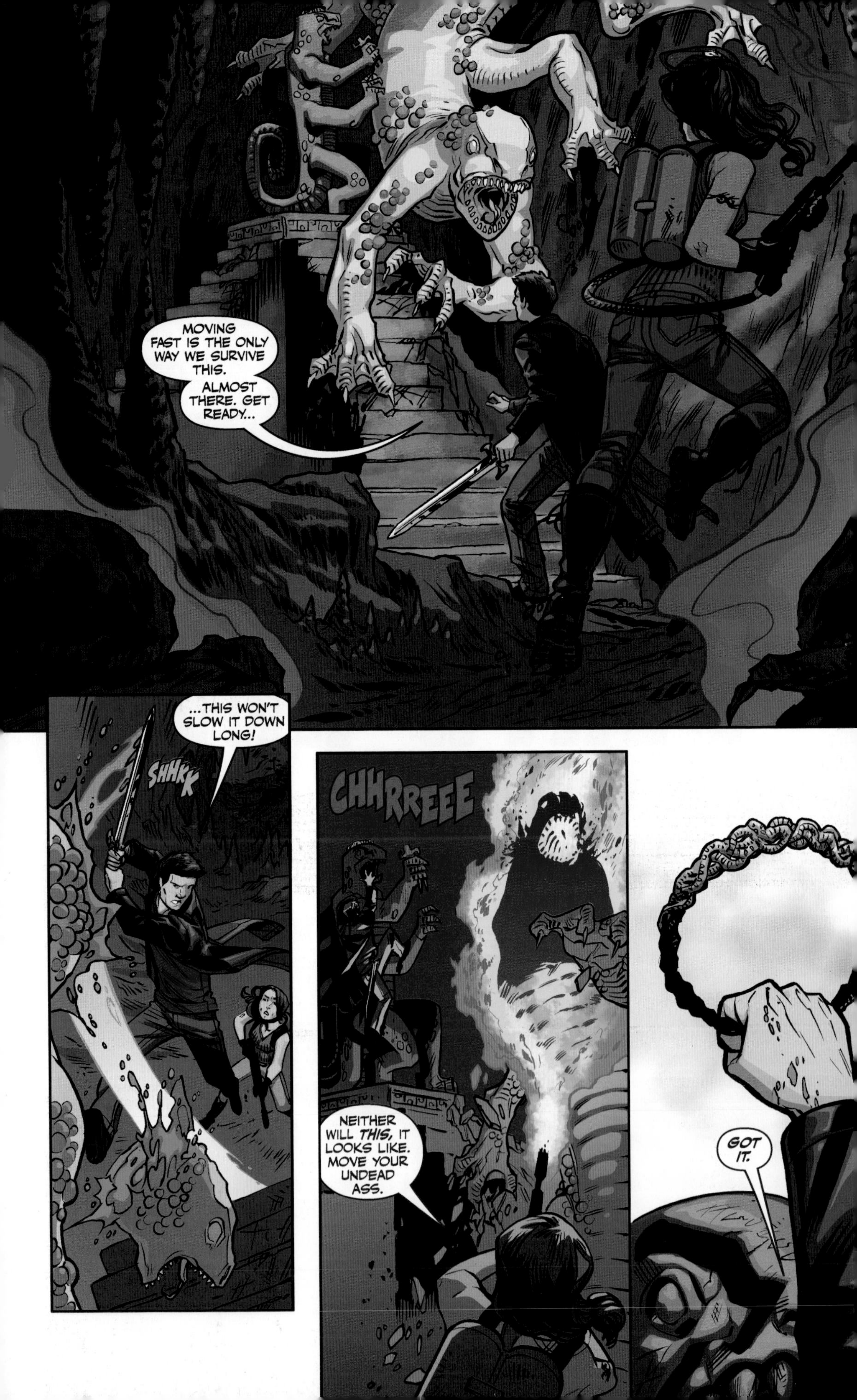
MOVING FAST IS THE ONLY WAY WE SURVIVE THIS.
ALMOST THERE. GET READY...
...THIS WON'T SLOW IT DOWN LONG!
SHHKK
CHHRREEE
NEITHER WILL *THIS*, IT LOOKS LIKE. MOVE YOUR UNDEAD ASS.
GOT IT.

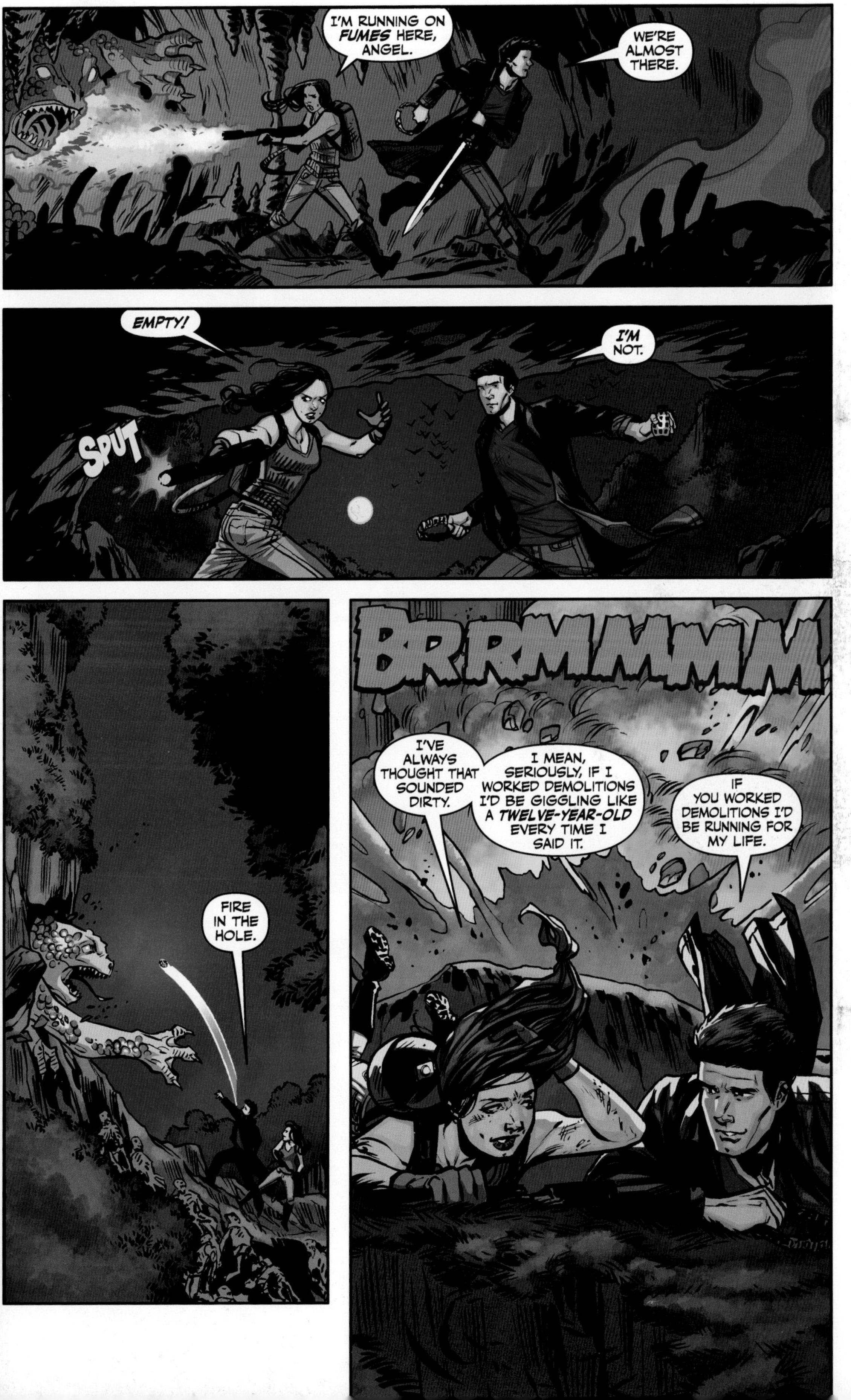
I'M RUNNING ON *FUMES* HERE, ANGEL.
WE'RE ALMOST THERE.
EMPTY!
I'M NOT.
SPUT
FIRE IN THE HOLE.
BRRMMMM
I'VE ALWAYS THOUGHT THAT SOUNDED DIRTY.
I MEAN, SERIOUSLY, IF I WORKED DEMOLITIONS I'D BE GIGGLING LIKE A *TWELVE-YEAR-OLD* EVERY TIME I SAID IT.
IF YOU WORKED DEMOLITIONS I'D BE RUNNING FOR MY LIFE.

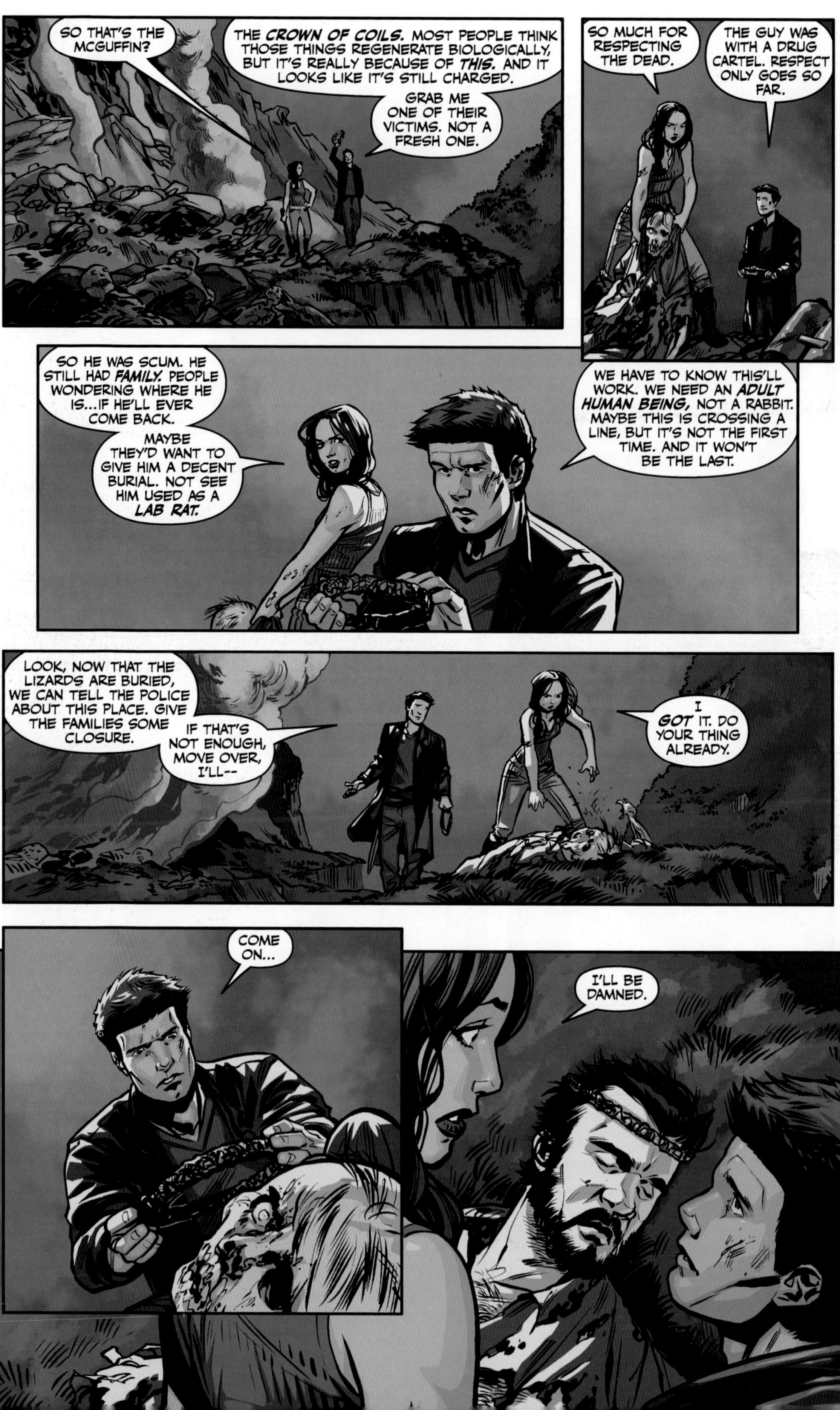
SO THAT'S THE MCGUFFIN?
THE CROWN OF COILS. MOST PEOPLE THINK THOSE THINGS REGENERATE BIOLOGICALLY, BUT IT'S REALLY BECAUSE OF THIS. AND IT LOOKS LIKE IT'S STILL CHARGED.
GRAB ME ONE OF THEIR VICTIMS. NOT A FRESH ONE.
SO MUCH FOR RESPECTING THE DEAD.
THE GUY WAS WITH A DRUG CARTEL. RESPECT ONLY GOES SO FAR.
SO HE WAS SCUM. HE STILL HAD FAMILY. PEOPLE WONDERING WHERE HE IS...IF HE'LL EVER COME BACK.
MAYBE THEY'D WANT TO GIVE HIM A DECENT BURIAL. NOT SEE HIM USED AS A LAB RAT.
WE HAVE TO KNOW THIS'LL WORK. WE NEED AN ADULT HUMAN BEING, NOT A RABBIT. MAYBE THIS IS CROSSING A LINE, BUT IT'S NOT THE FIRST TIME. AND IT WON'T BE THE LAST.
LOOK, NOW THAT THE LIZARDS ARE BURIED, WE CAN TELL THE POLICE ABOUT THIS PLACE. GIVE THE FAMILIES SOME CLOSURE.
IF THAT'S NOT ENOUGH, MOVE OVER, I'LL--
I GOT IT. DO YOUR THING ALREADY.
COME ON...
I'LL BE DAMNED.

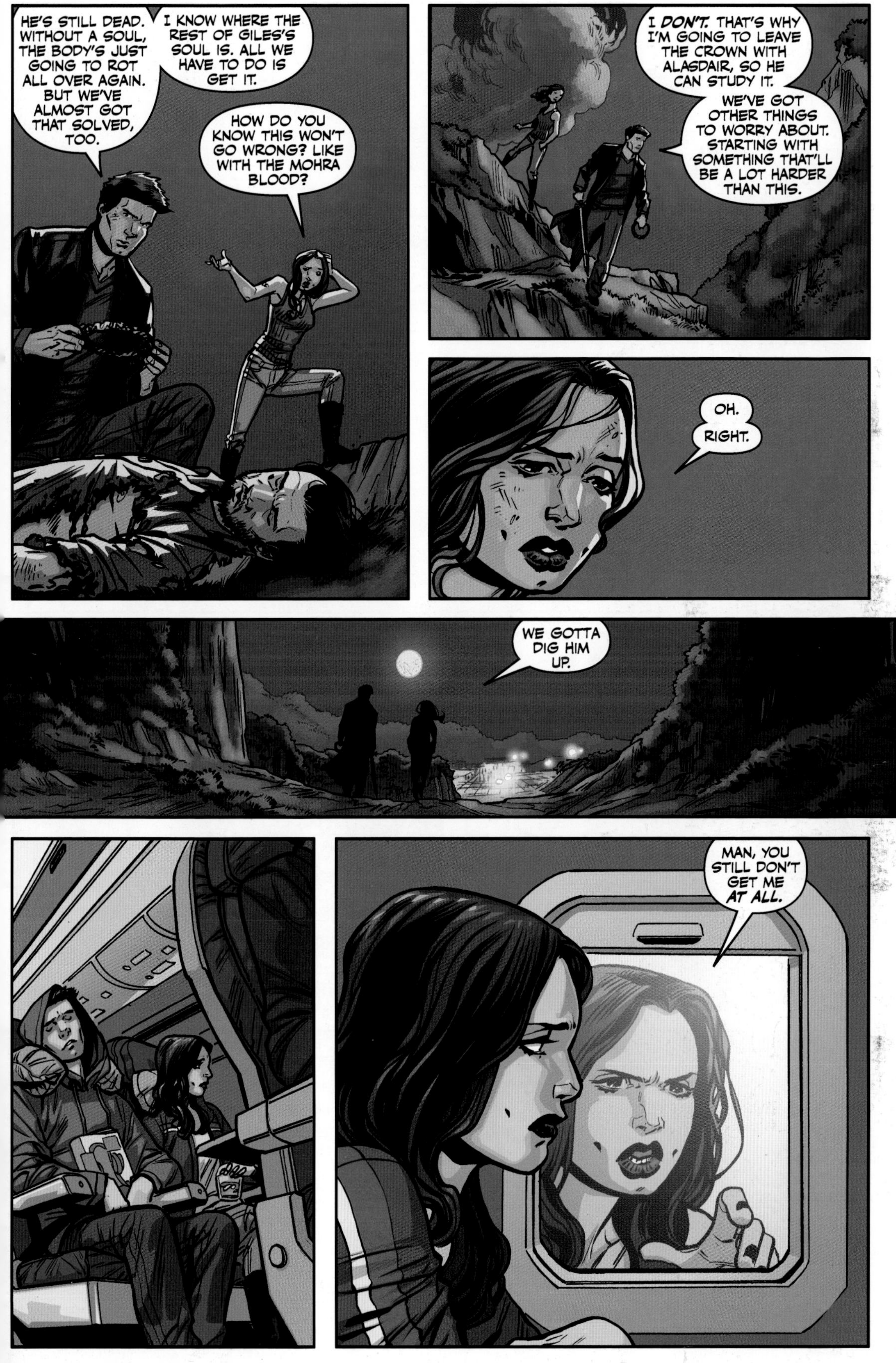
HE'S STILL DEAD. WITHOUT A SOUL, THE BODY'S JUST GOING TO ROT ALL OVER AGAIN. BUT WE'VE ALMOST GOT THAT SOLVED, TOO.
I KNOW WHERE THE REST OF GILES'S SOUL IS. ALL WE HAVE TO DO IS GET IT.
HOW DO YOU KNOW THIS WON'T GO WRONG? LIKE WITH THE MOHRA BLOOD?
I *DON'T.* THAT'S WHY I'M GOING TO LEAVE THE CROWN WITH ALASDAIR, SO HE CAN STUDY IT.
WE'VE GOT OTHER THINGS TO WORRY ABOUT. STARTING WITH SOMETHING THAT'LL BE A LOT HARDER THAN THIS.
OH.
RIGHT.
WE GOTTA DIG HIM UP.
MAN, YOU STILL DON'T GET ME *AT ALL.*

AH, YES. THE AGGRIEVED LAMENT OF YOUTH STRETCHING BACK TO *JAMES DEAN.*

FAITH, I WAS NOT INSULTING YOU.

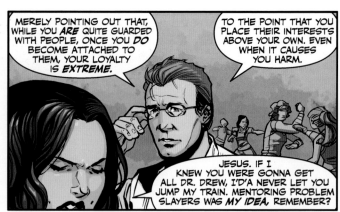

MERELY POINTING OUT THAT, WHILE YOU *ARE* QUITE GUARDED WITH PEOPLE, ONCE YOU *DO* BECOME ATTACHED TO THEM, YOUR LOYALTY IS *EXTREME.*

TO THE POINT THAT YOU PLACE THEIR INTERESTS ABOVE YOUR OWN. EVEN WHEN IT CAUSES YOU HARM.

JESUS. IF I KNEW YOU WERE GONNA GET ALL *DR. DREW,* I'D'A NEVER LET YOU JUMP MY TRAIN. MENTORING PROBLEM SLAYERS WAS *MY IDEA,* REMEMBER?

INDEED IT WAS, AND A *GOOD* ONE. GIVEN THE STATE OF THE WORLD, I STILL BELIEVE IT IS *CRUCIAL* THESE GIRLS RECEIVE GUIDANCE.

BUT YOU'VE SEEN FIRSTHAND THERE ARE THOSE WHO *CAN'T BE HELPED.* AS ONE WHO'S WORKED WITH SLAYERS FOR...WELL, THE EXACT AMOUNT OF TIME ISN'T RELEVANT... I PROMISE YOU THERE *WILL BE MORE.*

THOSE SO *DAMAGED* THEY CAN ONLY DRAG ANYONE WHO SEEKS TO AID THEM INTO THEIR MORASS OF PAIN AND DYSFUNCTION.

FAITH, I WOULD NEVER FORGIVE MYSELF IF I ALLOWED THAT TO HAPPEN TO YOU.

DAMN, G. YOU ARE, LIKE, THE *PRINCE* OF DRAGGING A TWO-SECOND CONVO INTO A SIX-HOUR MINISERIES.

LEMME SAVE SOME TIME. YOU--"WATCH YOUR ASS." ME--"COPY THAT." YOU--"GOOD. I'LL SHUT UP NOW."

WE COOL?

YES. WE ARE MOST DEFINITELY COOL.

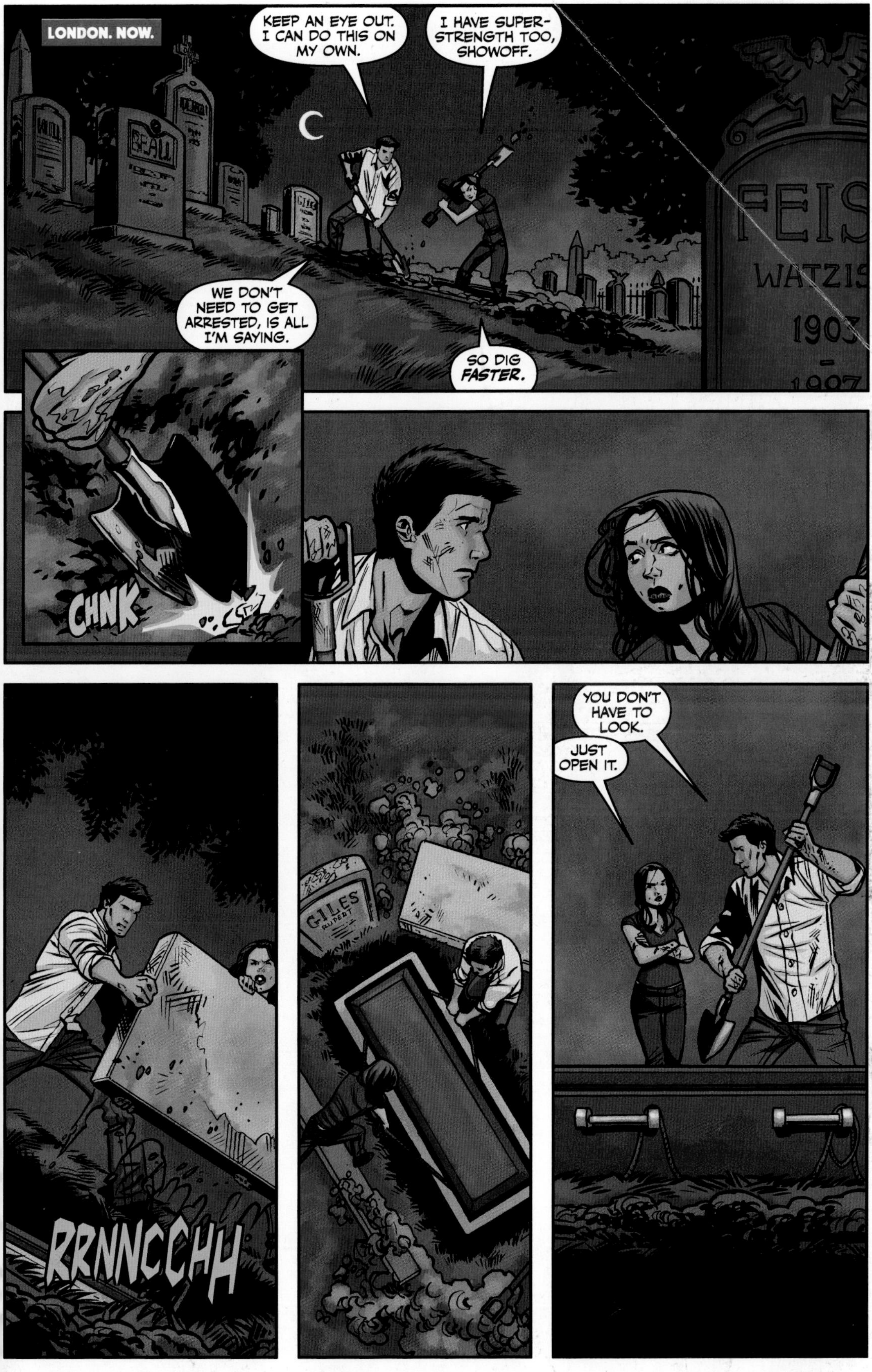
LONDON. NOW.
KEEP AN EYE OUT. I CAN DO THIS ON MY OWN.
I HAVE SUPER-STRENGTH TOO, SHOWOFF.
WE DON'T NEED TO GET ARRESTED, IS ALL I'M SAYING.
SO DIG *FASTER.*
FEIS
WATZIS
1903
–
CHNK
RRNNCCHH
GILES
RUPERT
YOU DON'T HAVE TO LOOK.
JUST OPEN IT.

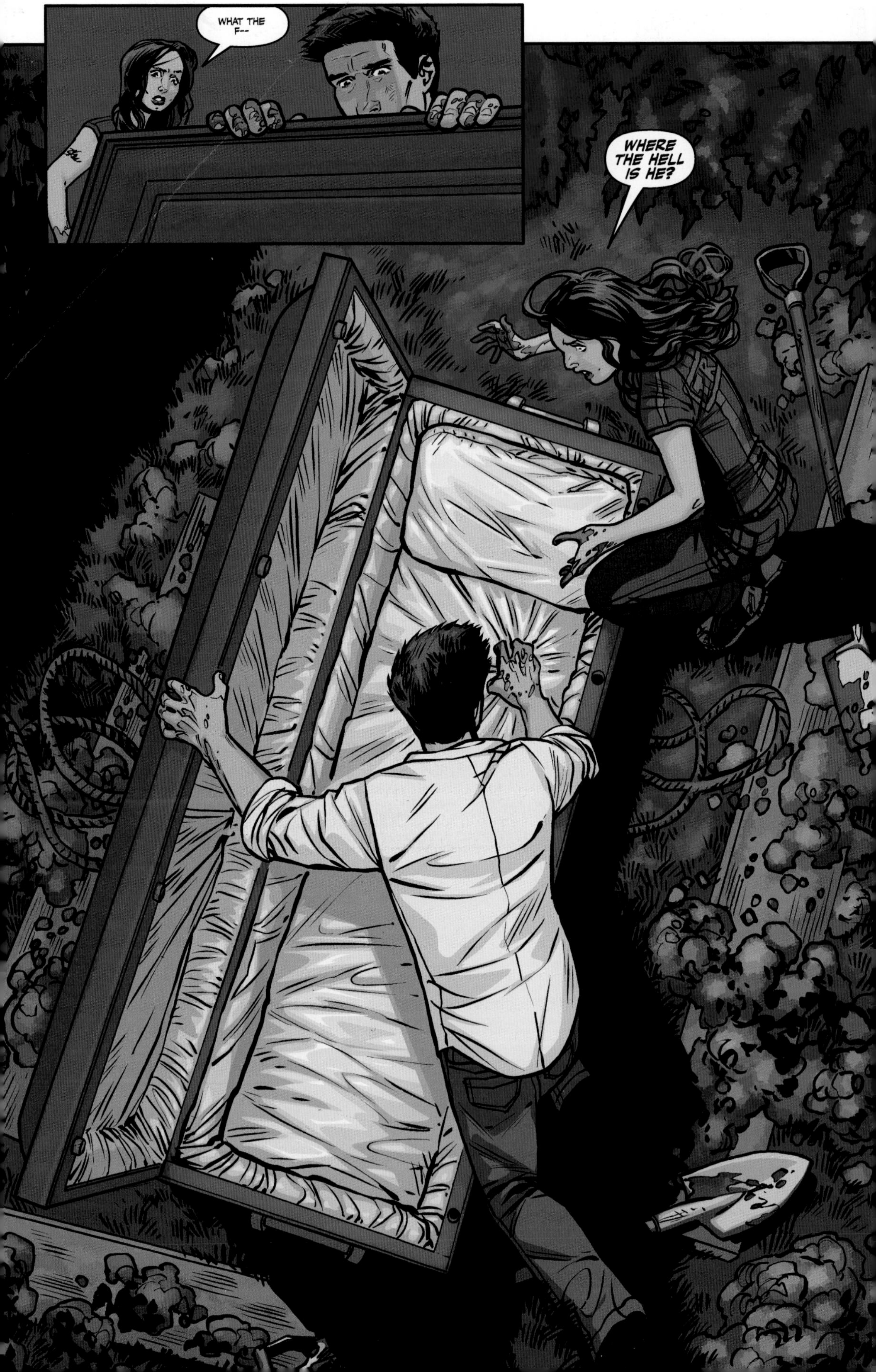
WHAT THE F--
WHERE THE HELL IS HE?

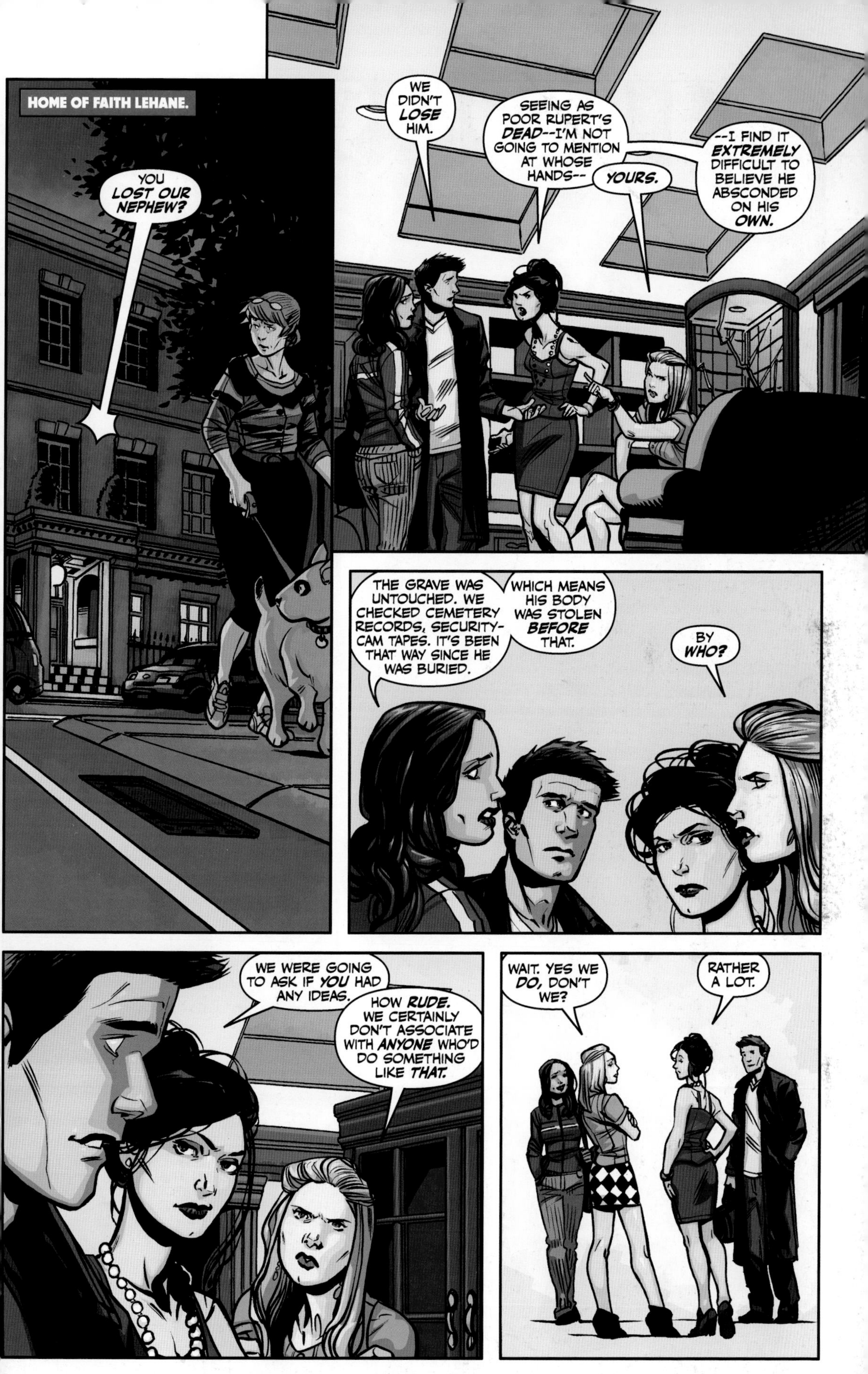
HOME OF FAITH LEHANE.
YOU LOST OUR NEPHEW?
WE DIDN'T LOSE HIM.
SEEING AS POOR RUPERT'S DEAD--I'M NOT GOING TO MENTION AT WHOSE HANDS--
YOURS.
--I FIND IT EXTREMELY DIFFICULT TO BELIEVE HE ABSCONDED ON HIS OWN.
THE GRAVE WAS UNTOUCHED. WE CHECKED CEMETERY RECORDS, SECURITY-CAM TAPES. IT'S BEEN THAT WAY SINCE HE WAS BURIED.
WHICH MEANS HIS BODY WAS STOLEN BEFORE THAT.
BY WHO?
WE WERE GOING TO ASK IF YOU HAD ANY IDEAS.
HOW RUDE. WE CERTAINLY DON'T ASSOCIATE WITH ANYONE WHO'D DO SOMETHING LIKE THAT.
WAIT. YES WE DO, DON'T WE?
RATHER A LOT.

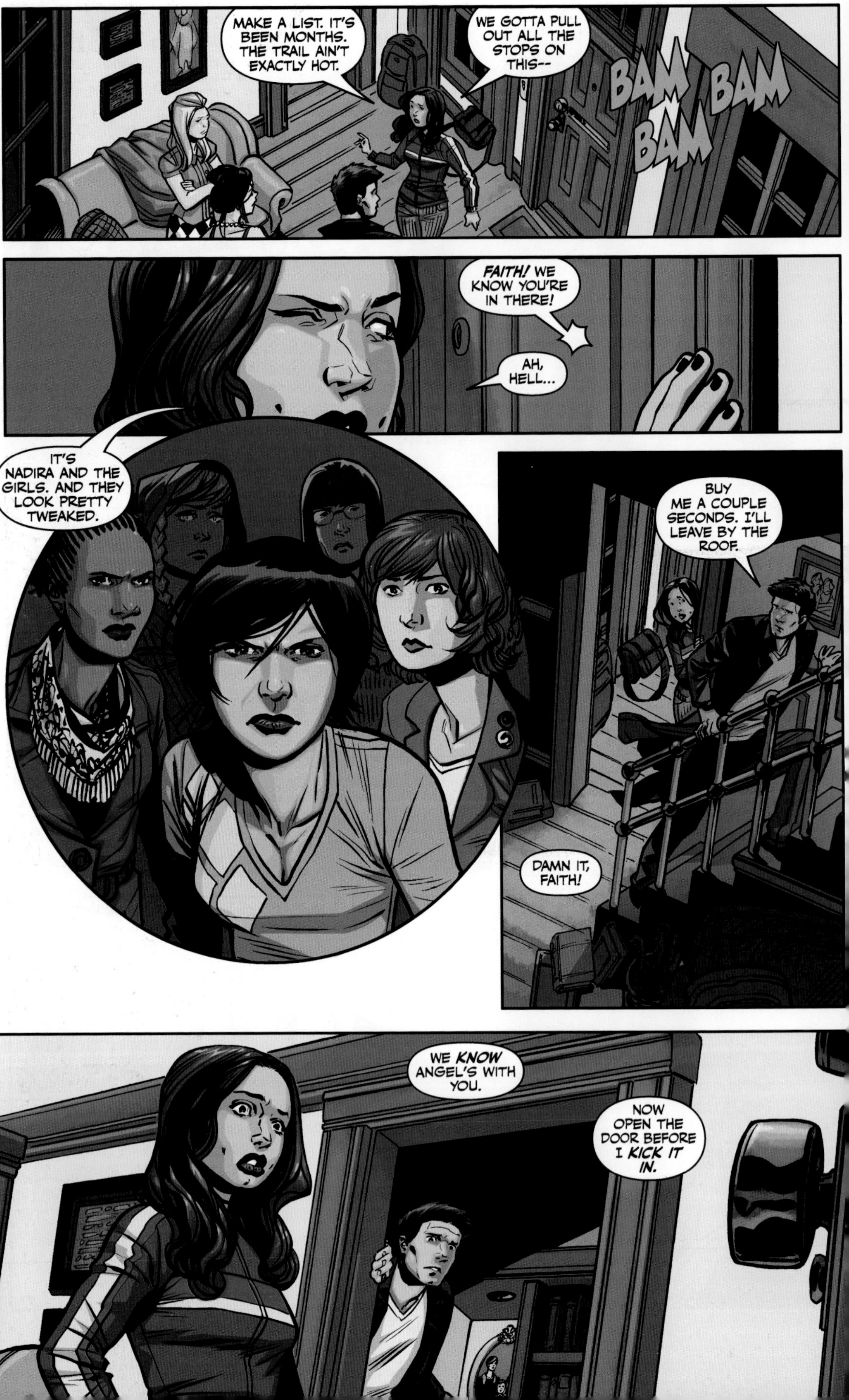
MAKE A LIST. IT'S BEEN MONTHS. THE TRAIL AIN'T EXACTLY HOT.
WE GOTTA PULL OUT ALL THE STOPS ON THIS--
BAM BAM BAM BAM
FAITH! WE KNOW YOU'RE IN THERE!
AH, HELL...
IT'S NADIRA AND THE GIRLS. AND THEY LOOK PRETTY TWEAKED.
BUY ME A COUPLE SECONDS. I'LL LEAVE BY THE ROOF.
DAMN IT, FAITH!
WE KNOW ANGEL'S WITH YOU.
NOW OPEN THE DOOR BEFORE I KICK IT IN.

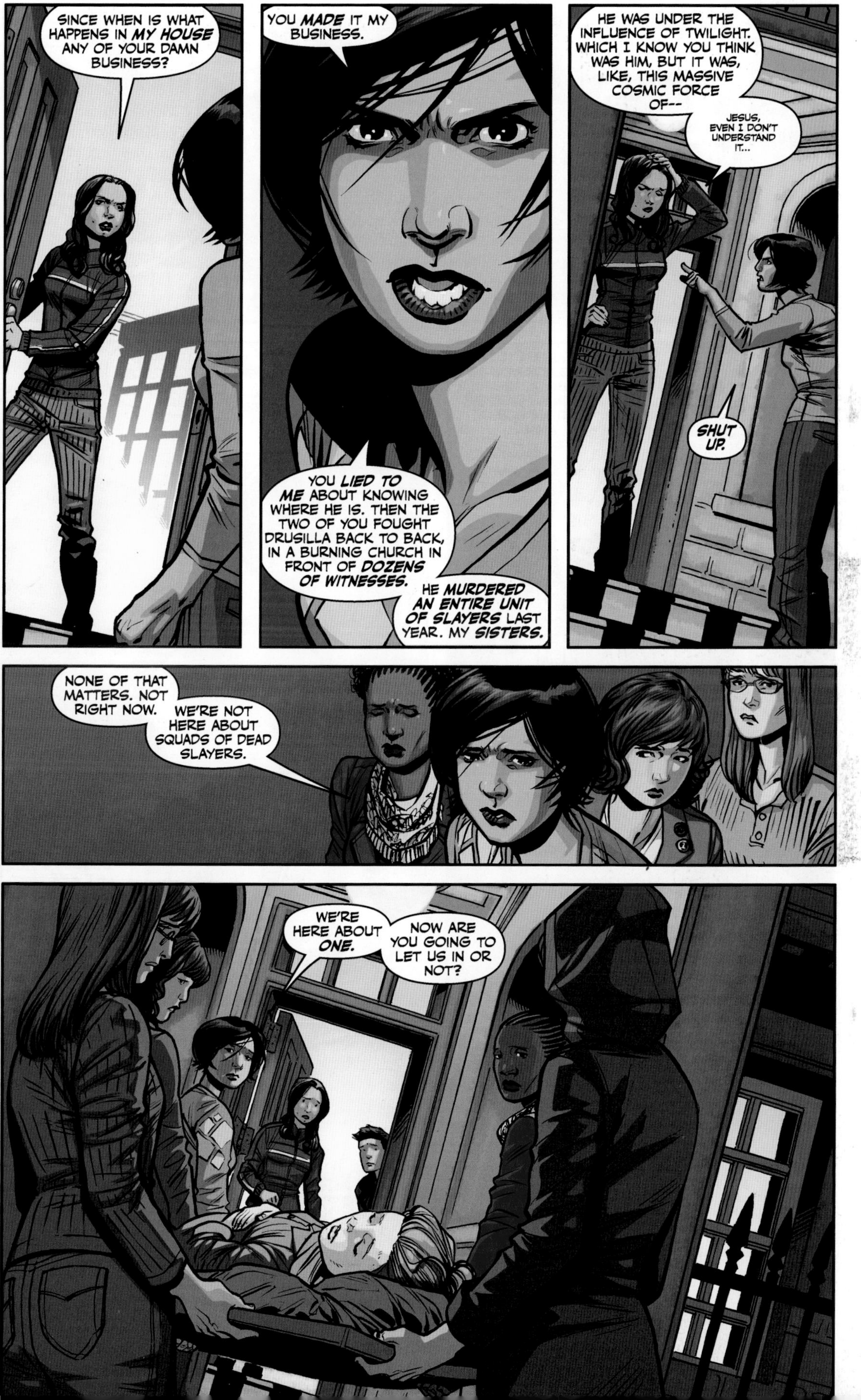
SINCE WHEN IS WHAT HAPPENS IN MY HOUSE ANY OF YOUR DAMN BUSINESS?
YOU MADE IT MY BUSINESS.
YOU LIED TO ME ABOUT KNOWING WHERE HE IS. THEN THE TWO OF YOU FOUGHT DRUSILLA BACK TO BACK, IN A BURNING CHURCH IN FRONT OF DOZENS OF WITNESSES.
HE MURDERED AN ENTIRE UNIT OF SLAYERS LAST YEAR. MY SISTERS.
HE WAS UNDER THE INFLUENCE OF TWILIGHT. WHICH I KNOW YOU THINK WAS HIM, BUT IT WAS, LIKE, THIS MASSIVE COSMIC FORCE OF--
JESUS, EVEN I DON'T UNDERSTAND IT...
SHUT UP.
NONE OF THAT MATTERS. NOT RIGHT NOW.
WE'RE NOT HERE ABOUT SQUADS OF DEAD SLAYERS.
WE'RE HERE ABOUT ONE.
NOW ARE YOU GOING TO LET US IN OR NOT?

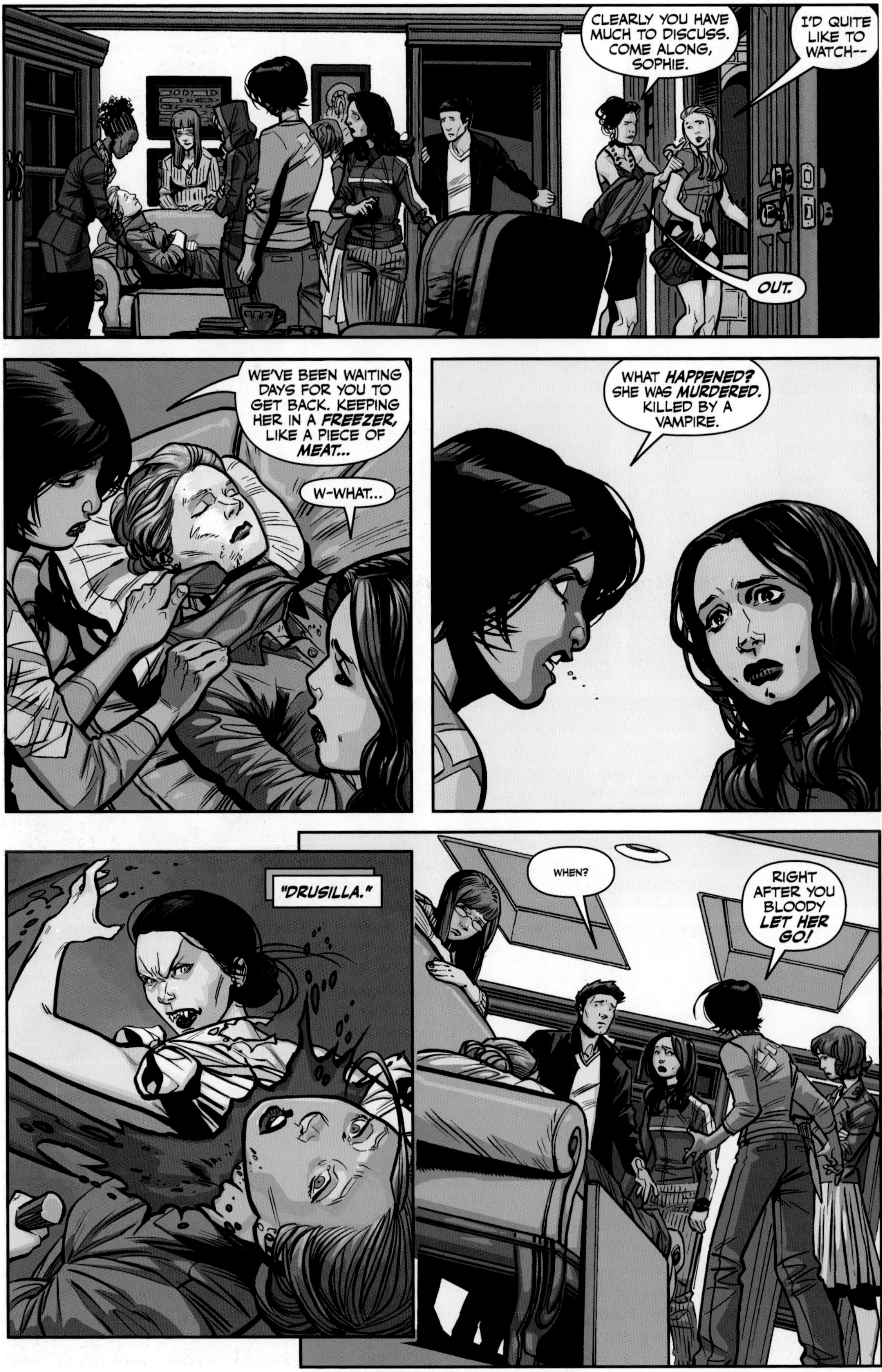
CLEARLY YOU HAVE MUCH TO DISCUSS. COME ALONG, SOPHIE.
I'D QUITE LIKE TO WATCH--
OUT.
WE'VE BEEN WAITING DAYS FOR YOU TO GET BACK. KEEPING HER IN A FREEZER, LIKE A PIECE OF MEAT...
W-WHAT...
WHAT HAPPENED? SHE WAS MURDERED. KILLED BY A VAMPIRE.
"DRUSILLA."
WHEN?
RIGHT AFTER YOU BLOODY LET HER GO!

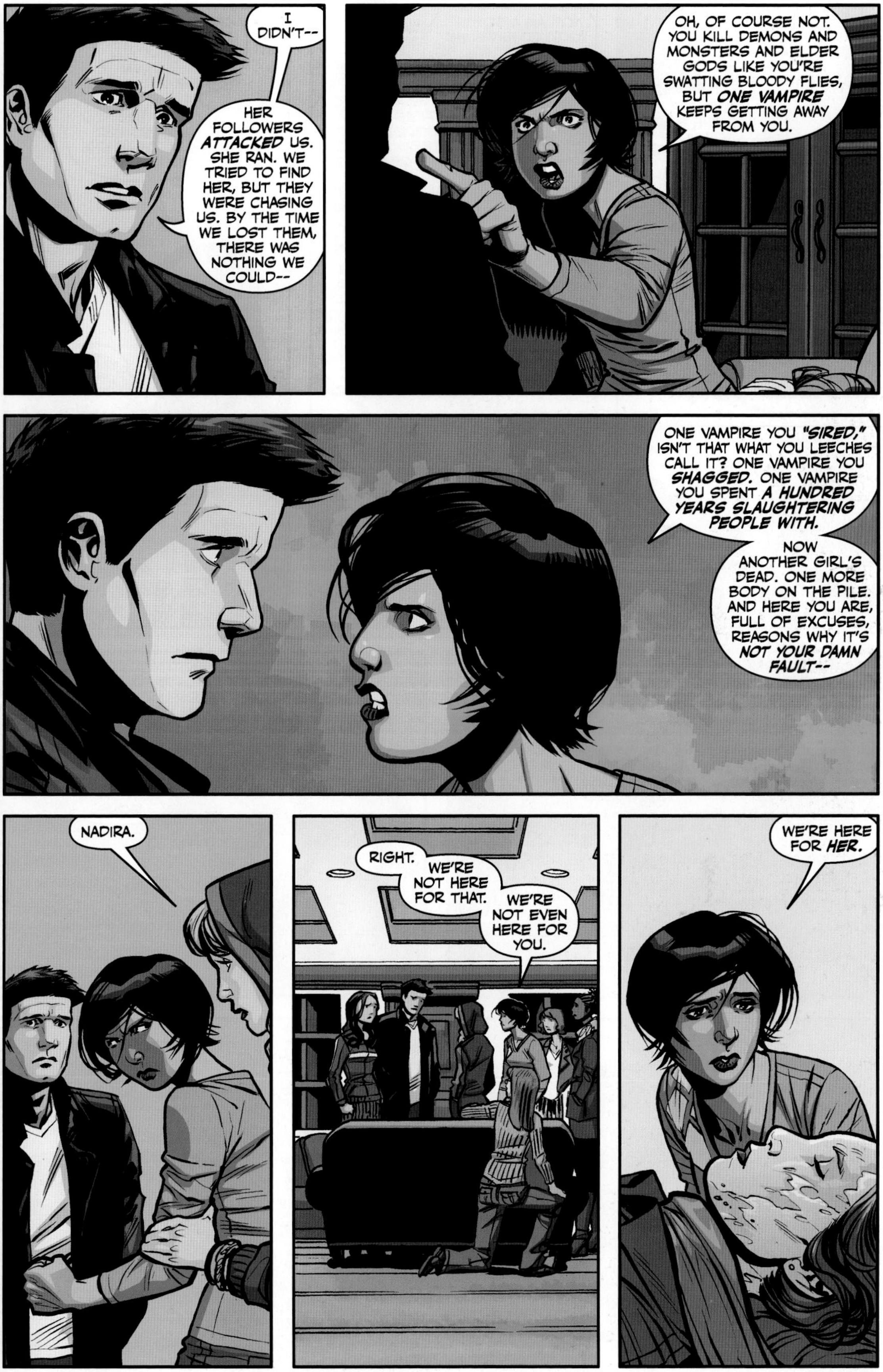

I DIDN'T--
HER FOLLOWERS ATTACKED US. SHE RAN. WE TRIED TO FIND HER, BUT THEY WERE CHASING US. BY THE TIME WE LOST THEM, THERE WAS NOTHING WE COULD--
OH, OF COURSE NOT. YOU KILL DEMONS AND MONSTERS AND ELDER GODS LIKE YOU'RE SWATTING BLOODY FLIES, BUT ONE VAMPIRE KEEPS GETTING AWAY FROM YOU.
ONE VAMPIRE YOU "SIRED," ISN'T THAT WHAT YOU LEECHES CALL IT? ONE VAMPIRE YOU SHAGGED. ONE VAMPIRE YOU SPENT A HUNDRED YEARS SLAUGHTERING PEOPLE WITH.
NOW ANOTHER GIRL'S DEAD. ONE MORE BODY ON THE PILE. AND HERE YOU ARE, FULL OF EXCUSES, REASONS WHY IT'S NOT YOUR DAMN FAULT--
NADIRA.
RIGHT.
WE'RE NOT HERE FOR THAT.
WE'RE NOT EVEN HERE FOR YOU.
WE'RE HERE FOR HER.

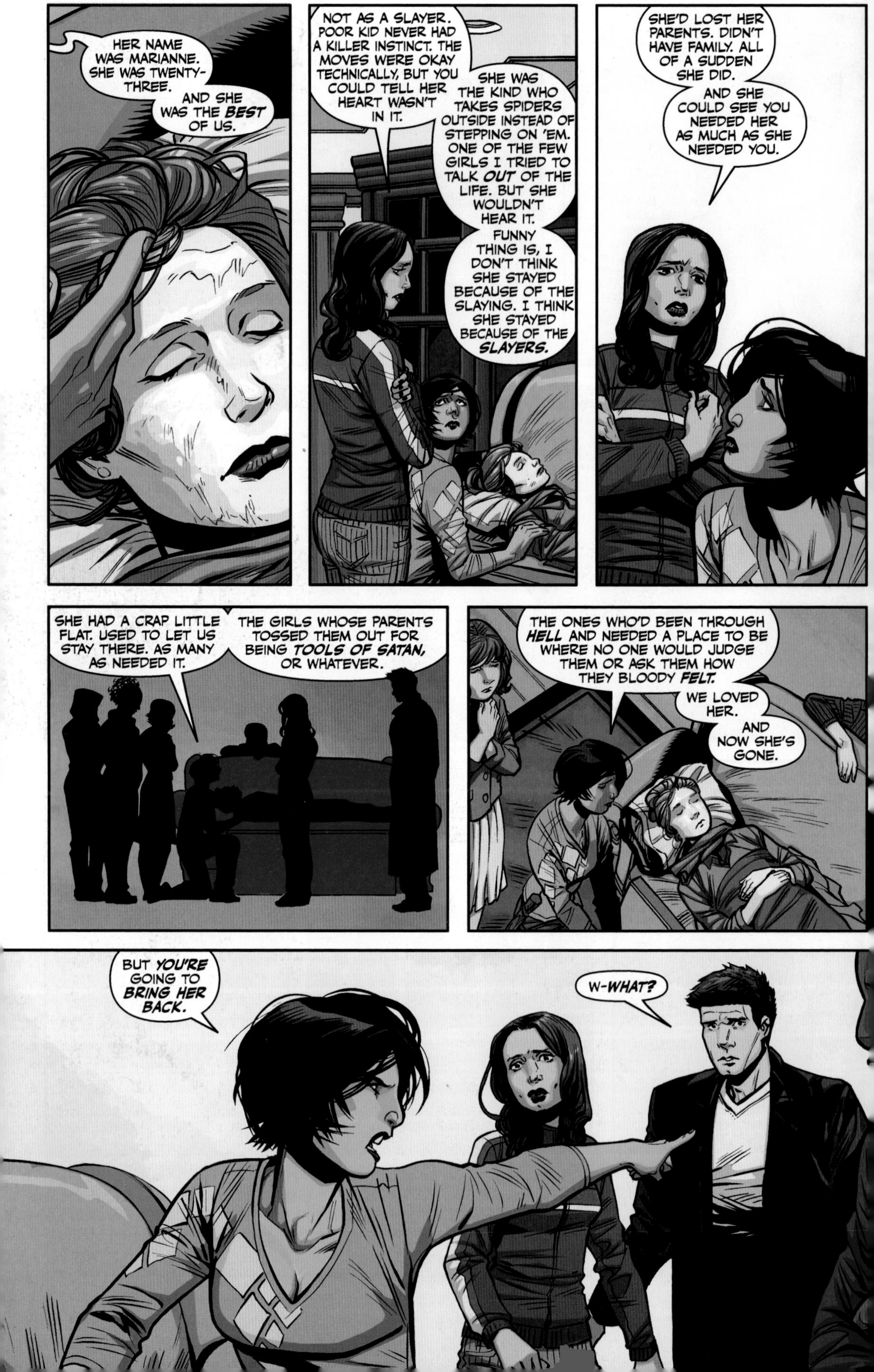
HER NAME WAS MARIANNE. SHE WAS TWENTY-THREE.
AND SHE WAS THE BEST OF US.
NOT AS A SLAYER. POOR KID NEVER HAD A KILLER INSTINCT. THE MOVES WERE OKAY TECHNICALLY, BUT YOU COULD TELL HER HEART WASN'T IN IT.
SHE WAS THE KIND WHO TAKES SPIDERS OUTSIDE INSTEAD OF STEPPING ON 'EM. ONE OF THE FEW GIRLS I TRIED TO TALK OUT OF THE LIFE. BUT SHE WOULDN'T HEAR IT.
FUNNY THING IS, I DON'T THINK SHE STAYED BECAUSE OF THE SLAYING. I THINK SHE STAYED BECAUSE OF THE SLAYERS.
SHE'D LOST HER PARENTS. DIDN'T HAVE FAMILY. ALL OF A SUDDEN SHE DID.
AND SHE COULD SEE YOU NEEDED HER AS MUCH AS SHE NEEDED YOU.
SHE HAD A CRAP LITTLE FLAT. USED TO LET US STAY THERE. AS MANY AS NEEDED IT.
THE GIRLS WHOSE PARENTS TOSSED THEM OUT FOR BEING TOOLS OF SATAN, OR WHATEVER.
THE ONES WHO'D BEEN THROUGH HELL AND NEEDED A PLACE TO BE WHERE NO ONE WOULD JUDGE THEM OR ASK THEM HOW THEY BLOODY FELT.
WE LOVED HER.
AND NOW SHE'S GONE.
BUT YOU'RE GOING TO BRING HER BACK.
W-WHAT?

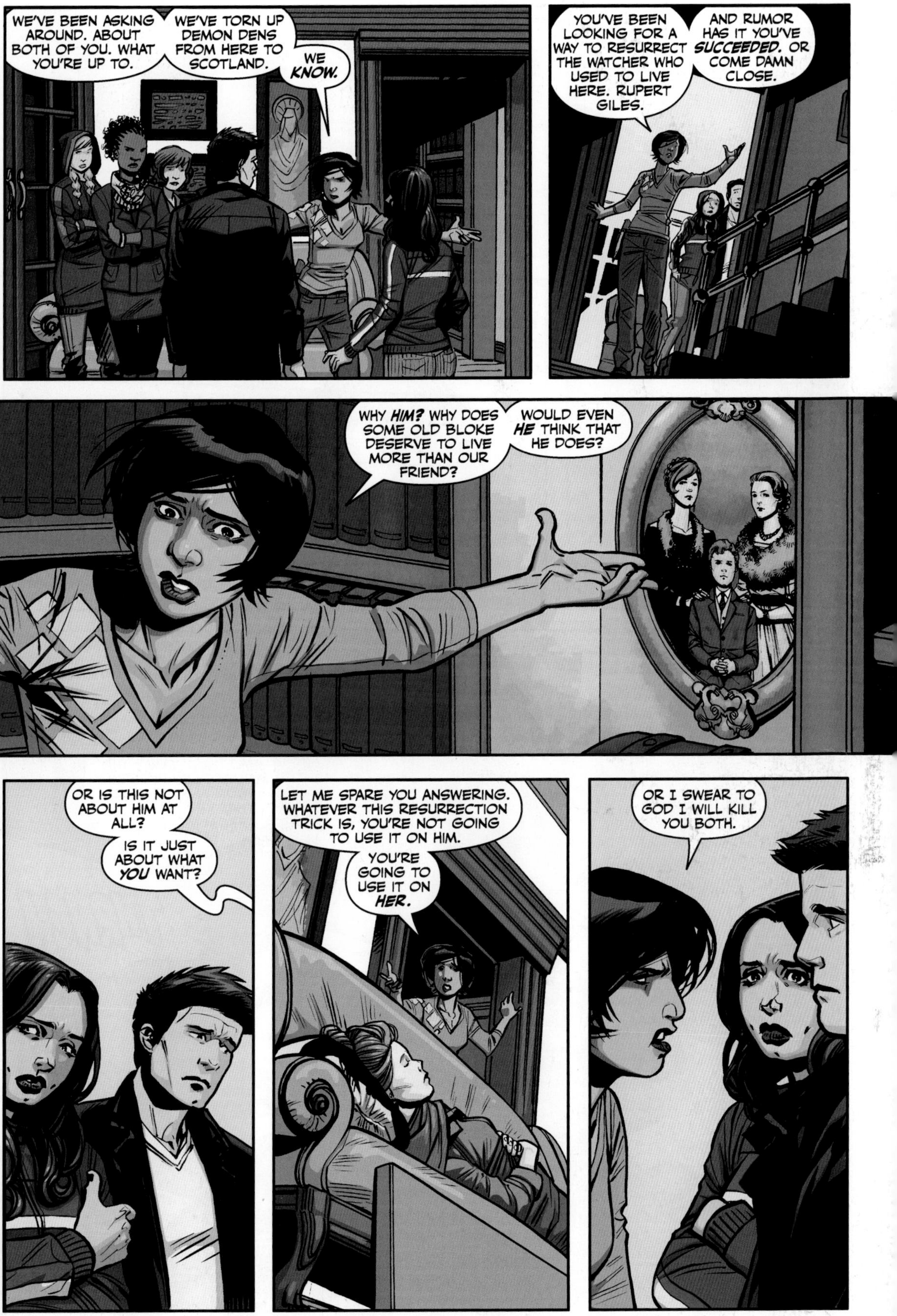
WE'VE BEEN ASKING AROUND. ABOUT BOTH OF YOU. WHAT YOU'RE UP TO.
WE'VE TORN UP DEMON DENS FROM HERE TO SCOTLAND.
WE *KNOW.*
YOU'VE BEEN LOOKING FOR A WAY TO RESURRECT THE WATCHER WHO USED TO LIVE HERE. RUPERT GILES.
AND RUMOR HAS IT YOU'VE *SUCCEEDED.* OR COME DAMN CLOSE.
WHY *HIM?* WHY DOES SOME OLD BLOKE DESERVE TO LIVE MORE THAN OUR FRIEND?
WOULD EVEN *HE* THINK THAT HE DOES?
OR IS THIS NOT ABOUT HIM AT ALL?
IS IT JUST ABOUT WHAT *YOU* WANT?
LET ME SPARE YOU ANSWERING. WHATEVER THIS RESURRECTION TRICK IS, YOU'RE NOT GOING TO USE IT ON HIM.
YOU'RE GOING TO USE IT ON *HER.*
OR I SWEAR TO GOD I WILL KILL YOU BOTH.

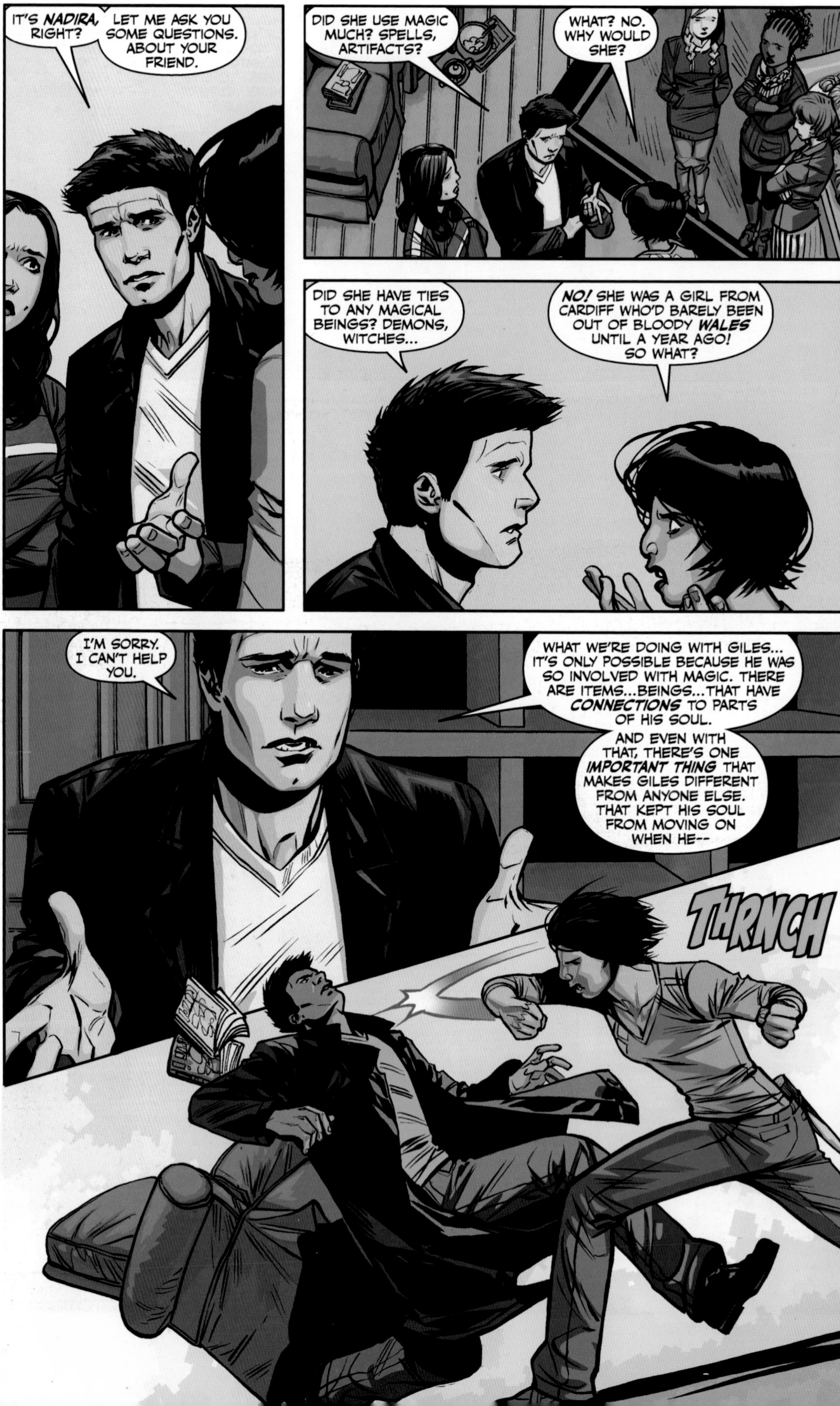
IT'S NADIRA, RIGHT?
LET ME ASK YOU SOME QUESTIONS. ABOUT YOUR FRIEND.
DID SHE USE MAGIC MUCH? SPELLS, ARTIFACTS?
WHAT? NO. WHY WOULD SHE?
DID SHE HAVE TIES TO ANY MAGICAL BEINGS? DEMONS, WITCHES...
NO! SHE WAS A GIRL FROM CARDIFF WHO'D BARELY BEEN OUT OF BLOODY WALES UNTIL A YEAR AGO! SO WHAT?
I'M SORRY. I CAN'T HELP YOU.
WHAT WE'RE DOING WITH GILES... IT'S ONLY POSSIBLE BECAUSE HE WAS SO INVOLVED WITH MAGIC. THERE ARE ITEMS...BEINGS...THAT HAVE CONNECTIONS TO PARTS OF HIS SOUL.
AND EVEN WITH THAT, THERE'S ONE IMPORTANT THING THAT MAKES GILES DIFFERENT FROM ANYONE ELSE. THAT KEPT HIS SOUL FROM MOVING ON WHEN HE--
THRNCH

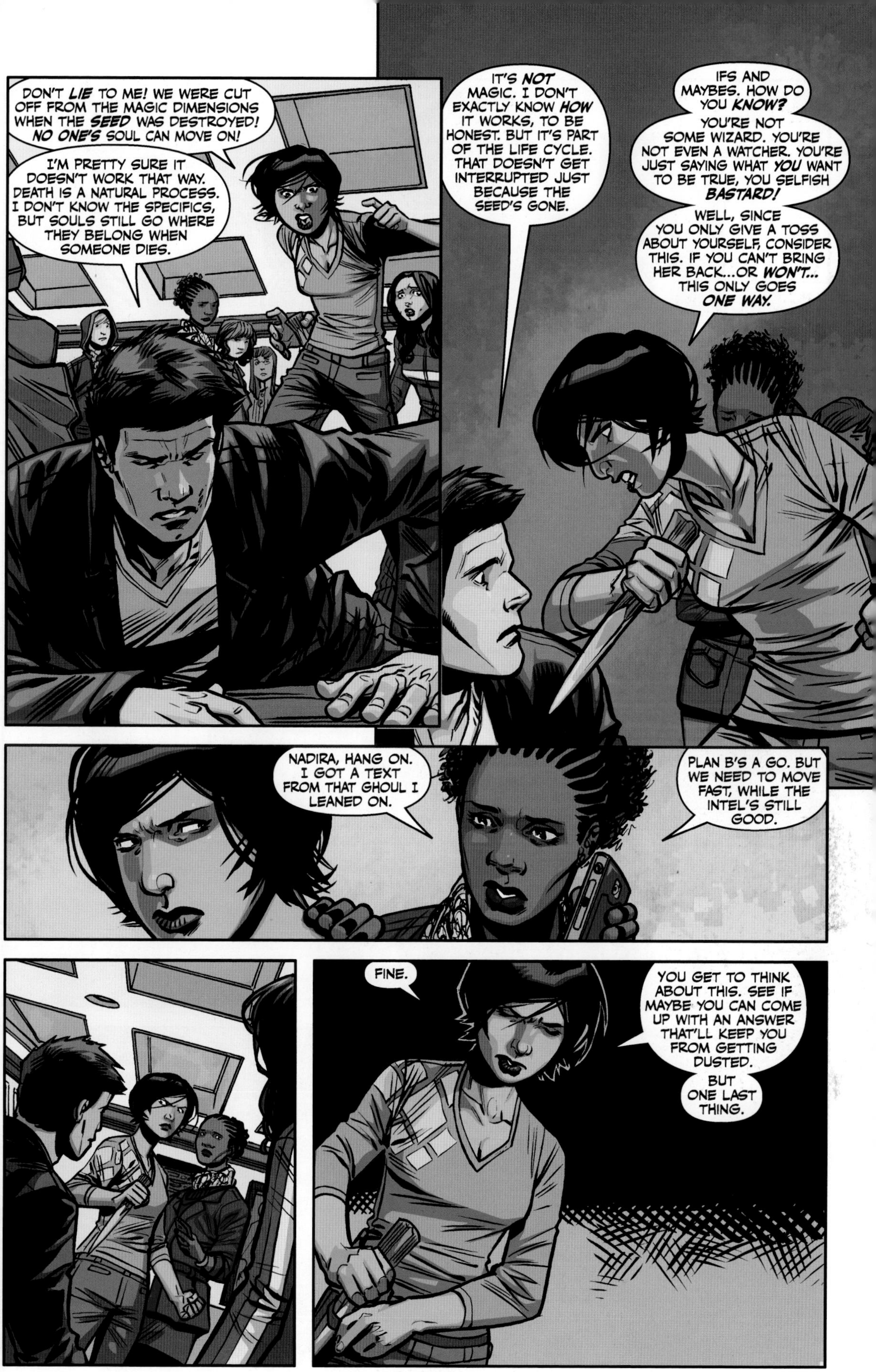
DON'T LIE TO ME! WE WERE CUT OFF FROM THE MAGIC DIMENSIONS WHEN THE SEED WAS DESTROYED! NO ONE'S SOUL CAN MOVE ON!
I'M PRETTY SURE IT DOESN'T WORK THAT WAY. DEATH IS A NATURAL PROCESS. I DON'T KNOW THE SPECIFICS, BUT SOULS STILL GO WHERE THEY BELONG WHEN SOMEONE DIES.
IT'S NOT MAGIC. I DON'T EXACTLY KNOW HOW IT WORKS, TO BE HONEST. BUT IT'S PART OF THE LIFE CYCLE. THAT DOESN'T GET INTERRUPTED JUST BECAUSE THE SEED'S GONE.
IFS AND MAYBES. HOW DO YOU KNOW?
YOU'RE NOT SOME WIZARD. YOU'RE NOT EVEN A WATCHER. YOU'RE JUST SAYING WHAT YOU WANT TO BE TRUE, YOU SELFISH BASTARD!
WELL, SINCE YOU ONLY GIVE A TOSS ABOUT YOURSELF, CONSIDER THIS. IF YOU CAN'T BRING HER BACK...OR WON'T... THIS ONLY GOES ONE WAY.
NADIRA, HANG ON. I GOT A TEXT FROM THAT GHOUL I LEANED ON.
PLAN B'S A GO. BUT WE NEED TO MOVE FAST, WHILE THE INTEL'S STILL GOOD.
FINE.
YOU GET TO THINK ABOUT THIS. SEE IF MAYBE YOU CAN COME UP WITH AN ANSWER THAT'LL KEEP YOU FROM GETTING DUSTED.
BUT ONE LAST THING.

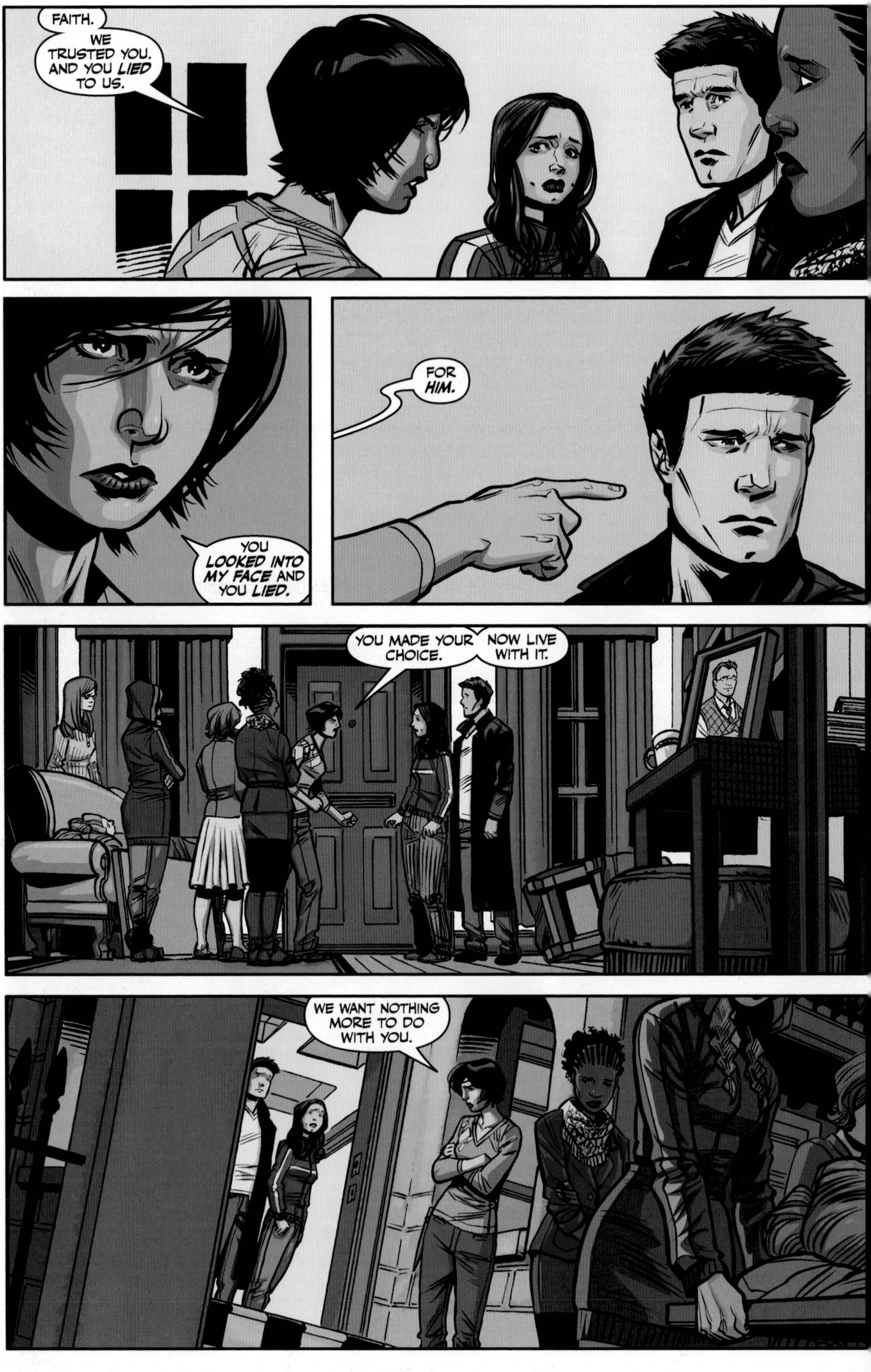
FAITH.
WE TRUSTED YOU. AND YOU *LIED* TO US.
YOU *LOOKED INTO MY FACE* AND YOU *LIED.*
FOR *HIM.*
YOU MADE YOUR CHOICE.
NOW LIVE WITH IT.
WE WANT NOTHING MORE TO DO WITH YOU.

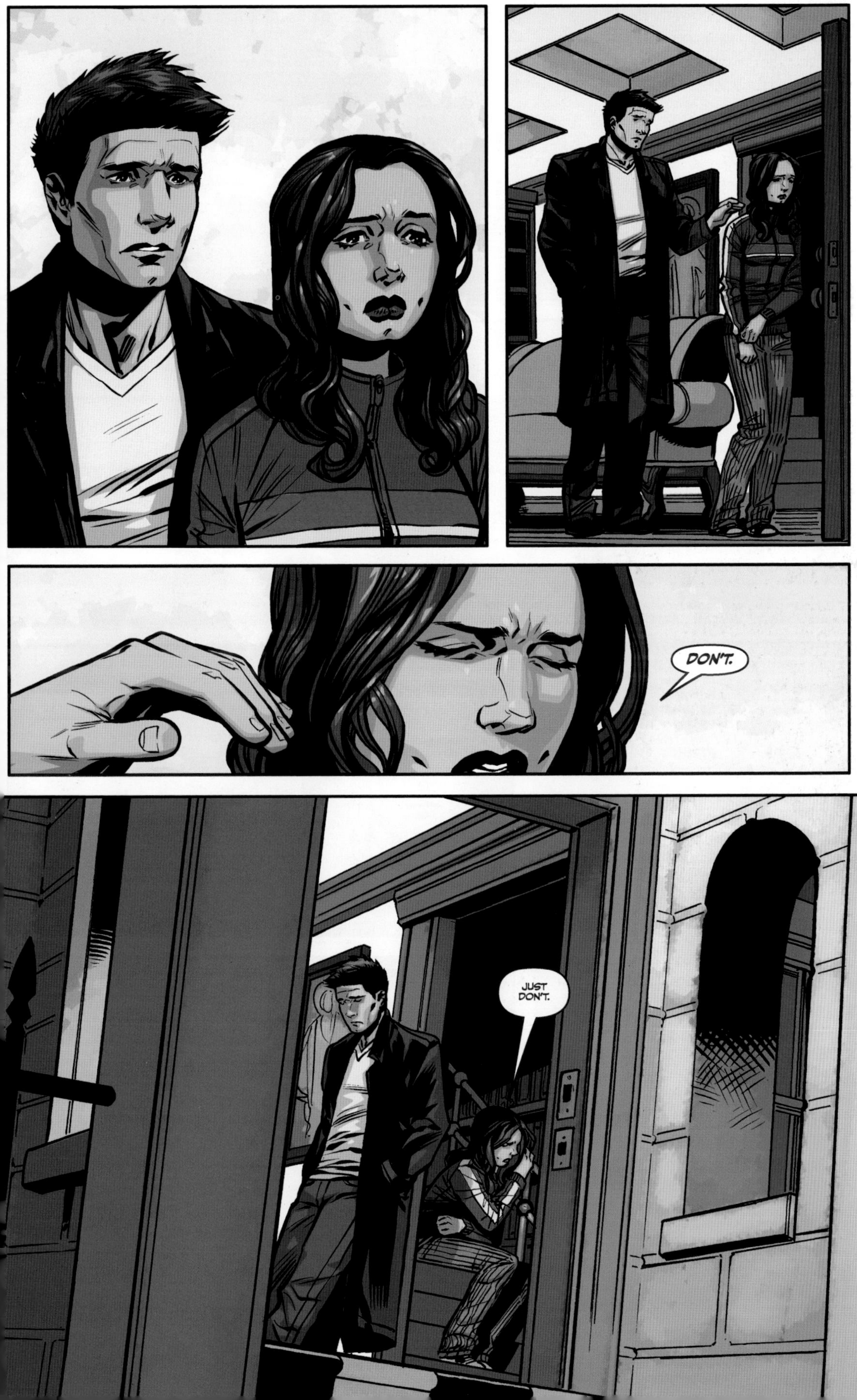
DON'T.
JUST DON'T.

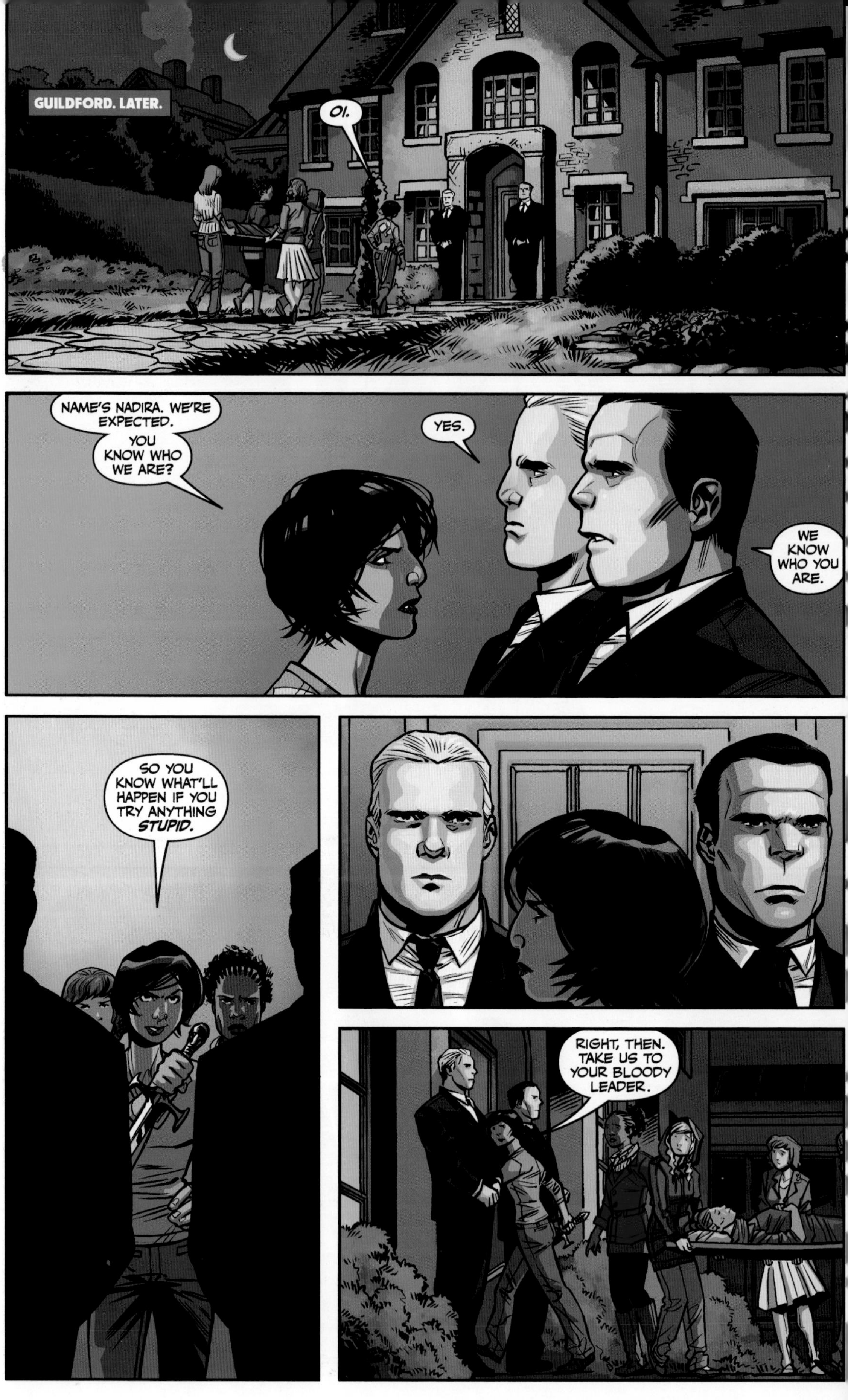
GUILDFORD. LATER.
OI.
NAME'S NADIRA. WE'RE EXPECTED.
YOU KNOW WHO WE ARE?
YES.
WE KNOW WHO YOU ARE.
SO YOU KNOW WHAT'LL HAPPEN IF YOU TRY ANYTHING *STUPID.*
RIGHT, THEN. TAKE US TO YOUR BLOODY LEADER.

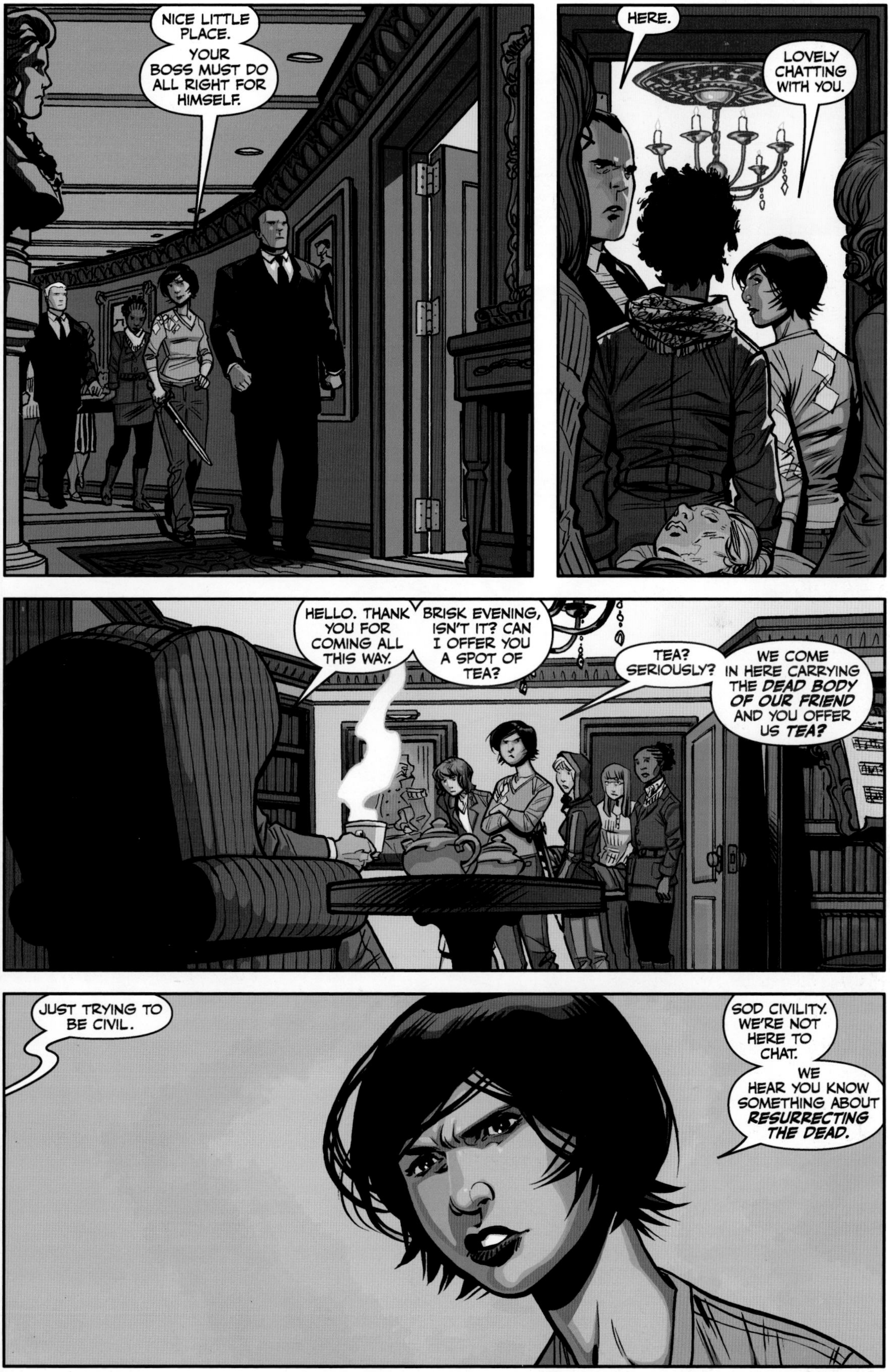
NICE LITTLE PLACE.
YOUR BOSS MUST DO ALL RIGHT FOR HIMSELF.
HERE.
LOVELY CHATTING WITH YOU.
HELLO. THANK YOU FOR COMING ALL THIS WAY.
BRISK EVENING, ISN'T IT? CAN I OFFER YOU A SPOT OF TEA?
TEA? SERIOUSLY?
WE COME IN HERE CARRYING THE *DEAD BODY OF OUR FRIEND* AND YOU OFFER US *TEA?*
JUST TRYING TO BE CIVIL.
SOD CIVILITY. WE'RE NOT HERE TO CHAT.
WE HEAR YOU KNOW SOMETHING ABOUT *RESURRECTING THE DEAD.*

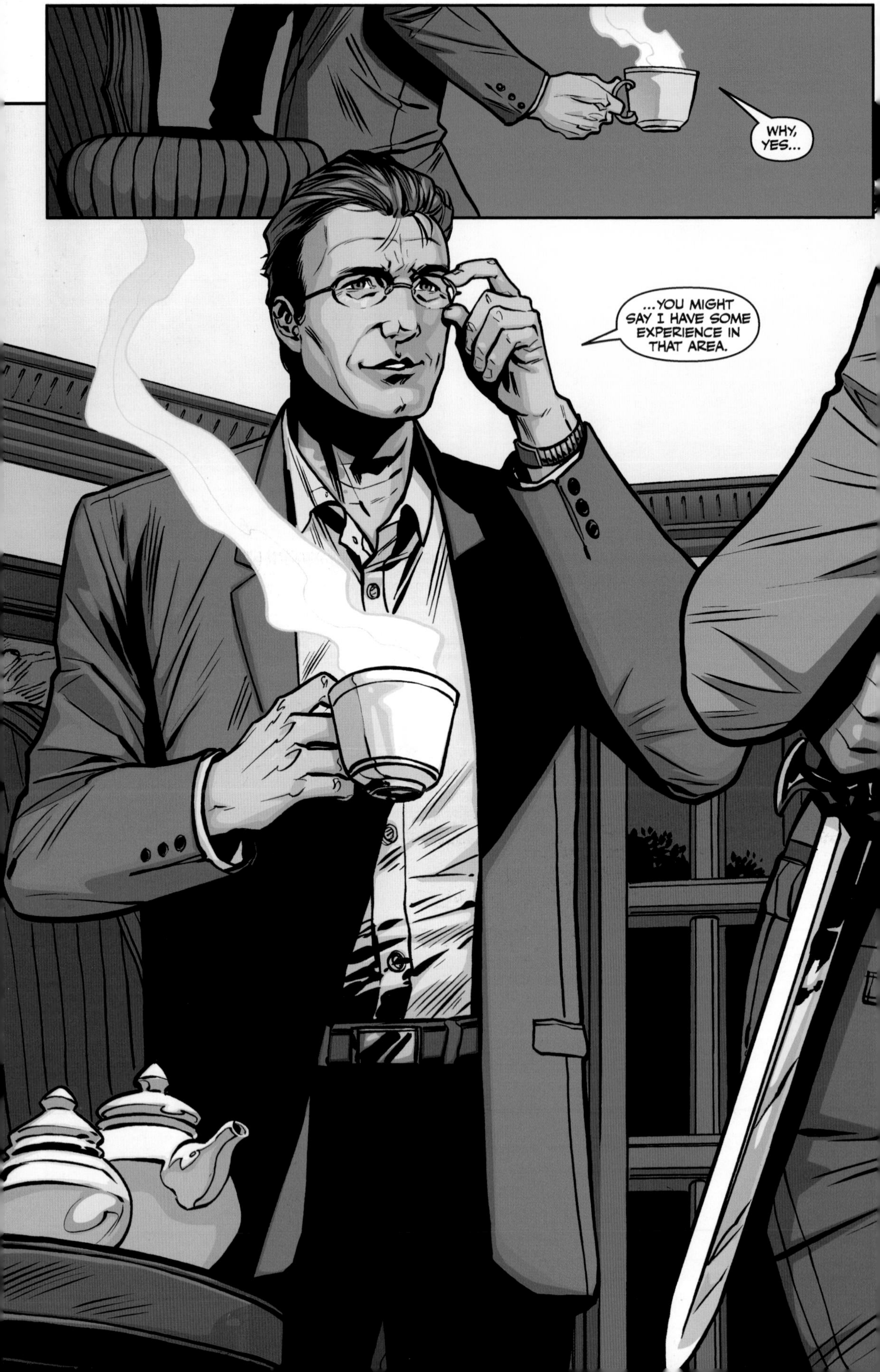
WHY, YES...
...YOU MIGHT SAY I HAVE SOME EXPERIENCE IN THAT AREA.

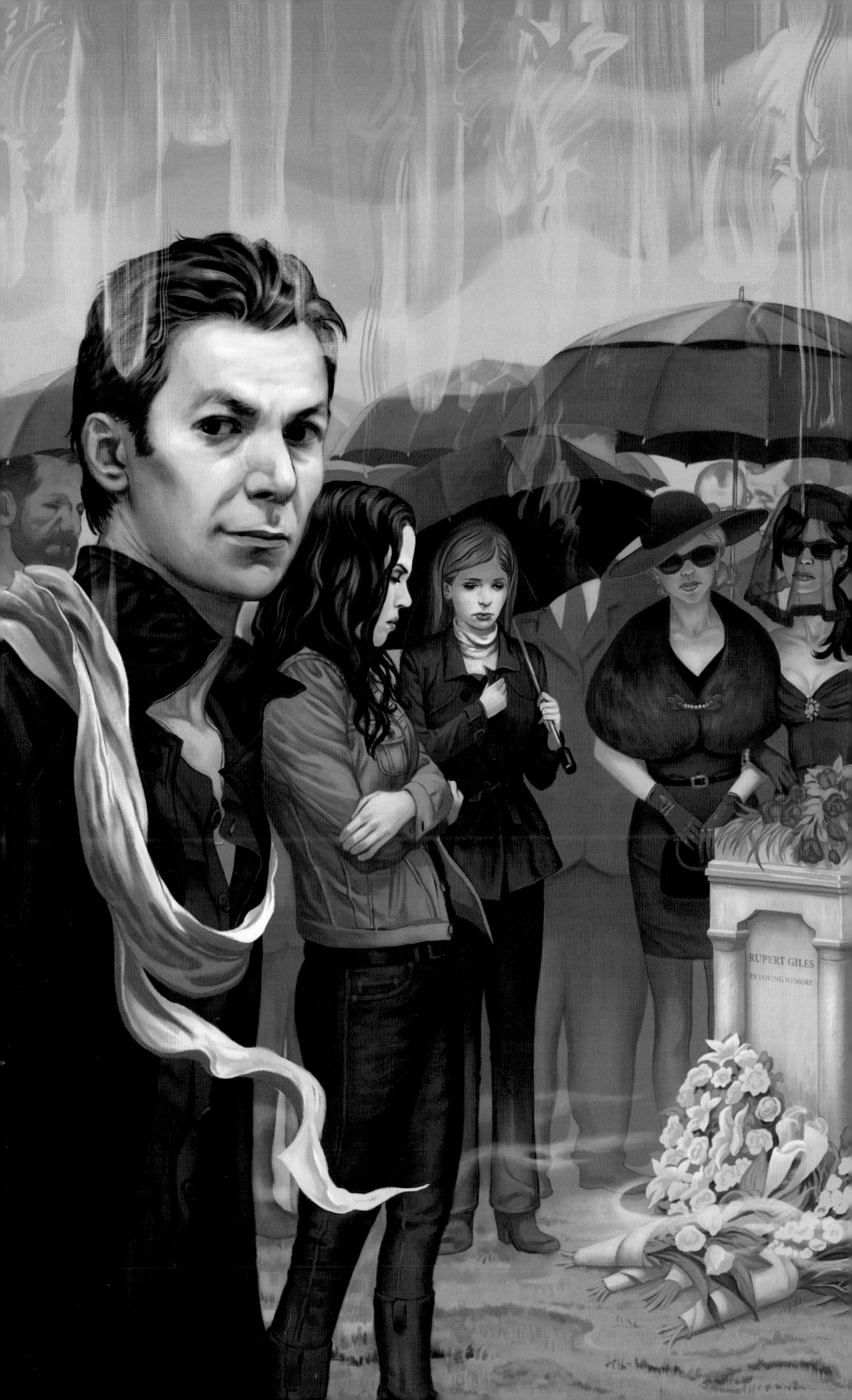
RUPERT GILES
IN LOVING MEMORY

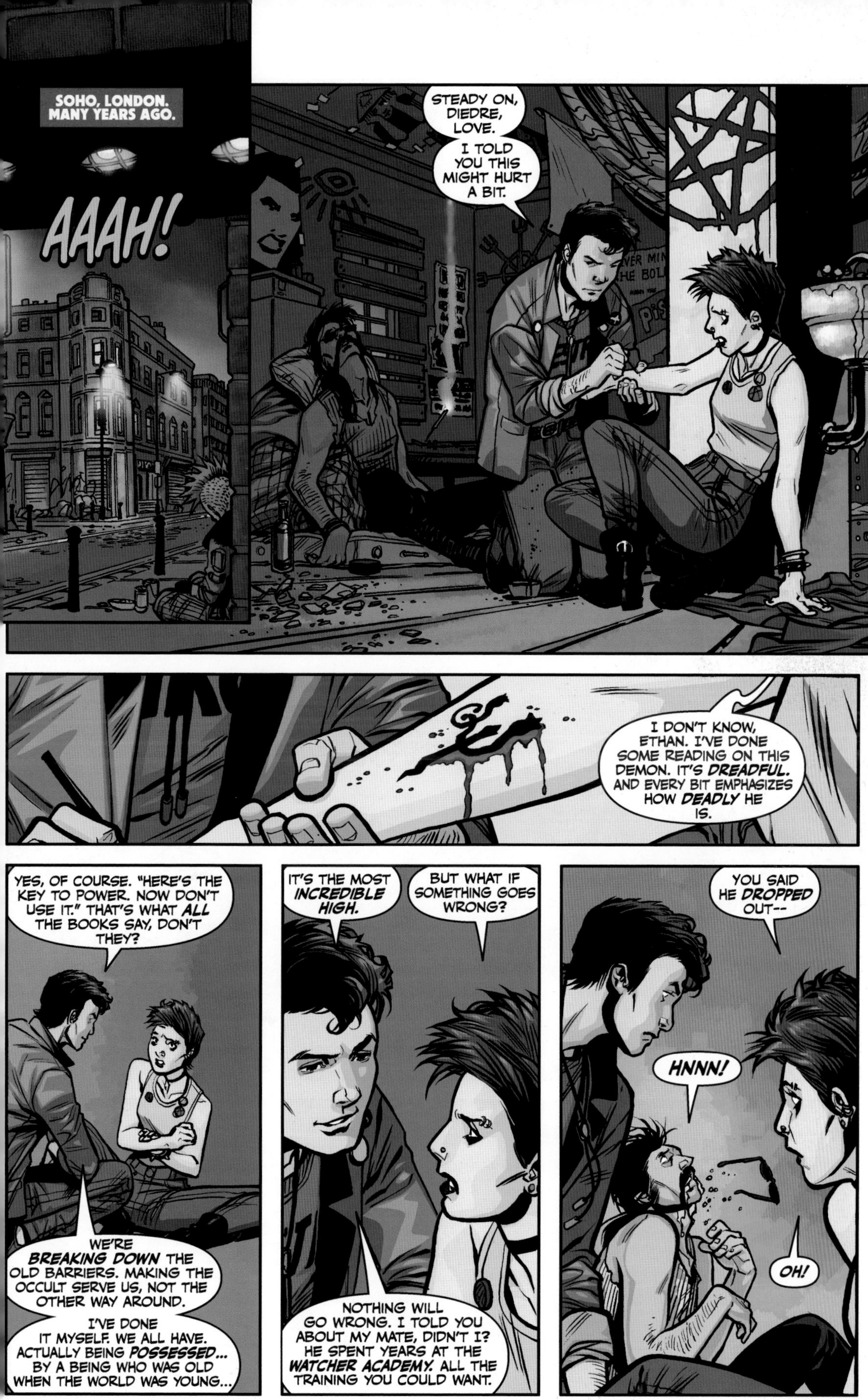
SOHO, LONDON. MANY YEARS AGO.
AAAH!
STEADY ON, DIEDRE, LOVE.
I TOLD YOU THIS MIGHT HURT A BIT.
I DON'T KNOW, ETHAN. I'VE DONE SOME READING ON THIS DEMON. IT'S DREADFUL. AND EVERY BIT EMPHASIZES HOW DEADLY HE IS.
YES, OF COURSE. "HERE'S THE KEY TO POWER. NOW DON'T USE IT." THAT'S WHAT ALL THE BOOKS SAY, DON'T THEY?
WE'RE BREAKING DOWN THE OLD BARRIERS. MAKING THE OCCULT SERVE US, NOT THE OTHER WAY AROUND.
I'VE DONE IT MYSELF. WE ALL HAVE. ACTUALLY BEING POSSESSED... BY A BEING WHO WAS OLD WHEN THE WORLD WAS YOUNG...
IT'S THE MOST INCREDIBLE HIGH.
BUT WHAT IF SOMETHING GOES WRONG?
NOTHING WILL GO WRONG. I TOLD YOU ABOUT MY MATE, DIDN'T I? HE SPENT YEARS AT THE WATCHER ACADEMY. ALL THE TRAINING YOU COULD WANT.
YOU SAID HE DROPPED OUT--
HNNN!
OH!

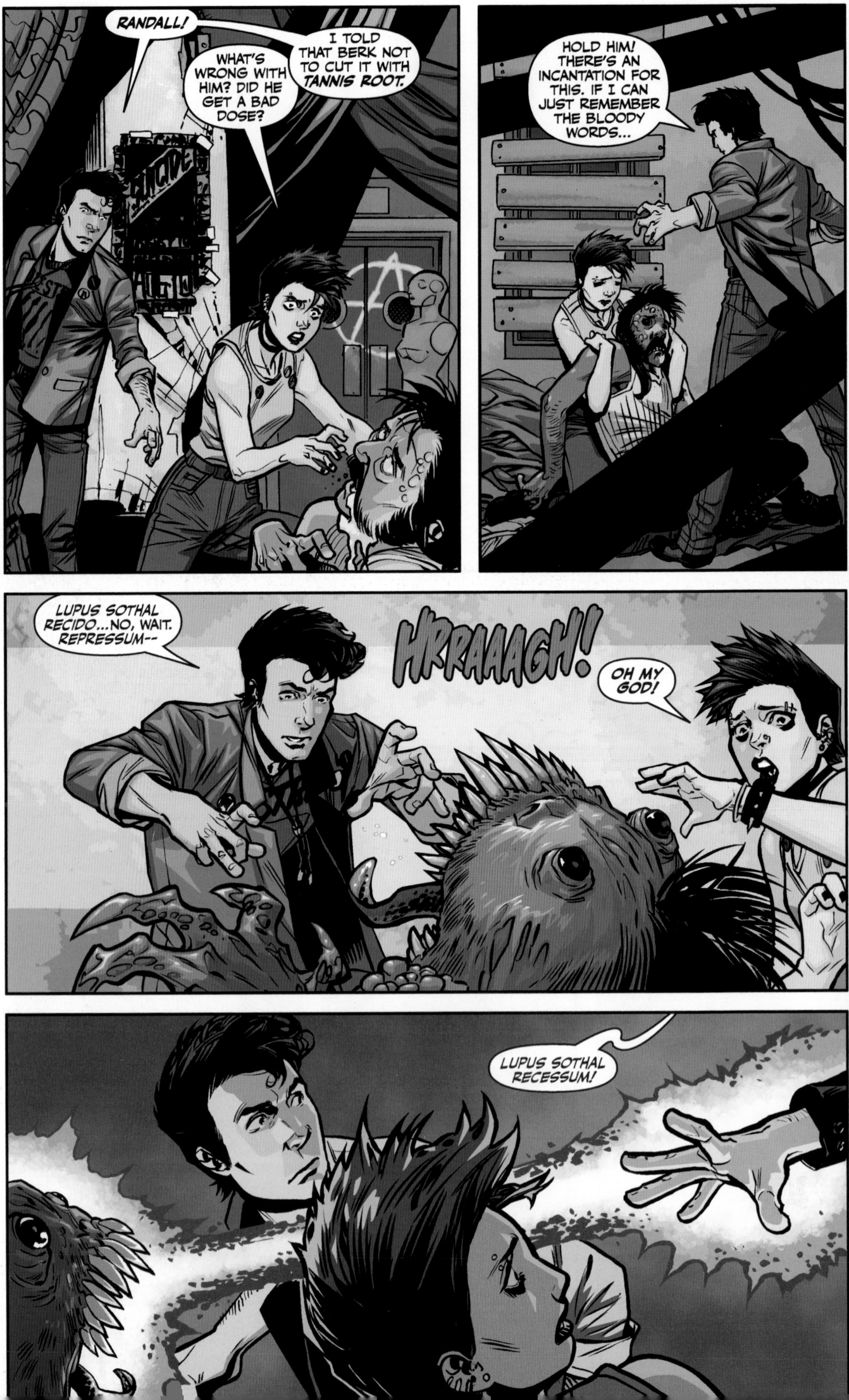

RANDALL!
WHAT'S WRONG WITH HIM? DID HE GET A BAD DOSE?
I TOLD THAT BERK NOT TO CUT IT WITH TANNIS ROOT.
HOLD HIM! THERE'S AN INCANTATION FOR THIS. IF I CAN JUST REMEMBER THE BLOODY WORDS...
LUPUS SOTHAL RECIDO...NO, WAIT. REPRESSUM--
HRRAAAGH!
OH MY GOD!
LUPUS SOTHAL RECESSUM!

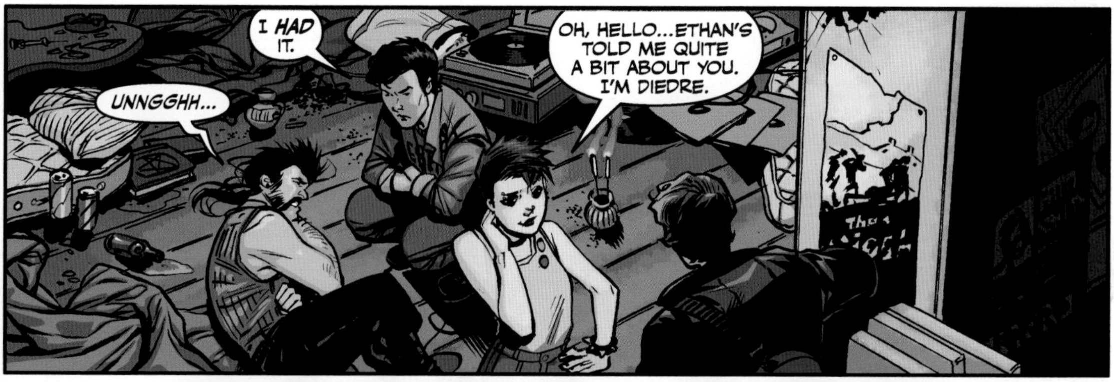
UNNGGHH...
I *HAD* IT.
OH, HELLO...ETHAN'S TOLD ME QUITE A BIT ABOUT YOU. I'M DIEDRE.

DEATH AND CONSEQUENCES

PART 2 OF 4

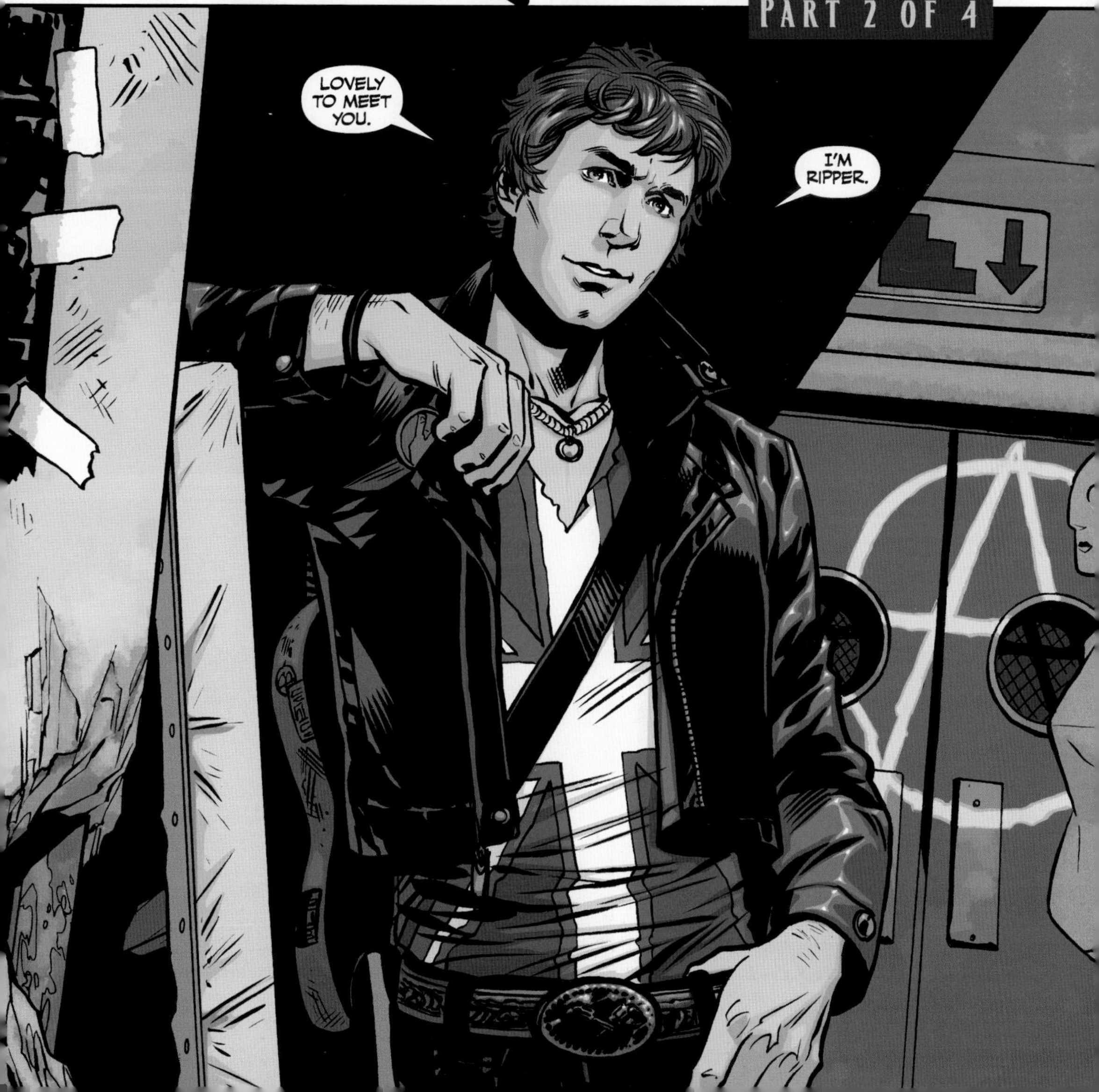
LOVELY TO MEET YOU.
I'M RIPPER.

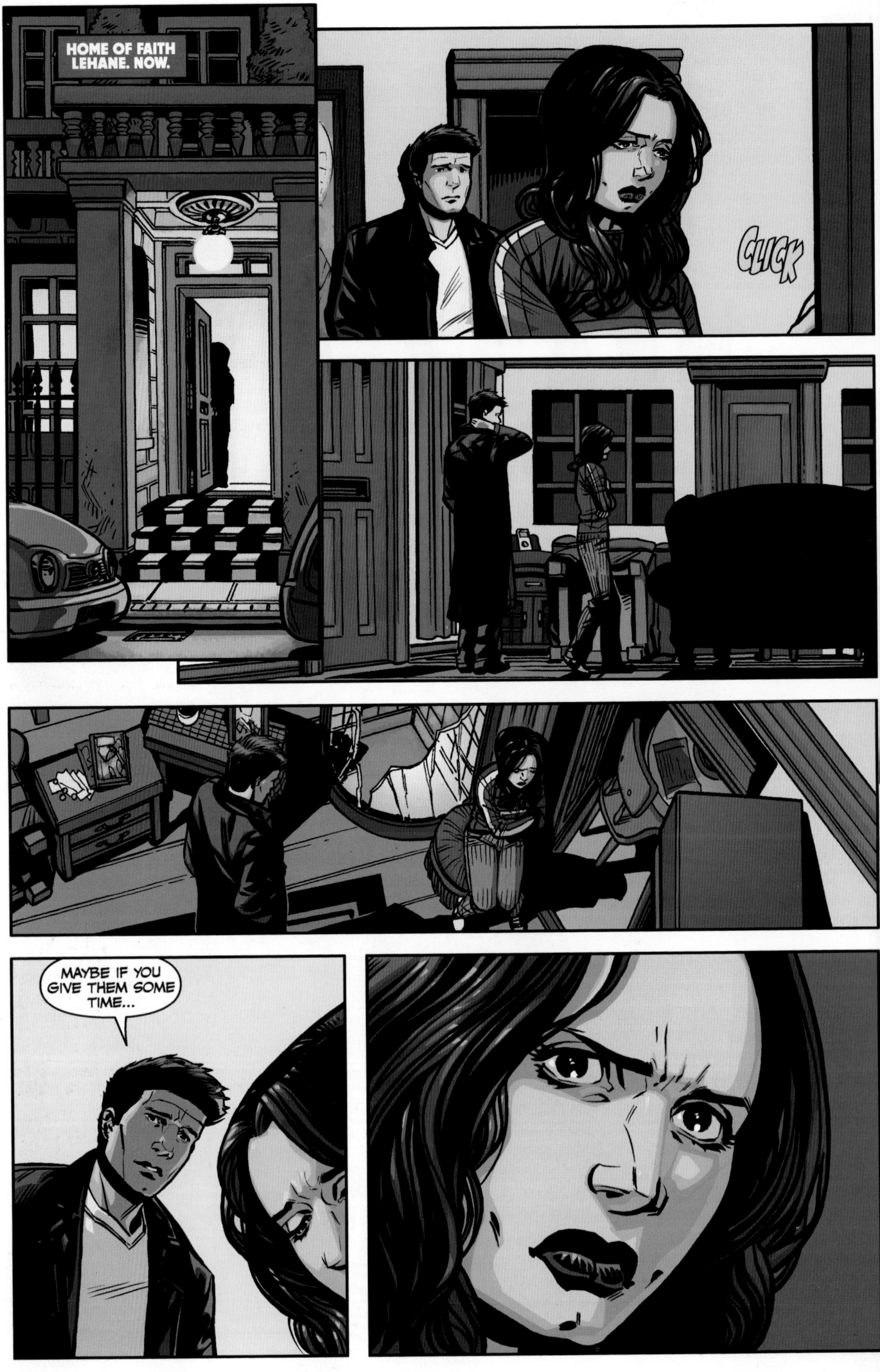
HOME OF FAITH LEHANE. NOW.
CLICK
MAYBE IF YOU GIVE THEM SOME TIME...

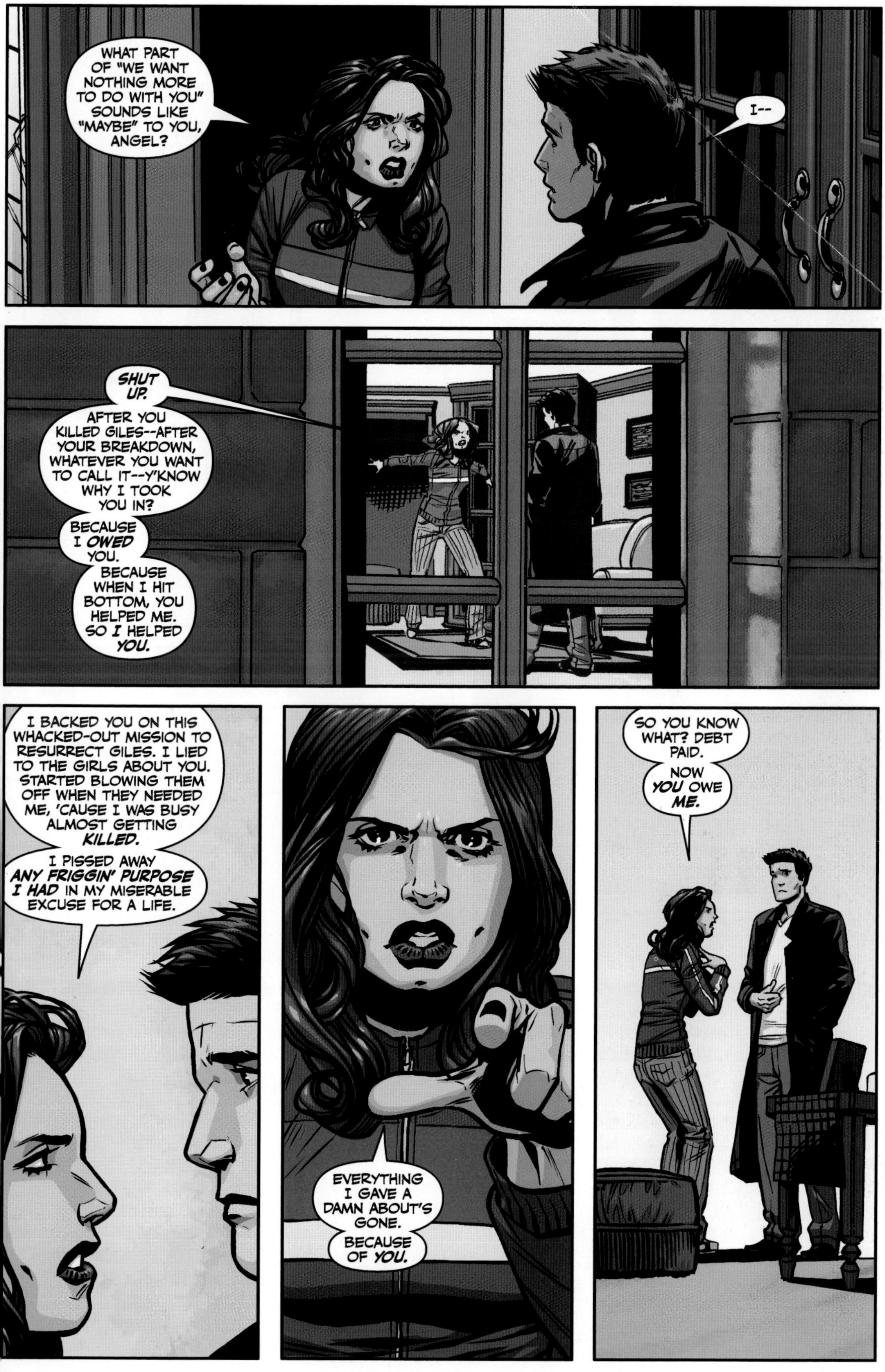

WHAT PART OF "WE WANT NOTHING MORE TO DO WITH YOU" SOUNDS LIKE "MAYBE" TO YOU, ANGEL?
I--
SHUT UP.
AFTER YOU KILLED GILES--AFTER YOUR BREAKDOWN, WHATEVER YOU WANT TO CALL IT--Y'KNOW WHY I TOOK YOU IN?
BECAUSE I OWED YOU.
BECAUSE WHEN I HIT BOTTOM, YOU HELPED ME. SO I HELPED YOU.
I BACKED YOU ON THIS WHACKED-OUT MISSION TO RESURRECT GILES. I LIED TO THE GIRLS ABOUT YOU. STARTED BLOWING THEM OFF WHEN THEY NEEDED ME, 'CAUSE I WAS BUSY ALMOST GETTING KILLED.
I PISSED AWAY ANY FRIGGIN' PURPOSE I HAD IN MY MISERABLE EXCUSE FOR A LIFE.
EVERYTHING I GAVE A DAMN ABOUT'S GONE.
BECAUSE OF YOU.
SO YOU KNOW WHAT? DEBT PAID.
NOW YOU OWE ME.

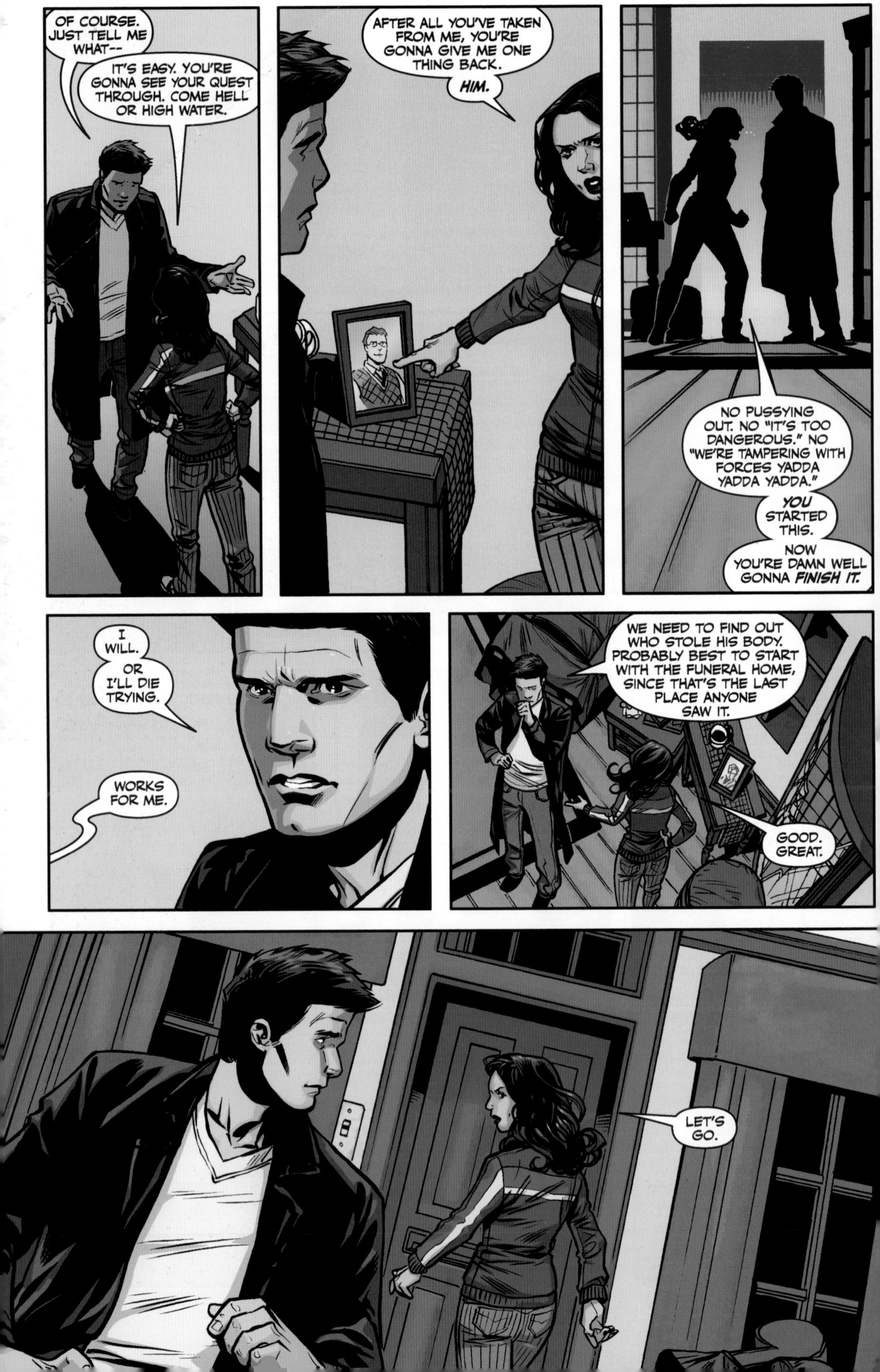
OF COURSE. JUST TELL ME WHAT--
IT'S EASY. YOU'RE GONNA SEE YOUR QUEST THROUGH. COME HELL OR HIGH WATER.
AFTER ALL YOU'VE TAKEN FROM ME, YOU'RE GONNA GIVE ME ONE THING BACK.
HIM.
NO PUSSYING OUT. NO "IT'S TOO DANGEROUS." NO "WE'RE TAMPERING WITH FORCES YADDA YADDA YADDA."
YOU STARTED THIS.
NOW YOU'RE DAMN WELL GONNA FINISH IT.
I WILL. OR I'LL DIE TRYING.
WORKS FOR ME.
WE NEED TO FIND OUT WHO STOLE HIS BODY. PROBABLY BEST TO START WITH THE FUNERAL HOME, SINCE THAT'S THE LAST PLACE ANYONE SAW IT.
GOOD. GREAT.
LET'S GO.

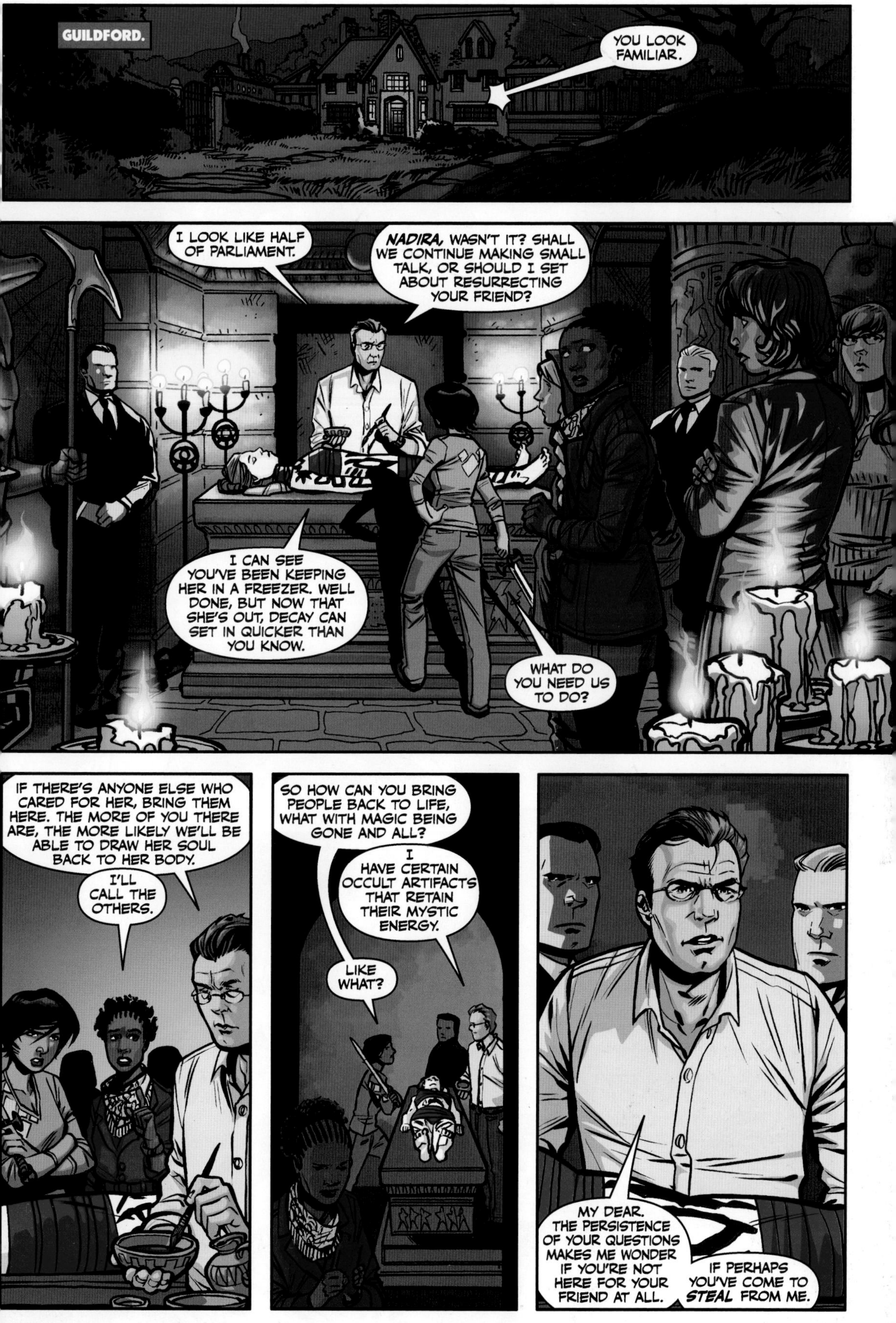
GUILDFORD.
YOU LOOK FAMILIAR.
I LOOK LIKE HALF OF PARLIAMENT.
NADIRA, WASN'T IT? SHALL WE CONTINUE MAKING SMALL TALK, OR SHOULD I SET ABOUT RESURRECTING YOUR FRIEND?
I CAN SEE YOU'VE BEEN KEEPING HER IN A FREEZER. WELL DONE, BUT NOW THAT SHE'S OUT, DECAY CAN SET IN QUICKER THAN YOU KNOW.
WHAT DO YOU NEED US TO DO?
IF THERE'S ANYONE ELSE WHO CARED FOR HER, BRING THEM HERE. THE MORE OF YOU THERE ARE, THE MORE LIKELY WE'LL BE ABLE TO DRAW HER SOUL BACK TO HER BODY.
I'LL CALL THE OTHERS.
SO HOW CAN YOU BRING PEOPLE BACK TO LIFE, WHAT WITH MAGIC BEING GONE AND ALL?
I HAVE CERTAIN OCCULT ARTIFACTS THAT RETAIN THEIR MYSTIC ENERGY.
LIKE WHAT?
MY DEAR. THE PERSISTENCE OF YOUR QUESTIONS MAKES ME WONDER IF YOU'RE NOT HERE FOR YOUR FRIEND AT ALL.
IF PERHAPS YOU'VE COME TO STEAL FROM ME.

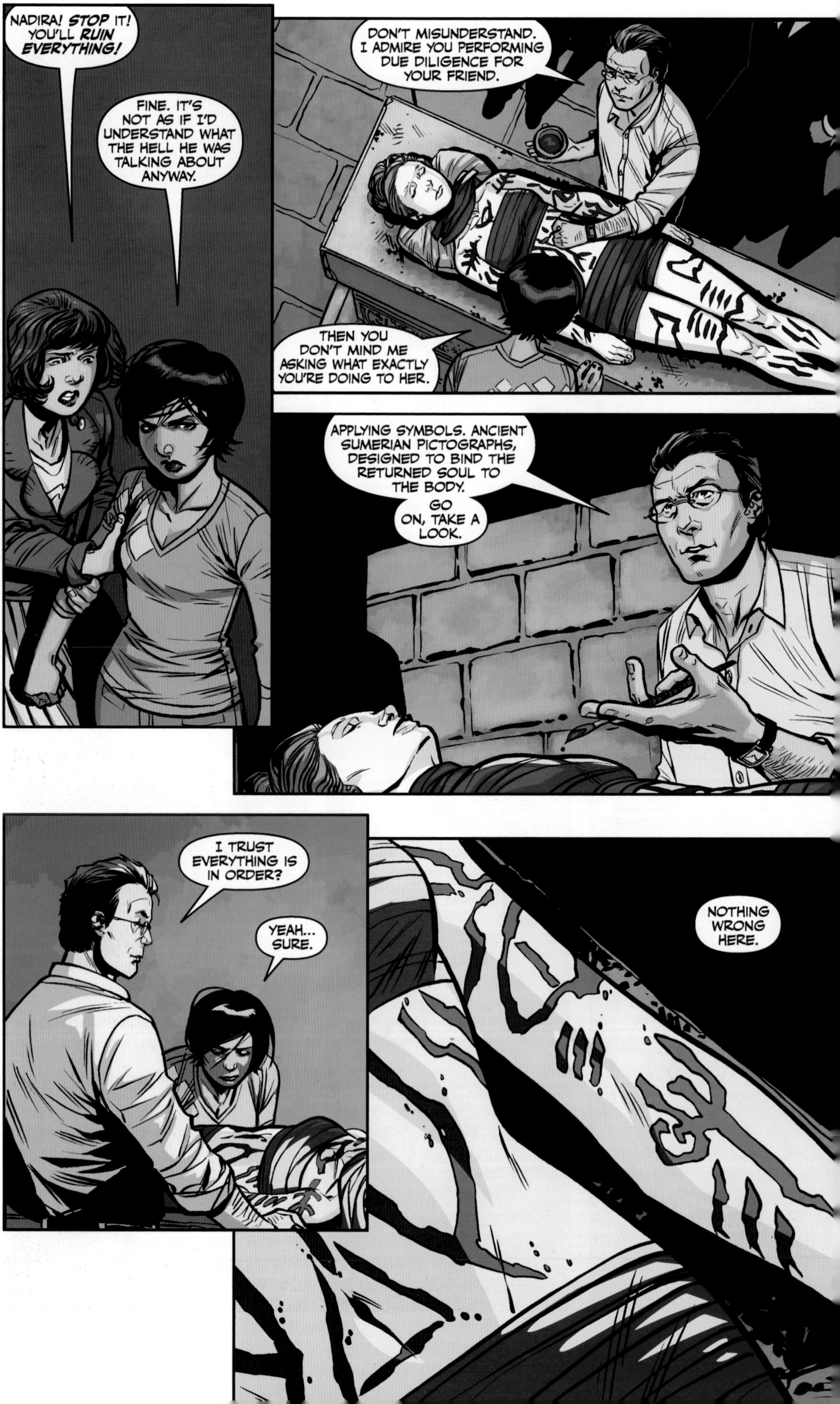
NADIRA! STOP IT! YOU'LL RUIN EVERYTHING!
FINE. IT'S NOT AS IF I'D UNDERSTAND WHAT THE HELL HE WAS TALKING ABOUT ANYWAY.
DON'T MISUNDERSTAND. I ADMIRE YOU PERFORMING DUE DILIGENCE FOR YOUR FRIEND.
THEN YOU DON'T MIND ME ASKING WHAT EXACTLY YOU'RE DOING TO HER.
APPLYING SYMBOLS. ANCIENT SUMERIAN PICTOGRAPHS, DESIGNED TO BIND THE RETURNED SOUL TO THE BODY.
GO ON, TAKE A LOOK.
I TRUST EVERYTHING IS IN ORDER?
YEAH... SURE.
NOTHING WRONG HERE.

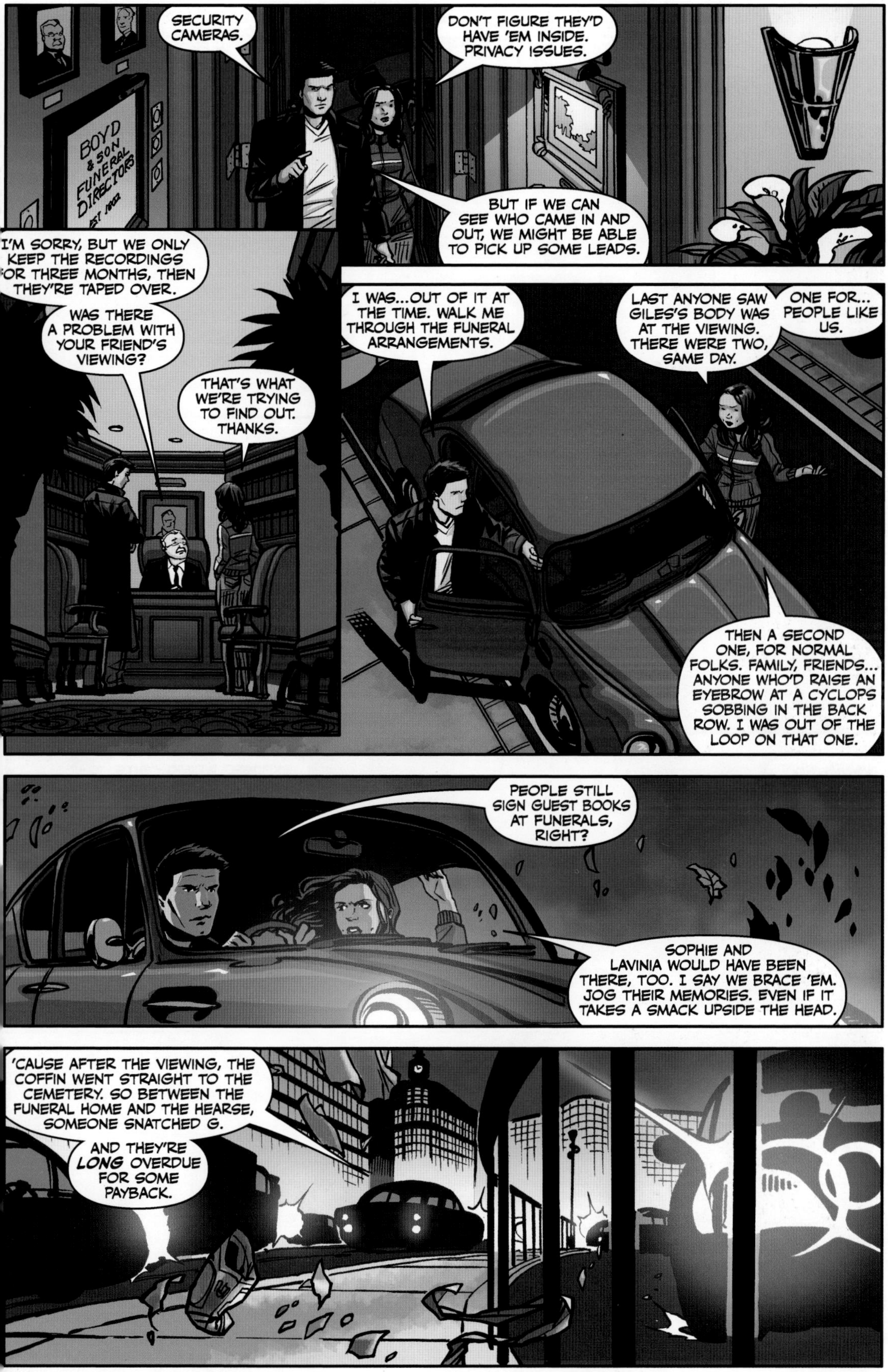
SECURITY CAMERAS.
DON'T FIGURE THEY'D HAVE 'EM INSIDE. PRIVACY ISSUES.
BOYD & SON FUNERAL DIRECTORS EST 1902
BUT IF WE CAN SEE WHO CAME IN AND OUT, WE MIGHT BE ABLE TO PICK UP SOME LEADS.
I'M SORRY, BUT WE ONLY KEEP THE RECORDINGS FOR THREE MONTHS, THEN THEY'RE TAPED OVER.
WAS THERE A PROBLEM WITH YOUR FRIEND'S VIEWING?
THAT'S WHAT WE'RE TRYING TO FIND OUT. THANKS.
I WAS...OUT OF IT AT THE TIME. WALK ME THROUGH THE FUNERAL ARRANGEMENTS.
LAST ANYONE SAW GILES'S BODY WAS AT THE VIEWING. THERE WERE TWO, SAME DAY.
ONE FOR... PEOPLE LIKE US.
THEN A SECOND ONE, FOR NORMAL FOLKS. FAMILY, FRIENDS... ANYONE WHO'D RAISE AN EYEBROW AT A CYCLOPS SOBBING IN THE BACK ROW. I WAS OUT OF THE LOOP ON THAT ONE.
PEOPLE STILL SIGN GUEST BOOKS AT FUNERALS, RIGHT?
SOPHIE AND LAVINIA WOULD HAVE BEEN THERE, TOO. I SAY WE BRACE 'EM. JOG THEIR MEMORIES. EVEN IF IT TAKES A SMACK UPSIDE THE HEAD.
'CAUSE AFTER THE VIEWING, THE COFFIN WENT STRAIGHT TO THE CEMETERY. SO BETWEEN THE FUNERAL HOME AND THE HEARSE, SOMEONE SNATCHED G.
AND THEY'RE *LONG* OVERDUE FOR SOME PAYBACK.

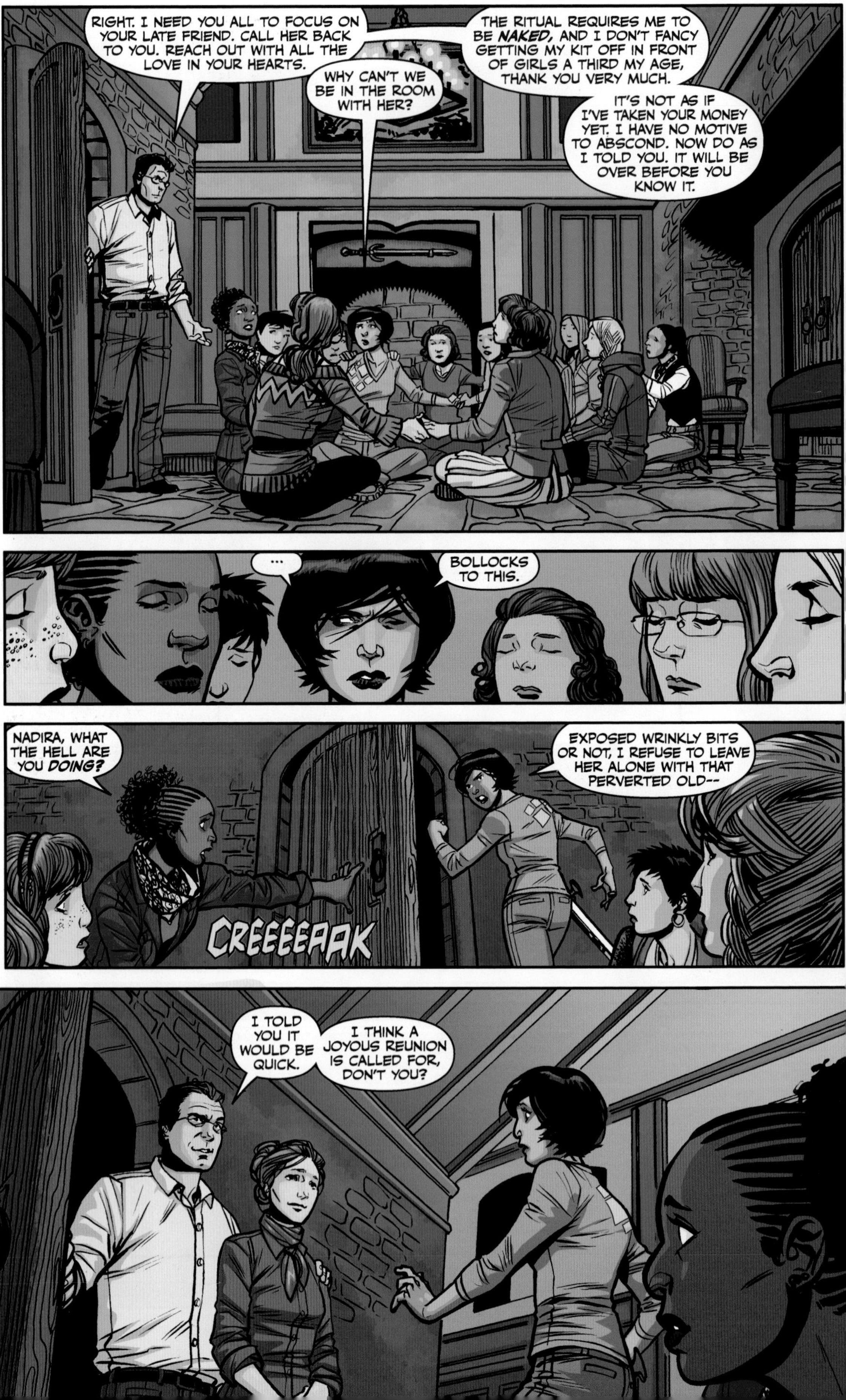
RIGHT. I NEED YOU ALL TO FOCUS ON YOUR LATE FRIEND. CALL HER BACK TO YOU. REACH OUT WITH ALL THE LOVE IN YOUR HEARTS.
WHY CAN'T WE BE IN THE ROOM WITH HER?
THE RITUAL REQUIRES ME TO BE NAKED, AND I DON'T FANCY GETTING MY KIT OFF IN FRONT OF GIRLS A THIRD MY AGE, THANK YOU VERY MUCH.
IT'S NOT AS IF I'VE TAKEN YOUR MONEY YET. I HAVE NO MOTIVE TO ABSCOND. NOW DO AS I TOLD YOU. IT WILL BE OVER BEFORE YOU KNOW IT.
...
BOLLOCKS TO THIS.
NADIRA, WHAT THE HELL ARE YOU DOING?
EXPOSED WRINKLY BITS OR NOT, I REFUSE TO LEAVE HER ALONE WITH THAT PERVERTED OLD--
CREEEEAAK
I TOLD YOU IT WOULD BE QUICK.
I THINK A JOYOUS REUNION IS CALLED FOR, DON'T YOU?

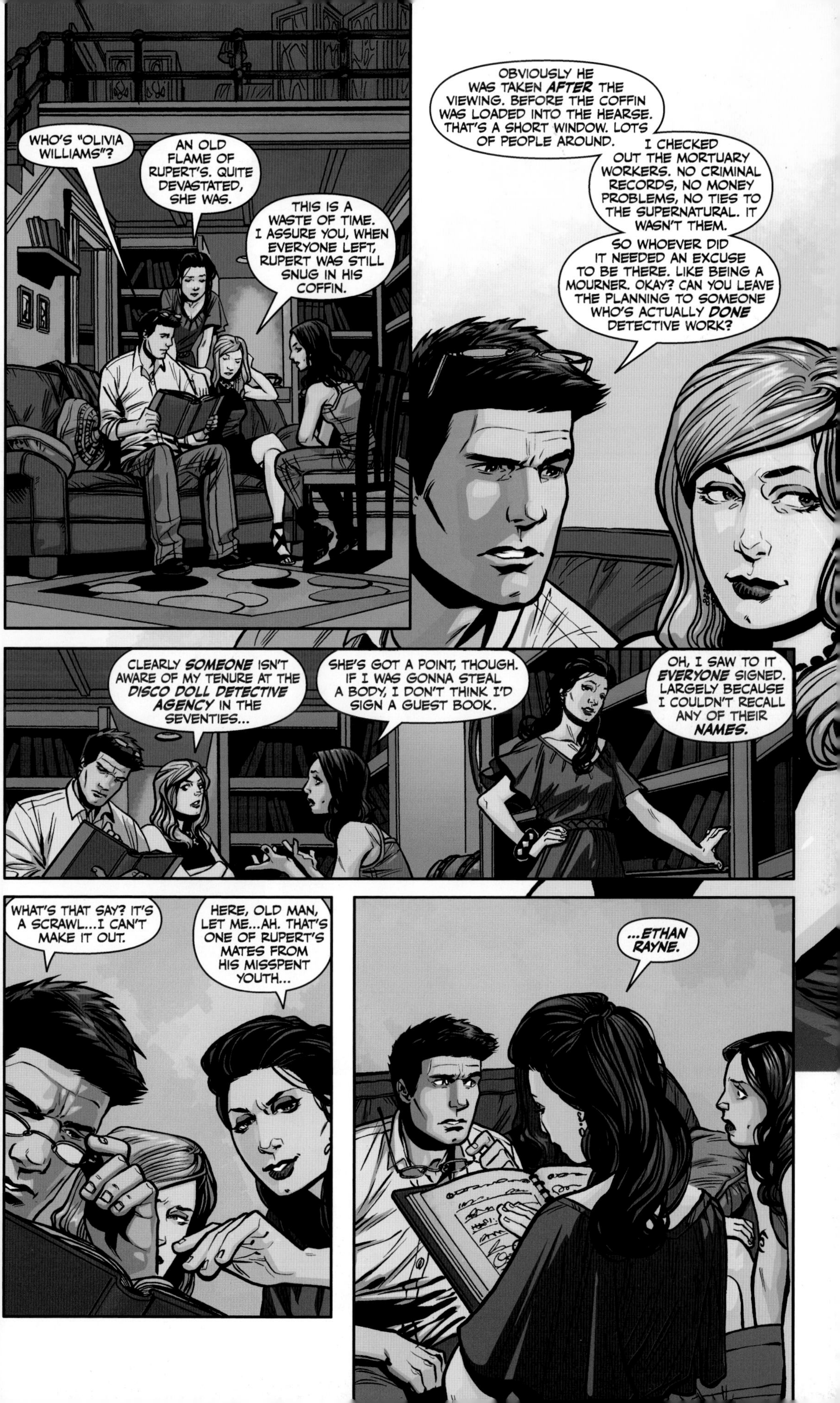
WHO'S "OLIVIA WILLIAMS"?
AN OLD FLAME OF RUPERT'S. QUITE DEVASTATED, SHE WAS.
THIS IS A WASTE OF TIME. I ASSURE YOU, WHEN EVERYONE LEFT, RUPERT WAS STILL SNUG IN HIS COFFIN.
OBVIOUSLY HE WAS TAKEN AFTER THE VIEWING. BEFORE THE COFFIN WAS LOADED INTO THE HEARSE. THAT'S A SHORT WINDOW. LOTS OF PEOPLE AROUND.
I CHECKED OUT THE MORTUARY WORKERS. NO CRIMINAL RECORDS, NO MONEY PROBLEMS, NO TIES TO THE SUPERNATURAL. IT WASN'T THEM.
SO WHOEVER DID IT NEEDED AN EXCUSE TO BE THERE. LIKE BEING A MOURNER. OKAY? CAN YOU LEAVE THE PLANNING TO SOMEONE WHO'S ACTUALLY DONE DETECTIVE WORK?
CLEARLY SOMEONE ISN'T AWARE OF MY TENURE AT THE DISCO DOLL DETECTIVE AGENCY IN THE SEVENTIES...
SHE'S GOT A POINT, THOUGH. IF I WAS GONNA STEAL A BODY, I DON'T THINK I'D SIGN A GUEST BOOK.
OH, I SAW TO IT EVERYONE SIGNED. LARGELY BECAUSE I COULDN'T RECALL ANY OF THEIR NAMES.
WHAT'S THAT SAY? IT'S A SCRAWL...I CAN'T MAKE IT OUT.
HERE, OLD MAN, LET ME...AH. THAT'S ONE OF RUPERT'S MATES FROM HIS MISSPENT YOUTH...
...ETHAN RAYNE.

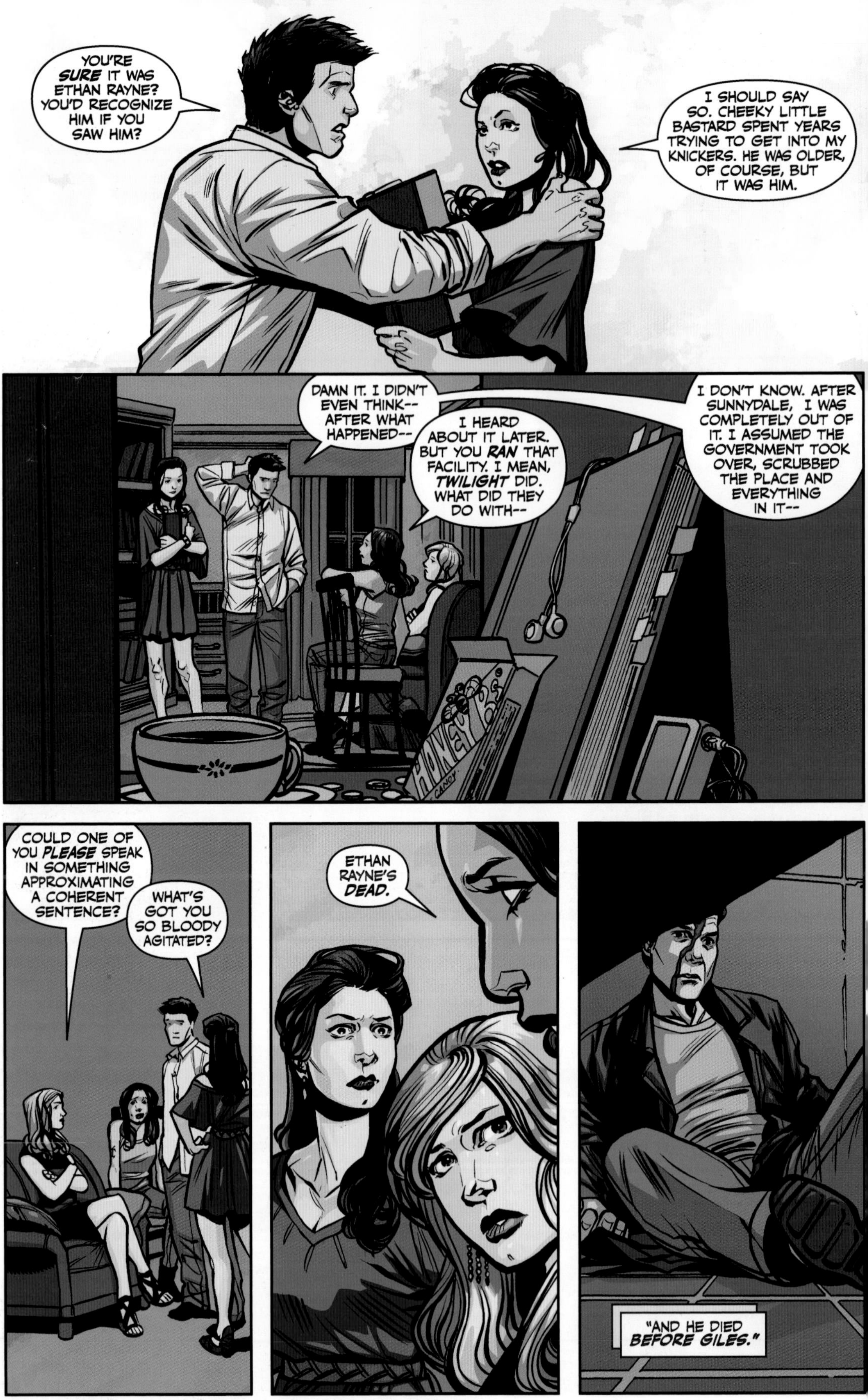
YOU'RE SURE IT WAS ETHAN RAYNE? YOU'D RECOGNIZE HIM IF YOU SAW HIM?
I SHOULD SAY SO. CHEEKY LITTLE BASTARD SPENT YEARS TRYING TO GET INTO MY KNICKERS. HE WAS OLDER, OF COURSE, BUT IT WAS HIM.
DAMN IT. I DIDN'T EVEN THINK-- AFTER WHAT HAPPENED--
I HEARD ABOUT IT LATER. BUT YOU RAN THAT FACILITY. I MEAN, TWILIGHT DID. WHAT DID THEY DO WITH--
I DON'T KNOW. AFTER SUNNYDALE, I WAS COMPLETELY OUT OF IT. I ASSUMED THE GOVERNMENT TOOK OVER, SCRUBBED THE PLACE AND EVERYTHING IN IT--
HONEY
COULD ONE OF YOU PLEASE SPEAK IN SOMETHING APPROXIMATING A COHERENT SENTENCE?
WHAT'S GOT YOU SO BLOODY AGITATED?
ETHAN RAYNE'S DEAD.
"AND HE DIED BEFORE GILES."

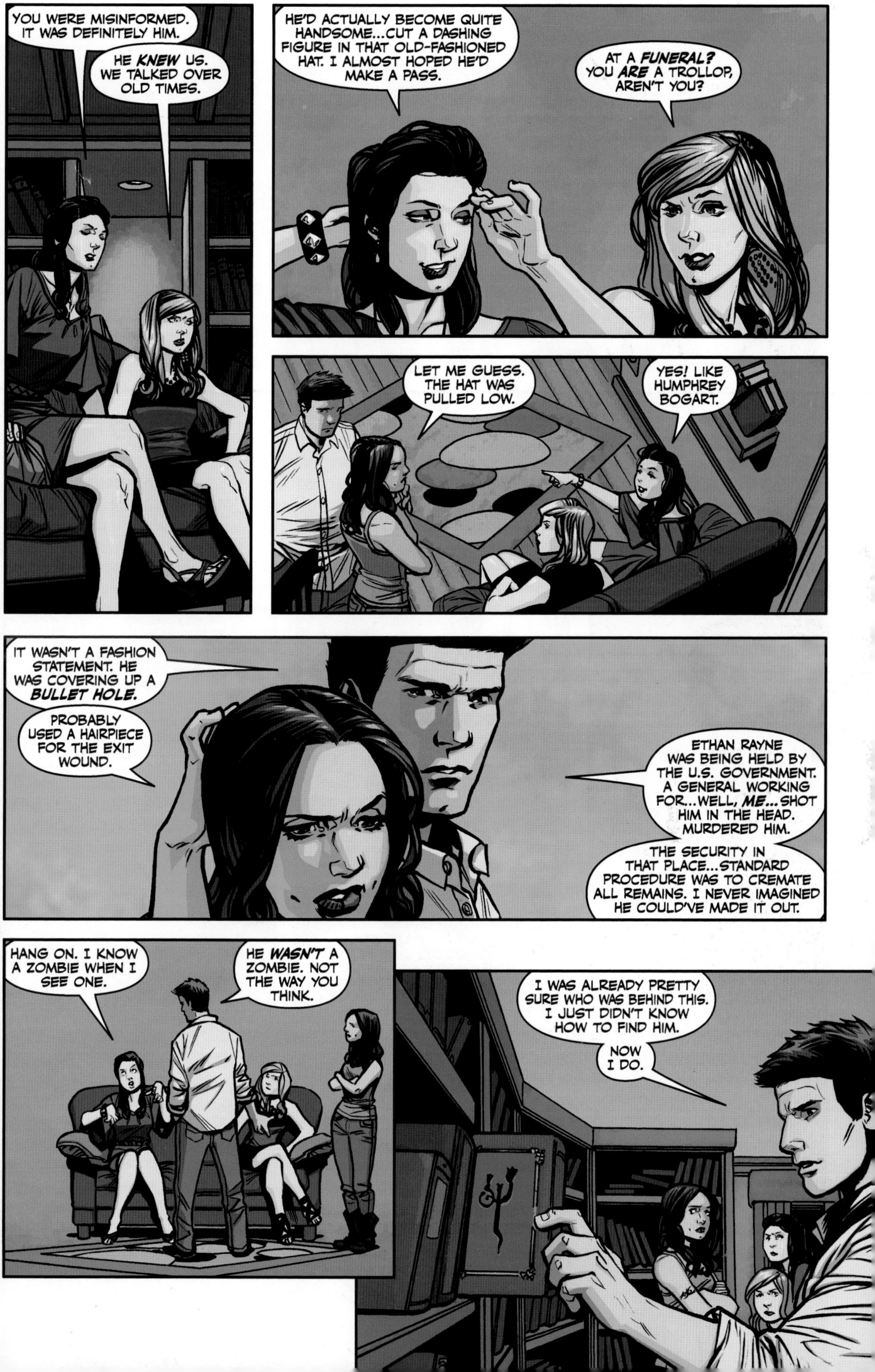
YOU WERE MISINFORMED. IT WAS DEFINITELY HIM.
HE KNEW US. WE TALKED OVER OLD TIMES.
HE'D ACTUALLY BECOME QUITE HANDSOME...CUT A DASHING FIGURE IN THAT OLD-FASHIONED HAT. I ALMOST HOPED HE'D MAKE A PASS.
AT A FUNERAL? YOU ARE A TROLLOP, AREN'T YOU?
LET ME GUESS. THE HAT WAS PULLED LOW.
YES! LIKE HUMPHREY BOGART.
IT WASN'T A FASHION STATEMENT. HE WAS COVERING UP A BULLET HOLE.
PROBABLY USED A HAIRPIECE FOR THE EXIT WOUND.
ETHAN RAYNE WAS BEING HELD BY THE U.S. GOVERNMENT. A GENERAL WORKING FOR...WELL, ME...SHOT HIM IN THE HEAD. MURDERED HIM.
THE SECURITY IN THAT PLACE...STANDARD PROCEDURE WAS TO CREMATE ALL REMAINS. I NEVER IMAGINED HE COULD'VE MADE IT OUT.
HANG ON. I KNOW A ZOMBIE WHEN I SEE ONE.
HE WASN'T A ZOMBIE. NOT THE WAY YOU THINK.
I WAS ALREADY PRETTY SURE WHO WAS BEHIND THIS. I JUST DIDN'T KNOW HOW TO FIND HIM.
NOW I DO.

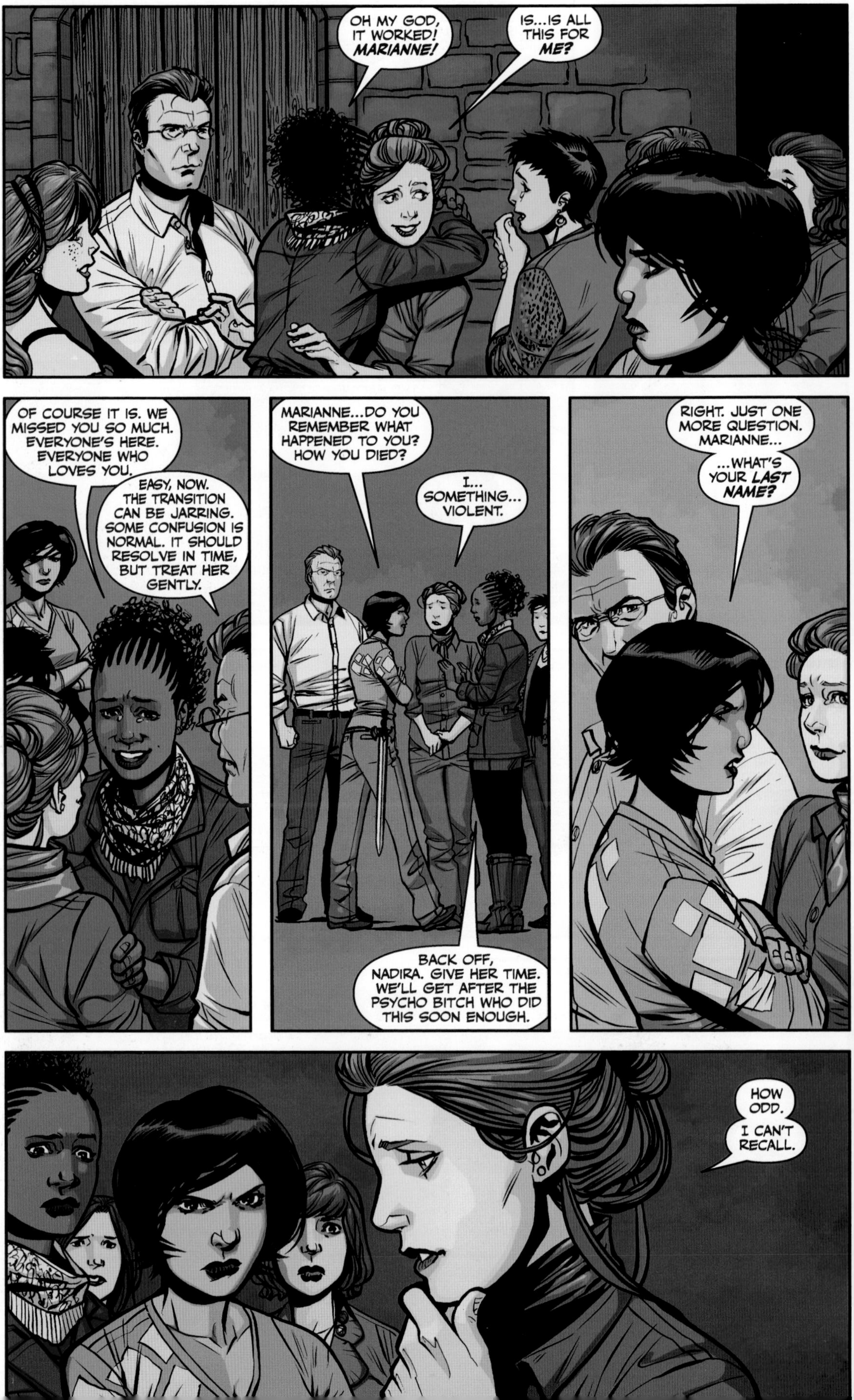
OH MY GOD, IT WORKED! MARIANNE!
IS...IS ALL THIS FOR ME?
OF COURSE IT IS. WE MISSED YOU SO MUCH. EVERYONE'S HERE. EVERYONE WHO LOVES YOU.
EASY, NOW. THE TRANSITION CAN BE JARRING. SOME CONFUSION IS NORMAL. IT SHOULD RESOLVE IN TIME, BUT TREAT HER GENTLY.
MARIANNE...DO YOU REMEMBER WHAT HAPPENED TO YOU? HOW YOU DIED?
I... SOMETHING... VIOLENT.
BACK OFF, NADIRA. GIVE HER TIME. WE'LL GET AFTER THE PSYCHO BITCH WHO DID THIS SOON ENOUGH.
RIGHT. JUST ONE MORE QUESTION. MARIANNE...
...WHAT'S YOUR LAST NAME?
HOW ODD.
I CAN'T RECALL.

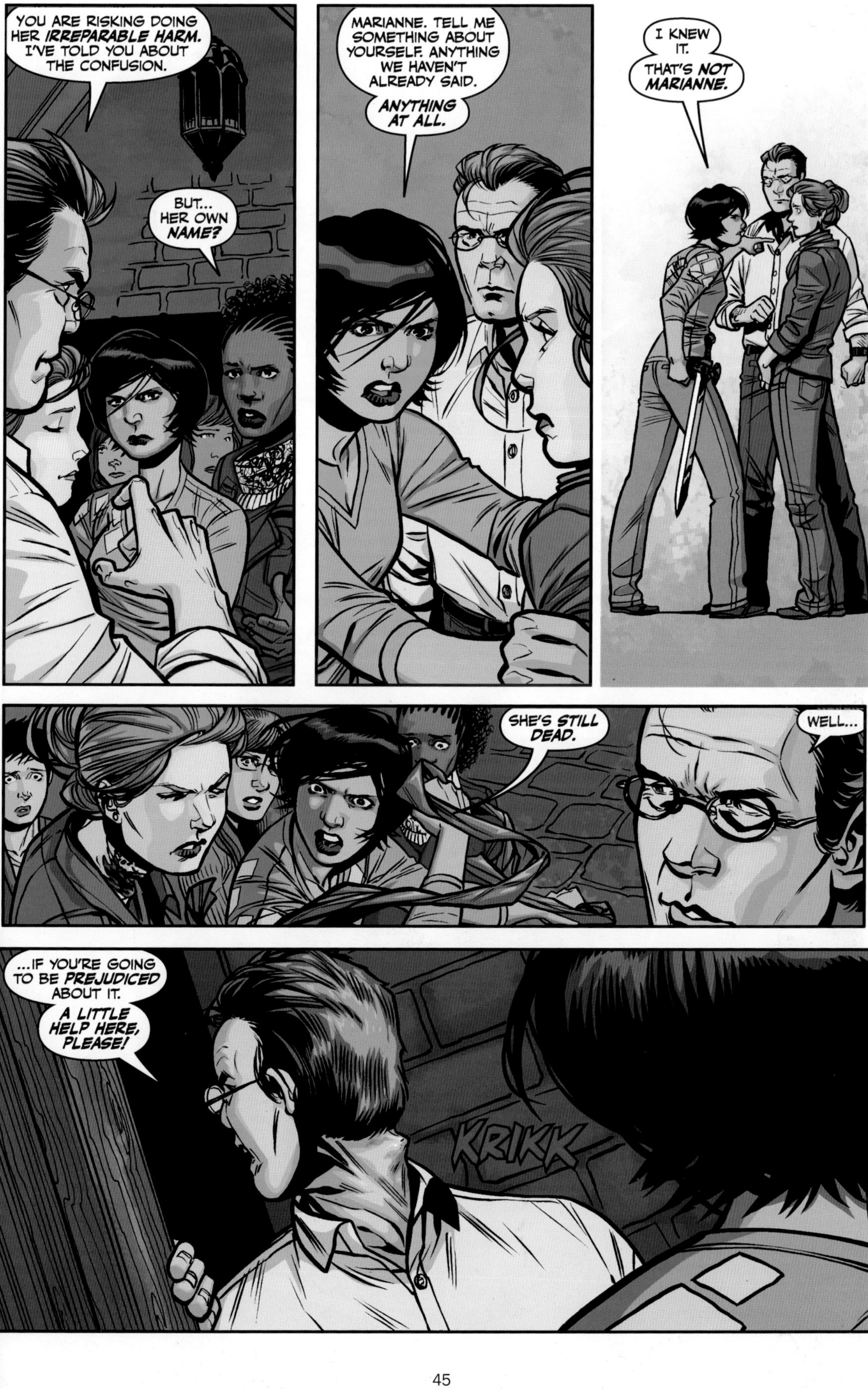
YOU ARE RISKING DOING HER IRREPARABLE HARM. I'VE TOLD YOU ABOUT THE CONFUSION.
BUT... HER OWN NAME?
MARIANNE. TELL ME SOMETHING ABOUT YOURSELF. ANYTHING WE HAVEN'T ALREADY SAID.
ANYTHING AT ALL.
I KNEW IT.
THAT'S NOT MARIANNE.
SHE'S STILL DEAD.
WELL...
...IF YOU'RE GOING TO BE PREJUDICED ABOUT IT.
A LITTLE HELP HERE, PLEASE!
KRIKK

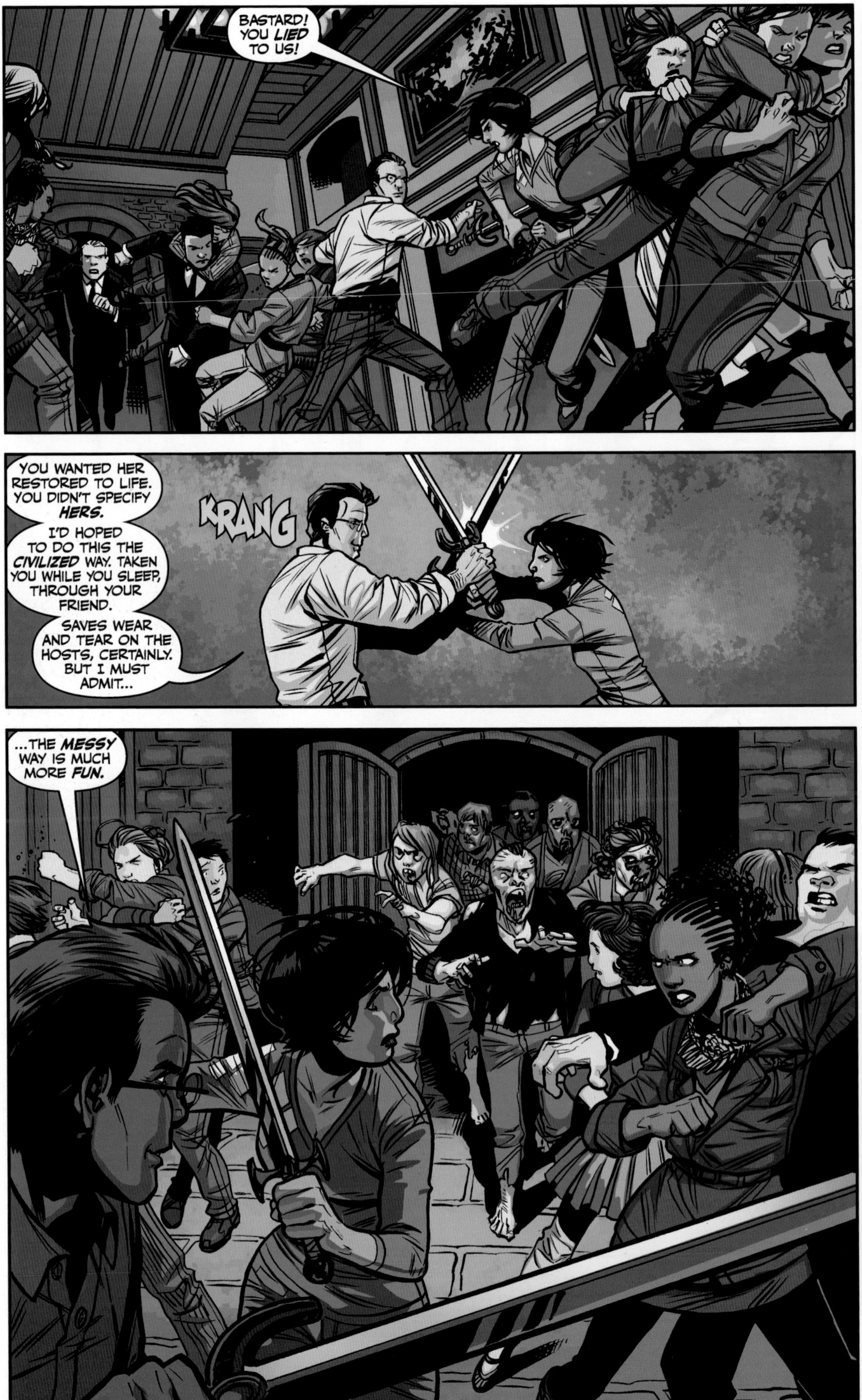
BASTARD! YOU LIED TO US!
YOU WANTED HER RESTORED TO LIFE. YOU DIDN'T SPECIFY HERS.
I'D HOPED TO DO THIS THE CIVILIZED WAY. TAKEN YOU WHILE YOU SLEEP, THROUGH YOUR FRIEND.
SAVES WEAR AND TEAR ON THE HOSTS, CERTAINLY. BUT I MUST ADMIT...
KRANG
...THE MESSY WAY IS MUCH MORE FUN.

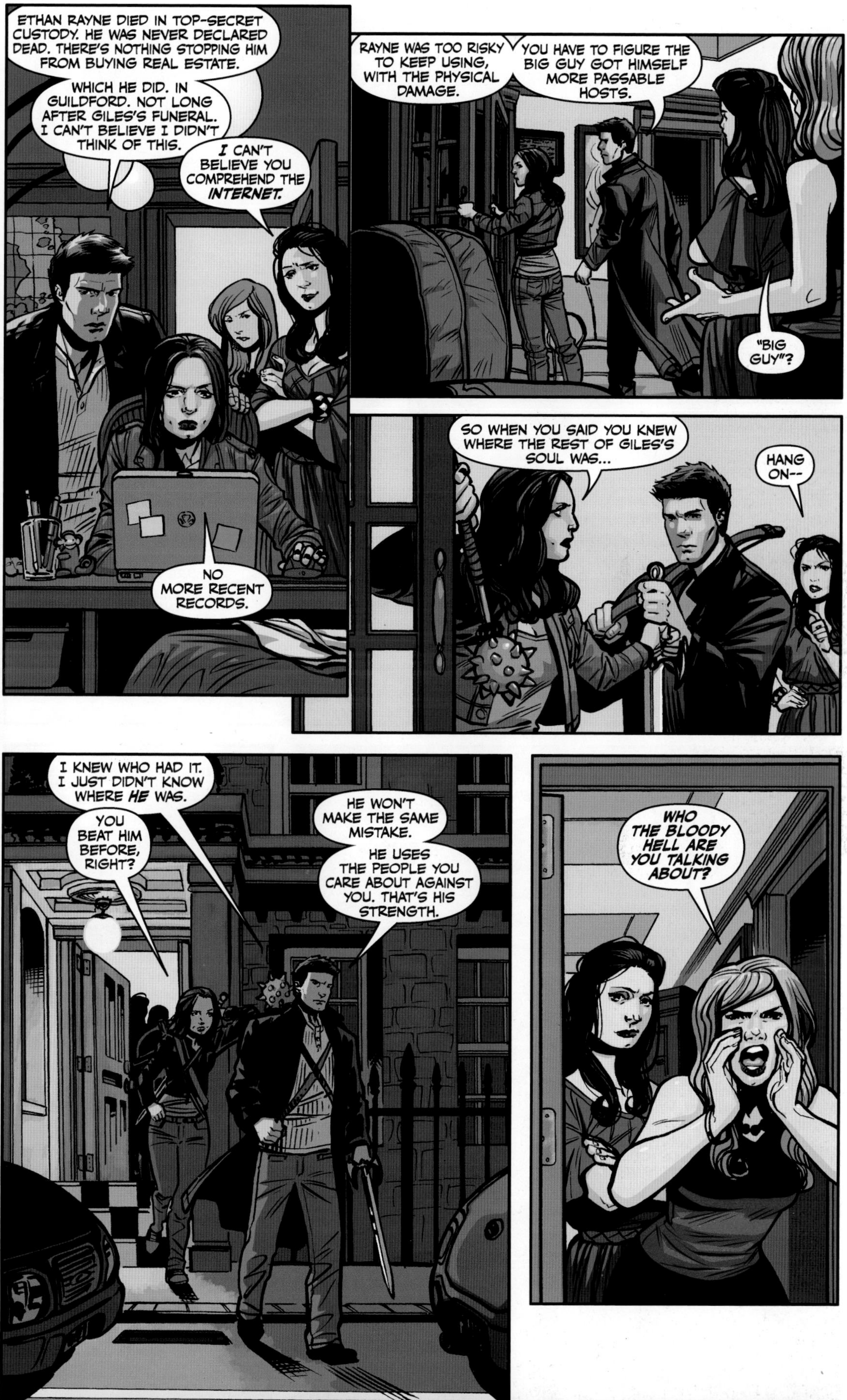

ETHAN RAYNE DIED IN TOP-SECRET CUSTODY. HE WAS NEVER DECLARED DEAD. THERE'S NOTHING STOPPING HIM FROM BUYING REAL ESTATE.
WHICH HE DID. IN GUILDFORD. NOT LONG AFTER GILES'S FUNERAL. I CAN'T BELIEVE I DIDN'T THINK OF THIS.
I CAN'T BELIEVE YOU COMPREHEND THE *INTERNET.*
NO MORE RECENT RECORDS.
RAYNE WAS TOO RISKY TO KEEP USING, WITH THE PHYSICAL DAMAGE.
YOU HAVE TO FIGURE THE BIG GUY GOT HIMSELF MORE PASSABLE HOSTS.
"BIG GUY"?
SO WHEN YOU SAID YOU KNEW WHERE THE REST OF GILES'S SOUL WAS...
HANG ON--
I KNEW WHO HAD IT. I JUST DIDN'T KNOW WHERE *HE* WAS.
YOU BEAT HIM BEFORE, RIGHT?
HE WON'T MAKE THE SAME MISTAKE.
HE USES THE PEOPLE YOU CARE ABOUT AGAINST YOU. THAT'S HIS STRENGTH.
WHO THE BLOODY HELL ARE YOU TALKING ABOUT?

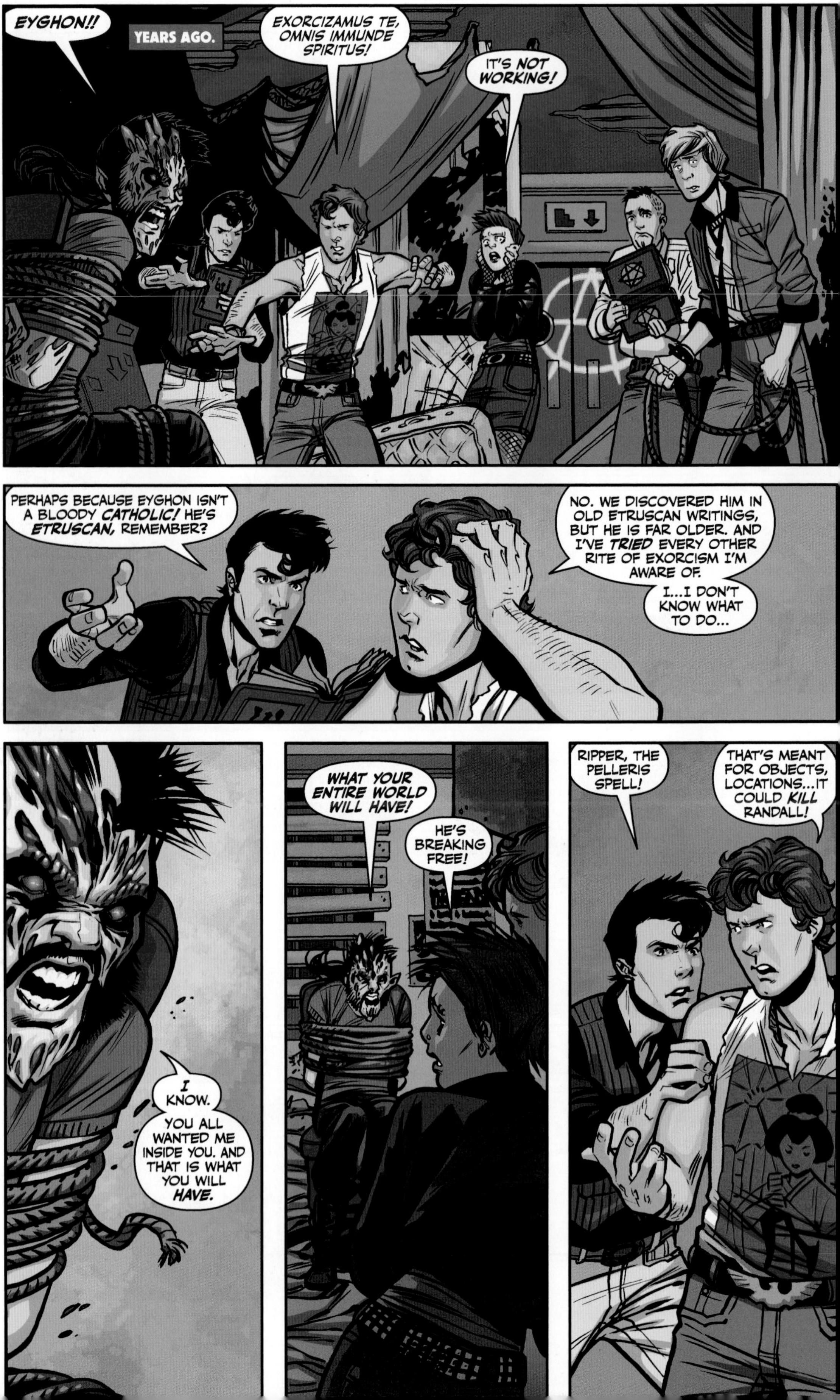
EYGHON!!
YEARS AGO.
EXORCIZAMUS TE, OMNIS IMMUNDE SPIRITUS!
IT'S NOT WORKING!
PERHAPS BECAUSE EYGHON ISN'T A BLOODY CATHOLIC! HE'S ETRUSCAN, REMEMBER?
NO. WE DISCOVERED HIM IN OLD ETRUSCAN WRITINGS, BUT HE IS FAR OLDER. AND I'VE TRIED EVERY OTHER RITE OF EXORCISM I'M AWARE OF.
I...I DON'T KNOW WHAT TO DO...
I KNOW.
YOU ALL WANTED ME INSIDE YOU. AND THAT IS WHAT YOU WILL HAVE.
WHAT YOUR ENTIRE WORLD WILL HAVE!
HE'S BREAKING FREE!
RIPPER, THE PELLERIS SPELL!
THAT'S MEANT FOR OBJECTS, LOCATIONS...IT COULD KILL RANDALL!

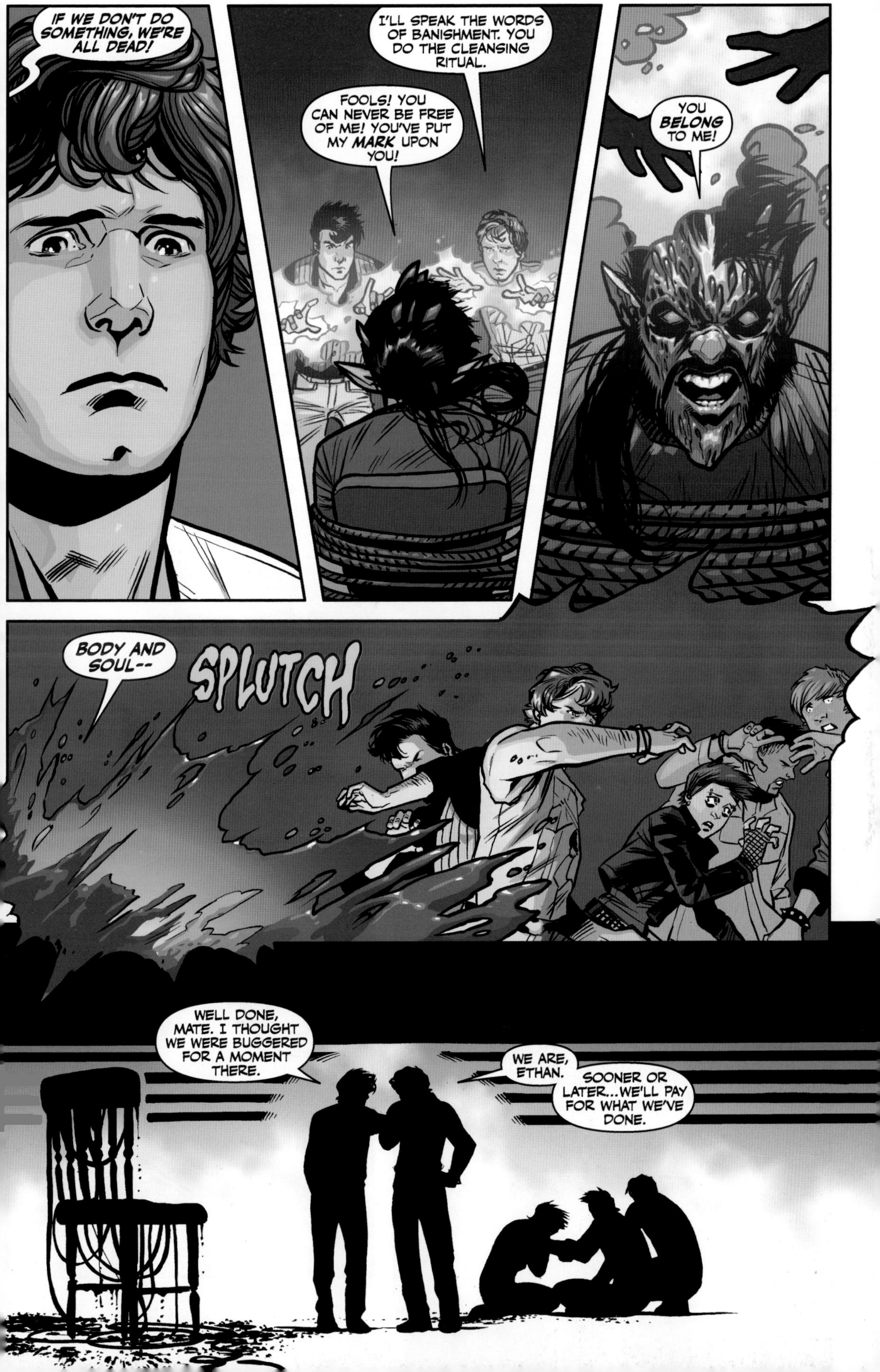

IF WE DON'T DO SOMETHING, WE'RE ALL DEAD!
I'LL SPEAK THE WORDS OF BANISHMENT. YOU DO THE CLEANSING RITUAL.
FOOLS! YOU CAN NEVER BE FREE OF ME! YOU'VE PUT MY MARK UPON YOU!
YOU BELONG TO ME!
BODY AND SOUL--
SPLUTCH
WELL DONE, MATE. I THOUGHT WE WERE BUGGERED FOR A MOMENT THERE.
WE ARE, ETHAN.
SOONER OR LATER...WE'LL PAY FOR WHAT WE'VE DONE.

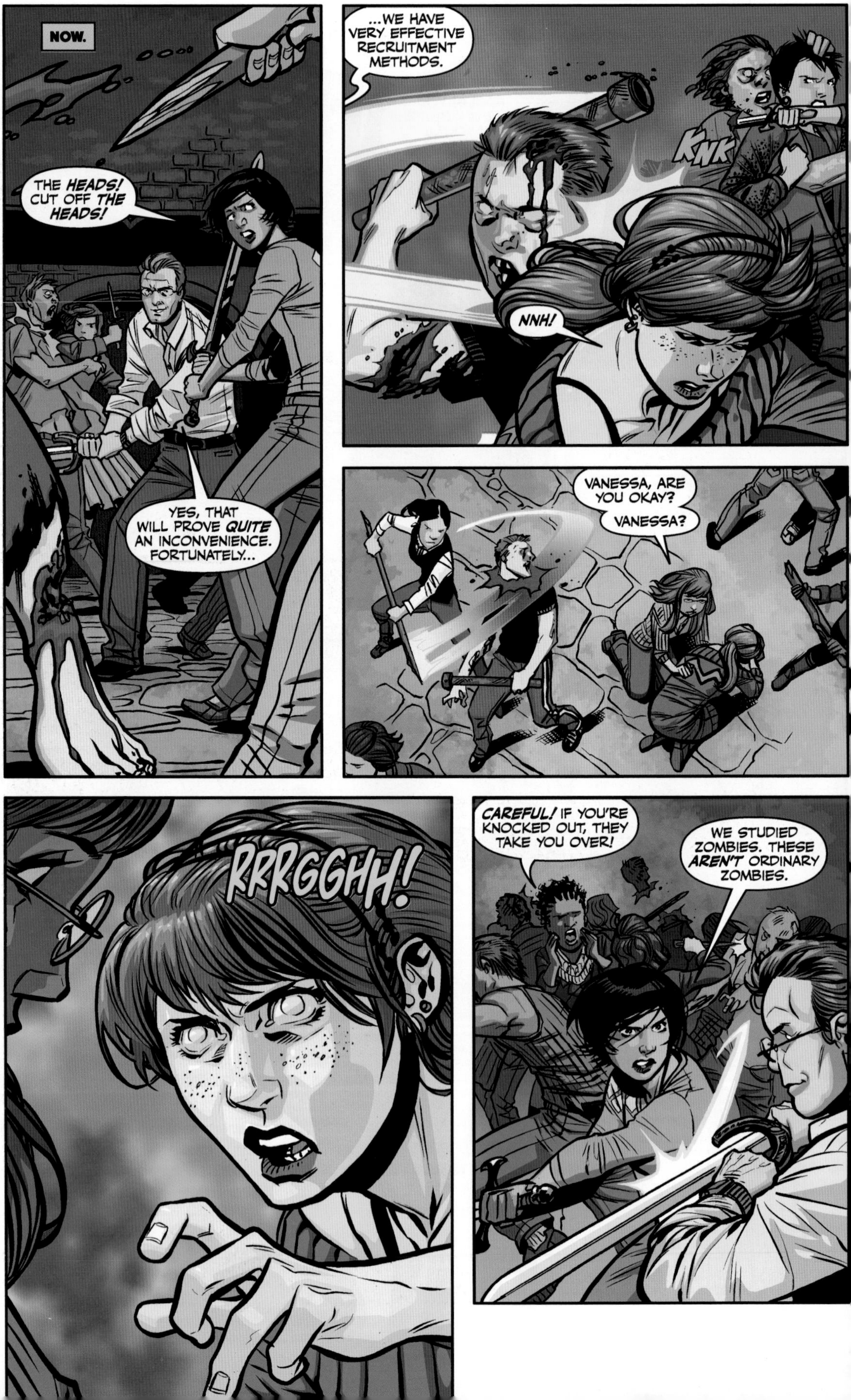
NOW.
THE HEADS! CUT OFF THE HEADS!
YES, THAT WILL PROVE QUITE AN INCONVENIENCE. FORTUNATELY...
...WE HAVE VERY EFFECTIVE RECRUITMENT METHODS.
KNK
NNH!
VANESSA, ARE YOU OKAY?
VANESSA?
RRRGGHH!
CAREFUL! IF YOU'RE KNOCKED OUT, THEY TAKE YOU OVER!
WE STUDIED ZOMBIES. THESE AREN'T ORDINARY ZOMBIES.

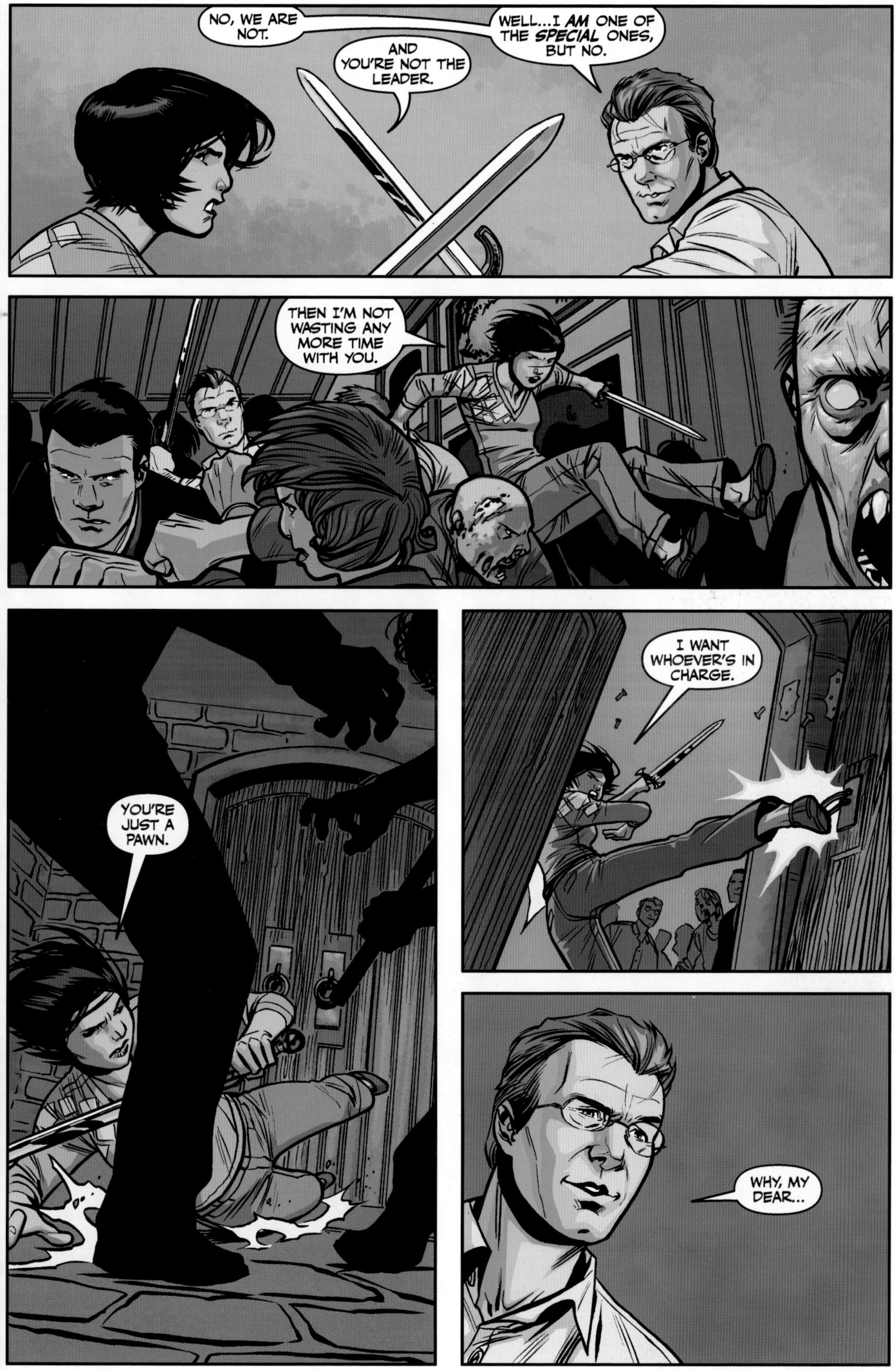
NO, WE ARE NOT.
AND YOU'RE NOT THE LEADER.
WELL...I AM ONE OF THE SPECIAL ONES, BUT NO.
THEN I'M NOT WASTING ANY MORE TIME WITH YOU.
YOU'RE JUST A PAWN.
I WANT WHOEVER'S IN CHARGE.
WHY, MY DEAR...

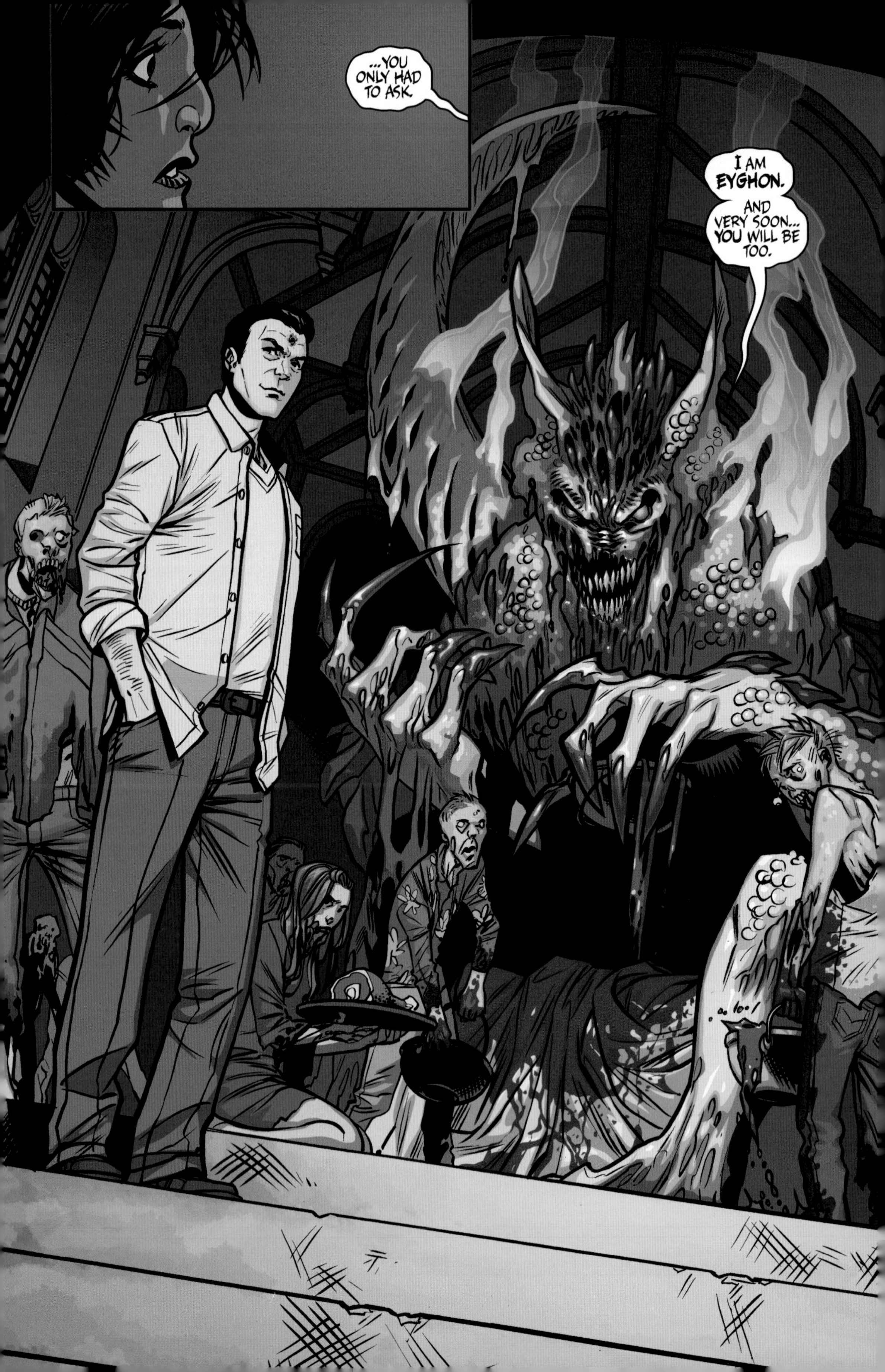
...YOU ONLY HAD TO ASK.
I AM EYGHON.
AND VERY SOON... YOU WILL BE TOO.

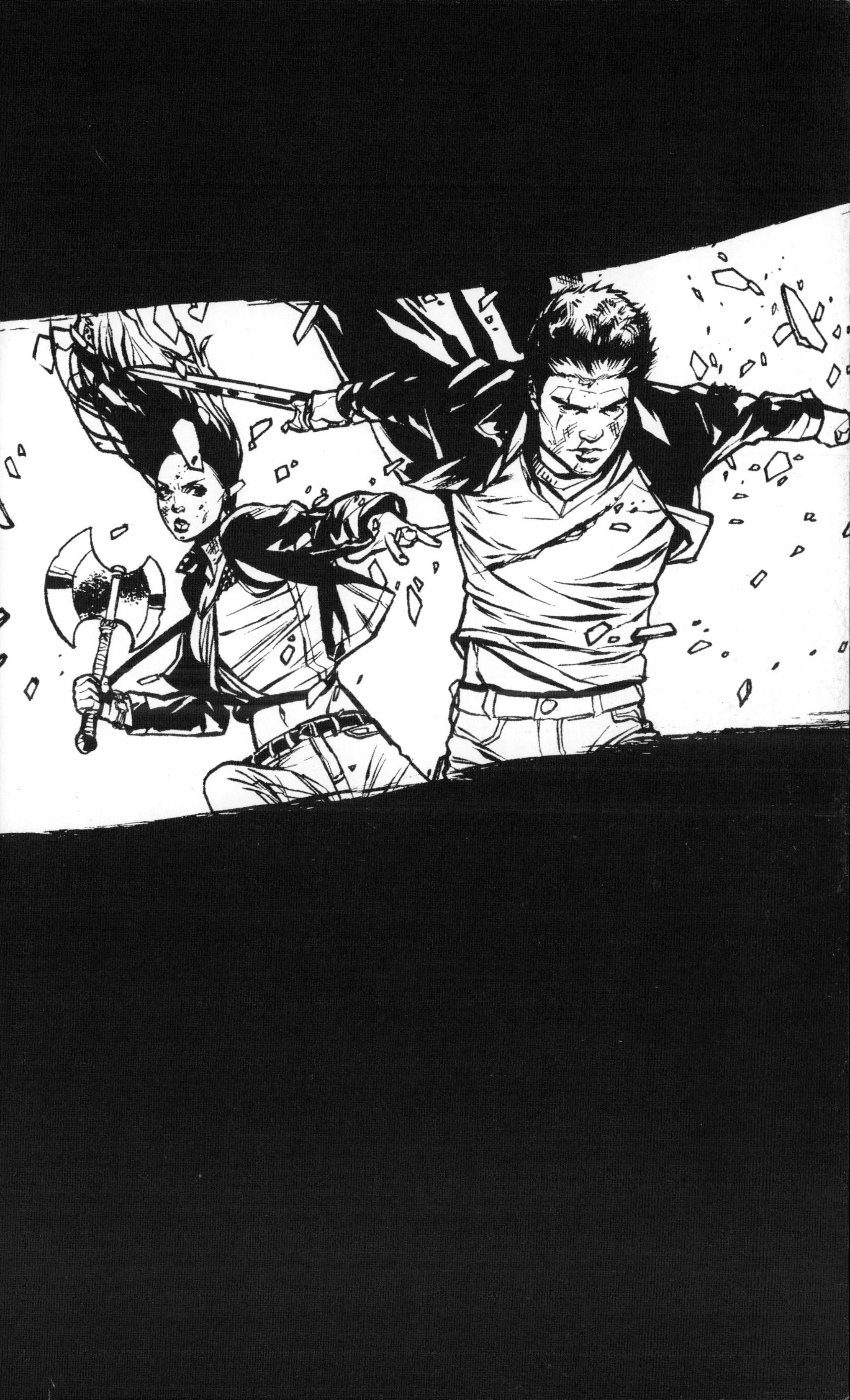

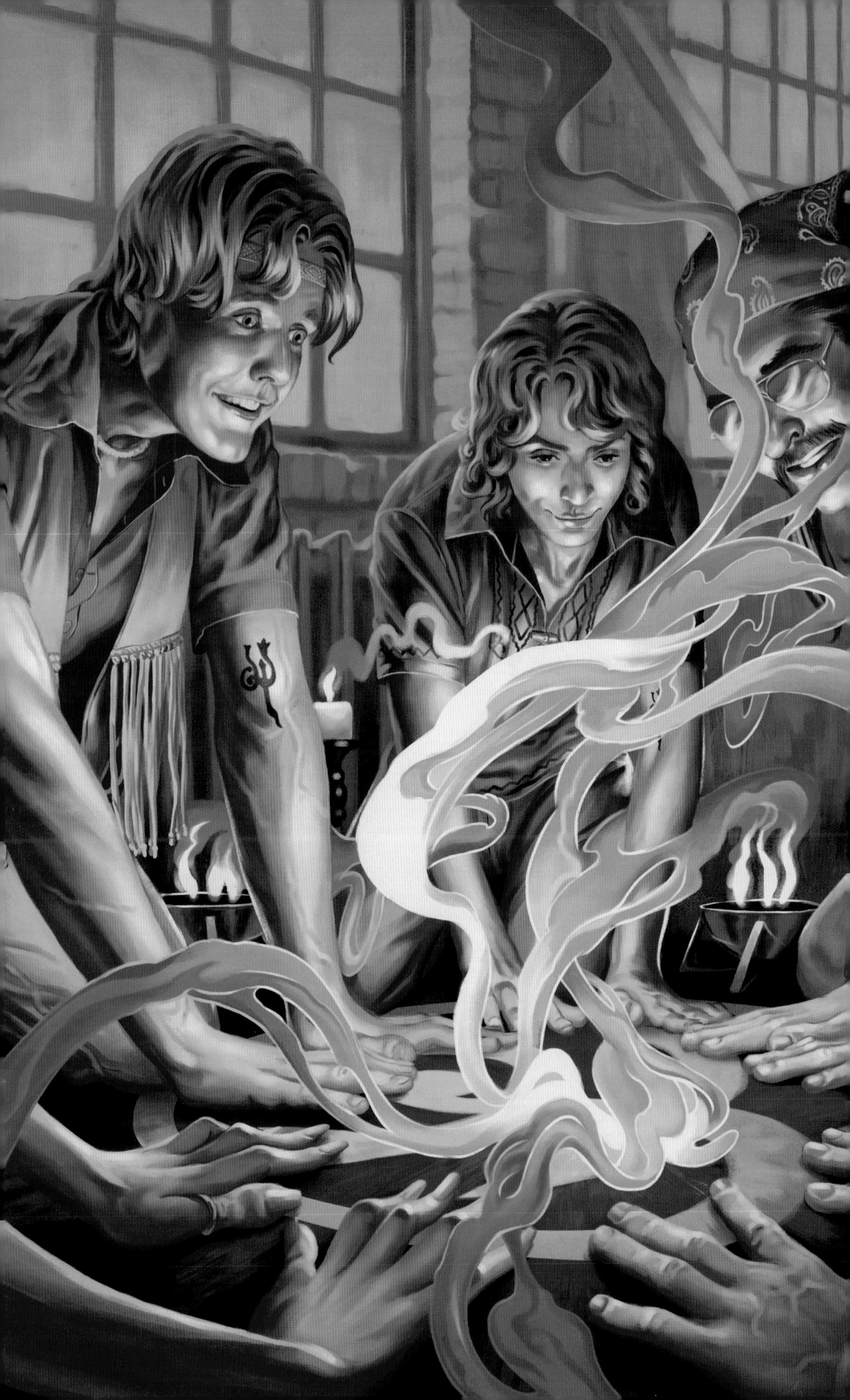

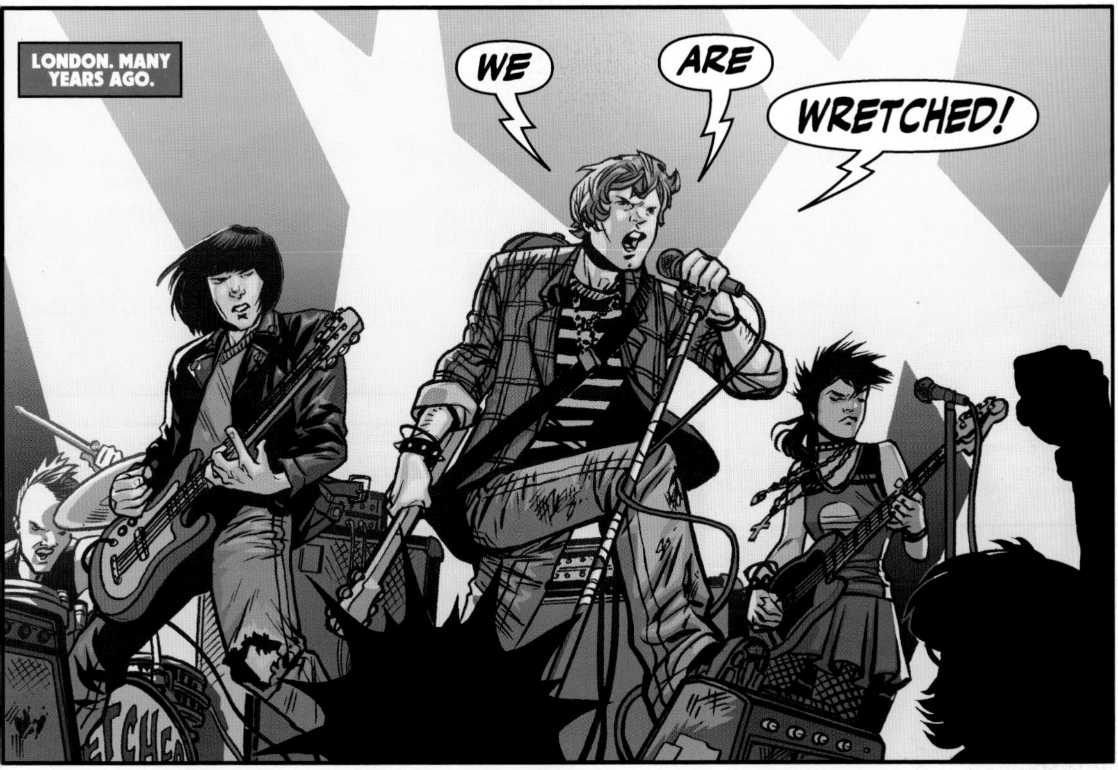
LONDON. MANY YEARS AGO.
WE
ARE
WRETCHED!

DEATH AND CONSEQUENCES

PART 3 OF 4

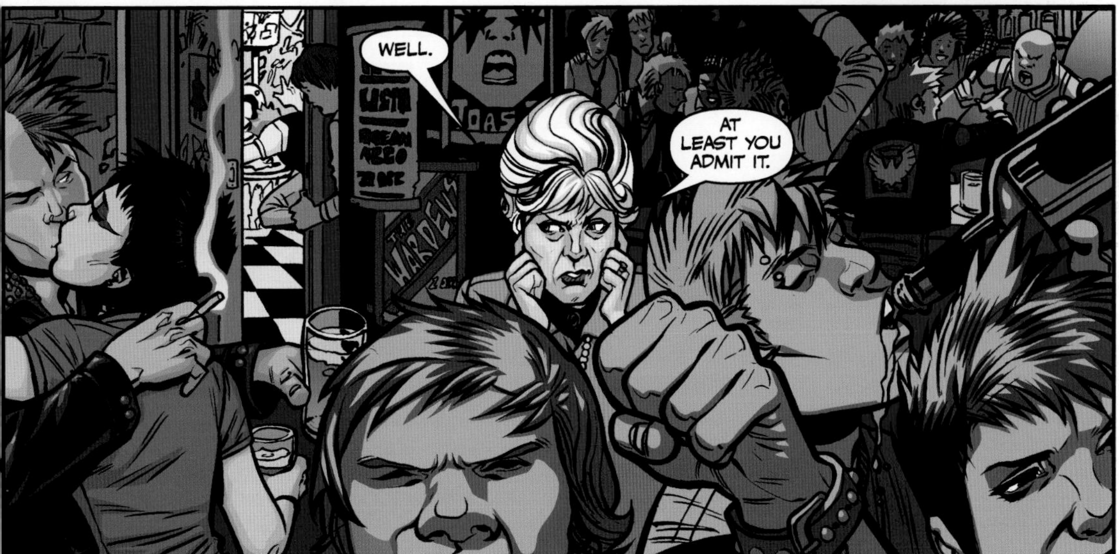
WELL.
AT LEAST YOU ADMIT IT.

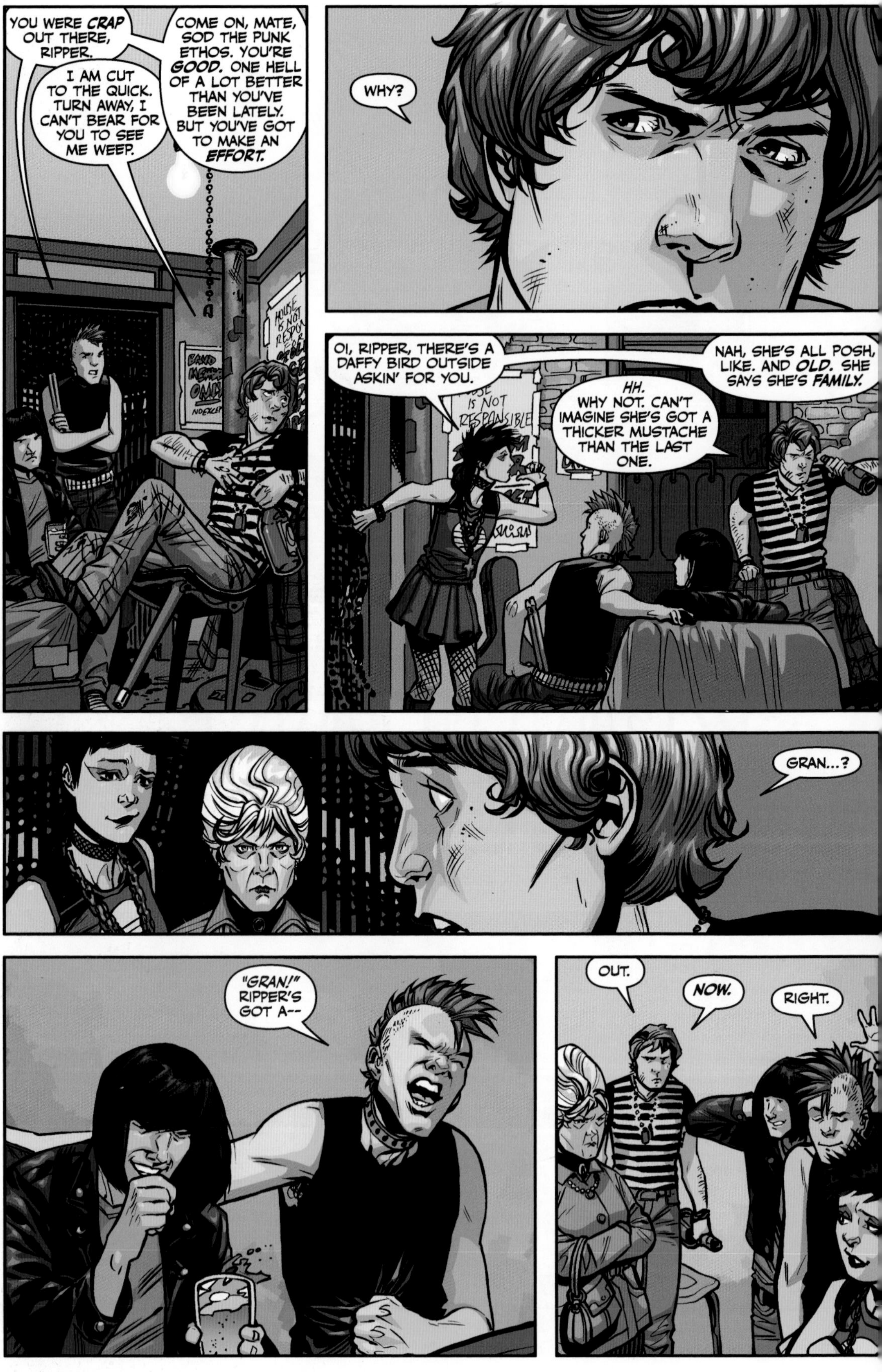
YOU WERE CRAP OUT THERE, RIPPER.
COME ON, MATE, SOD THE PUNK ETHOS. YOU'RE GOOD. ONE HELL OF A LOT BETTER THAN YOU'VE BEEN LATELY.
I AM CUT TO THE QUICK. TURN AWAY, I CAN'T BEAR FOR YOU TO SEE ME WEEP.
BUT YOU'VE GOT TO MAKE AN EFFORT.
WHY?
OI, RIPPER, THERE'S A DAFFY BIRD OUTSIDE ASKIN' FOR YOU.
HH. WHY NOT. CAN'T IMAGINE SHE'S GOT A THICKER MUSTACHE THAN THE LAST ONE.
NAH, SHE'S ALL POSH, LIKE. AND OLD. SHE SAYS SHE'S FAMILY.
HOUSE IS NOT RESPONSIBLE
GRAN...?
"GRAN!" RIPPER'S GOT A--
OUT.
NOW.
RIGHT.

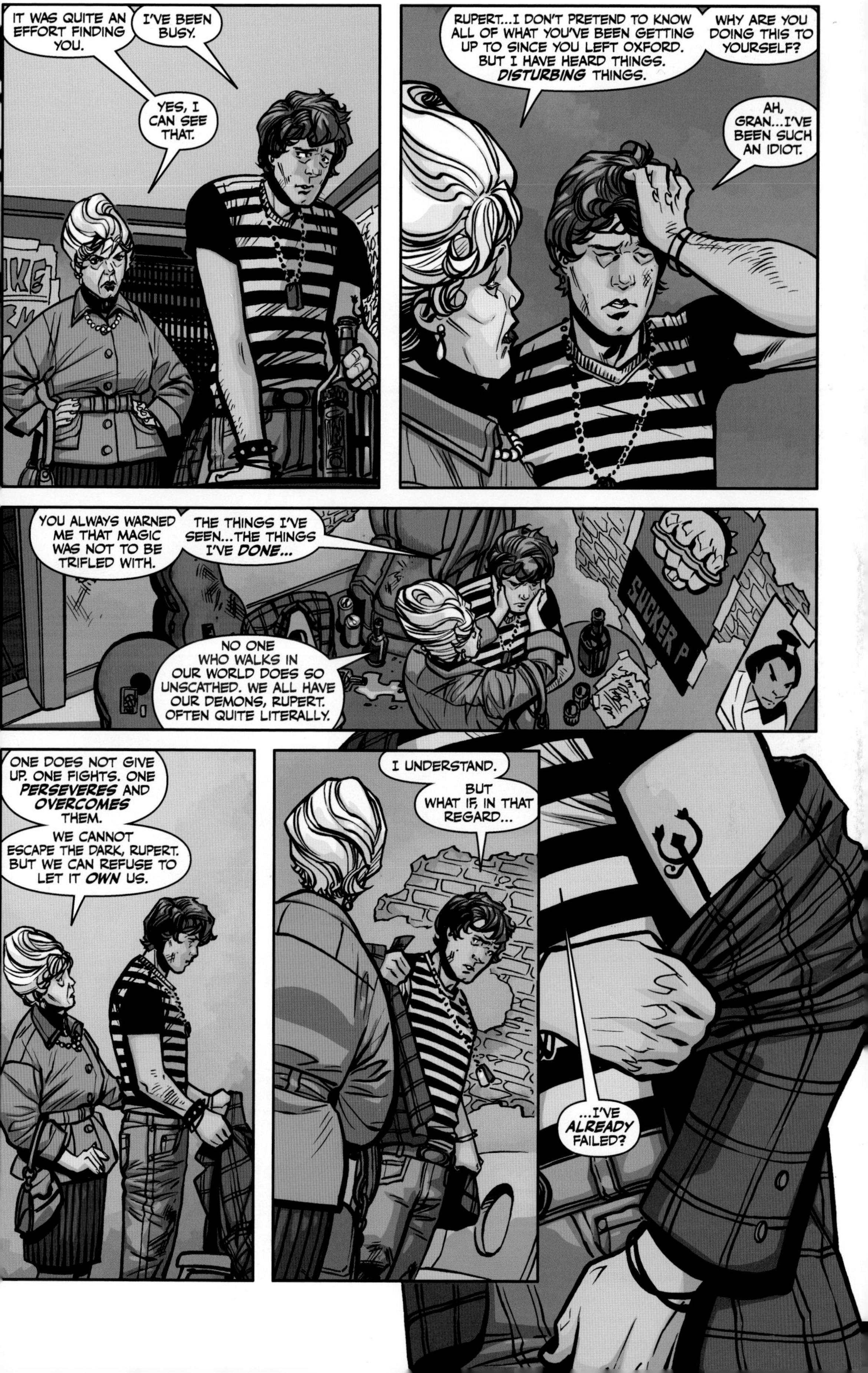

IT WAS QUITE AN EFFORT FINDING YOU.
I'VE BEEN BUSY.
YES, I CAN SEE THAT.
RUPERT...I DON'T PRETEND TO KNOW ALL OF WHAT YOU'VE BEEN GETTING UP TO SINCE YOU LEFT OXFORD. BUT I HAVE HEARD THINGS. *DISTURBING* THINGS.
WHY ARE YOU DOING THIS TO YOURSELF?
AH, GRAN...I'VE BEEN SUCH AN IDIOT.
YOU ALWAYS WARNED ME THAT MAGIC WAS NOT TO BE TRIFLED WITH.
THE THINGS I'VE SEEN...THE THINGS I'VE *DONE*...
NO ONE WHO WALKS IN OUR WORLD DOES SO UNSCATHED. WE ALL HAVE OUR DEMONS, RUPERT. OFTEN QUITE LITERALLY.
SUCKER P
ONE DOES NOT GIVE UP. ONE FIGHTS. ONE *PERSEVERES* AND *OVERCOMES* THEM.
WE CANNOT ESCAPE THE DARK, RUPERT. BUT WE CAN REFUSE TO LET IT *OWN* US.
I UNDERSTAND.
BUT WHAT IF, IN THAT REGARD...
...I'VE *ALREADY* FAILED?

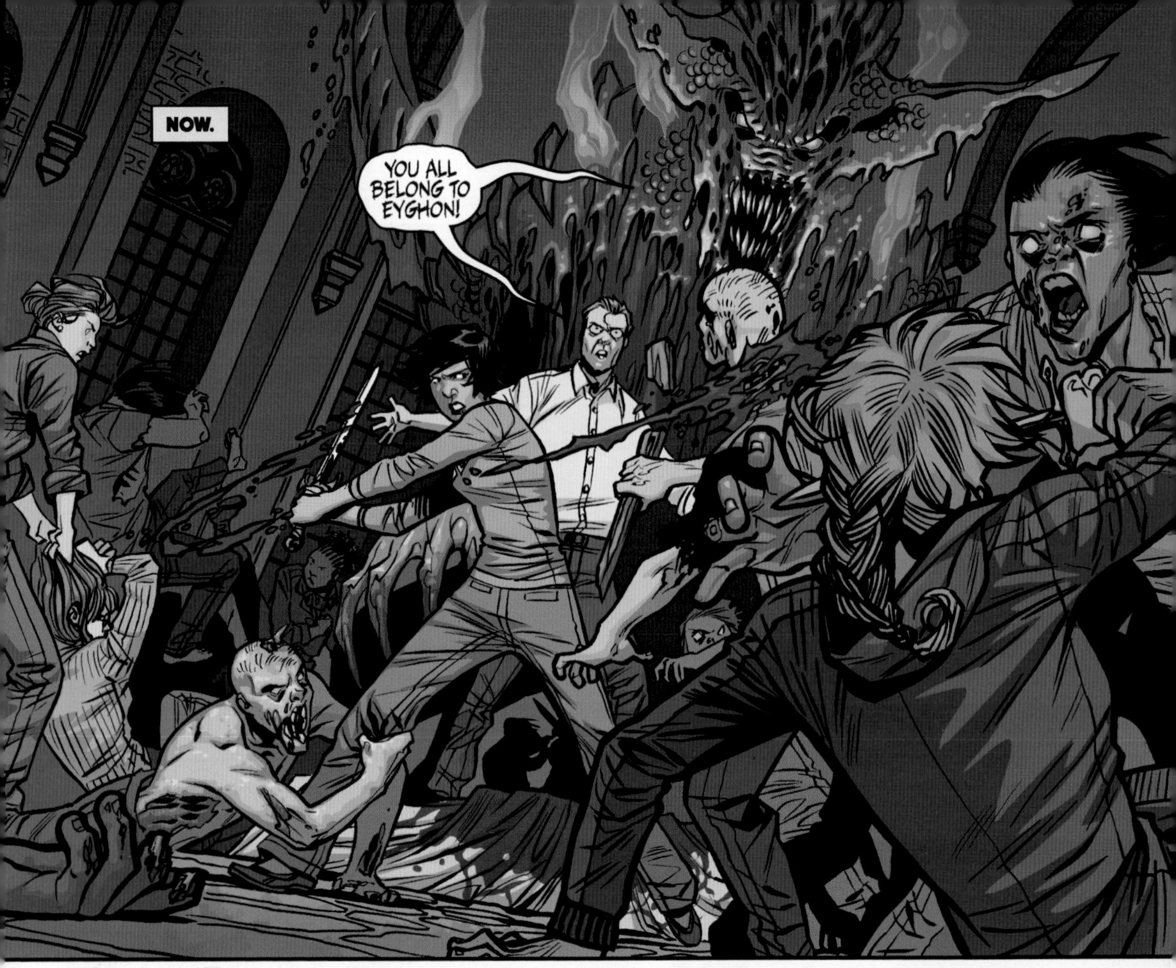
NOW.
YOU ALL BELONG TO EYGHON!

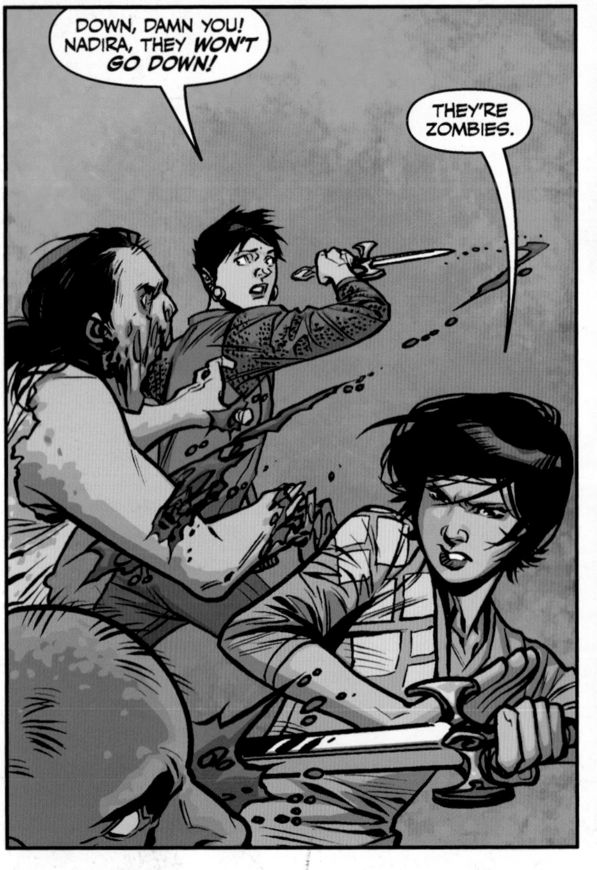
DOWN, DAMN YOU! NADIRA, THEY *WON'T GO DOWN!*
THEY'RE ZOMBIES.

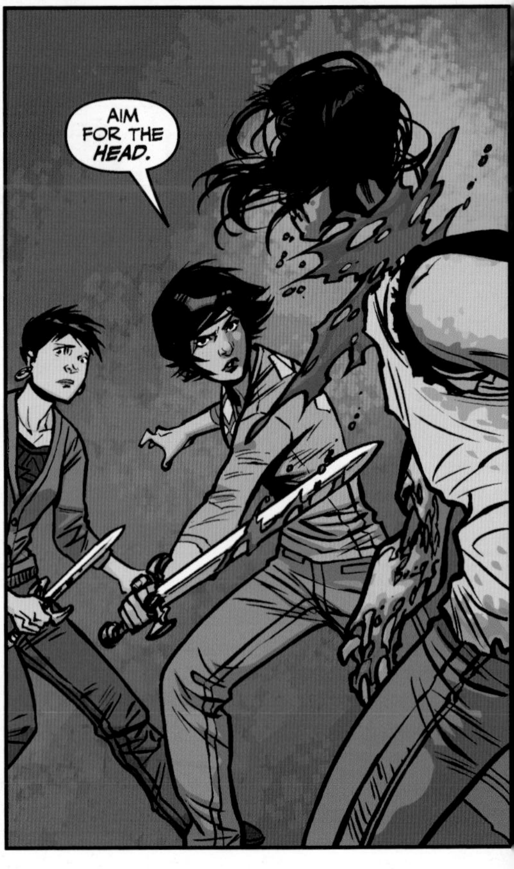
AIM FOR THE *HEAD.*

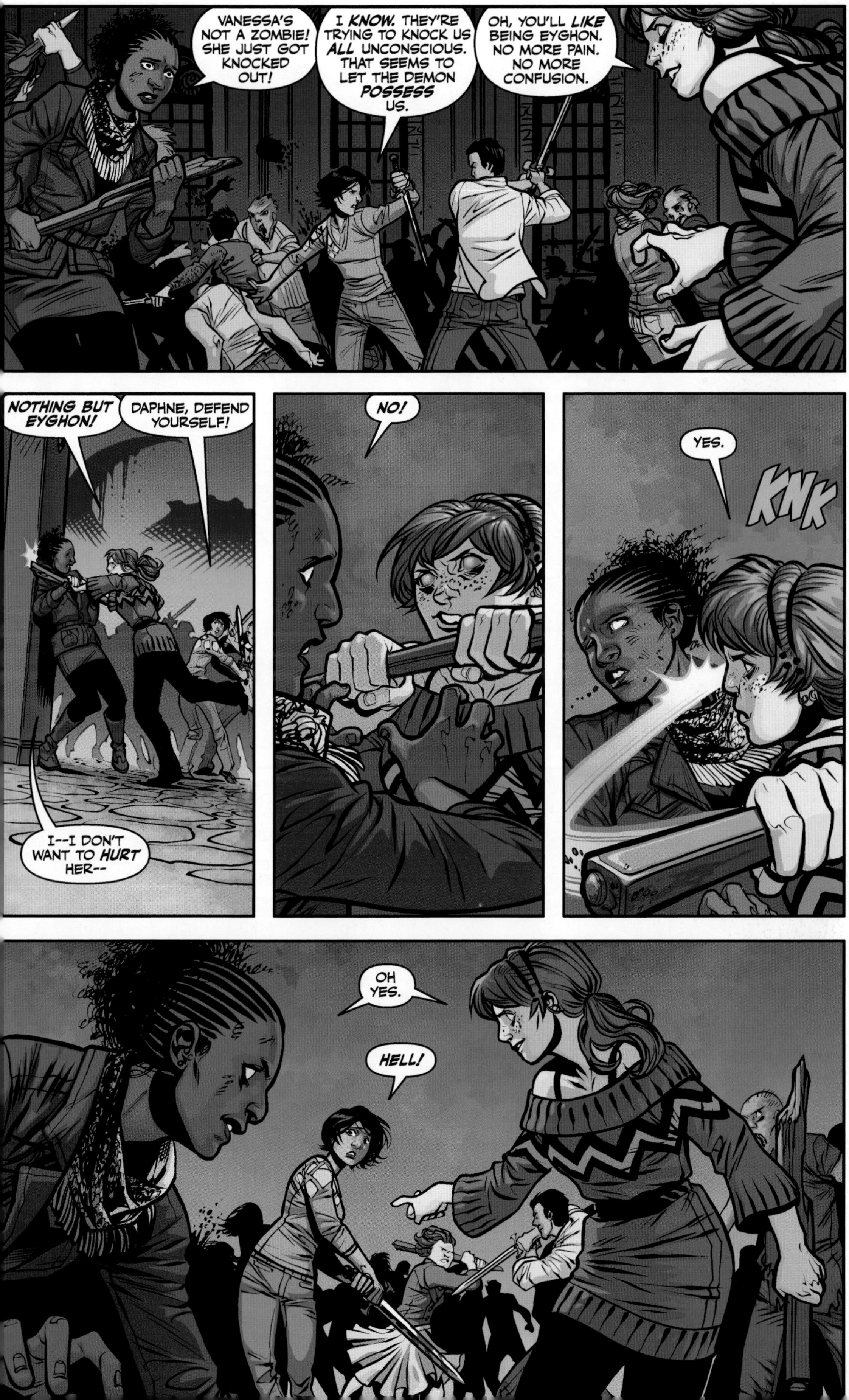
VANESSA'S NOT A ZOMBIE! SHE JUST GOT KNOCKED OUT!
I KNOW. THEY'RE TRYING TO KNOCK US ALL UNCONSCIOUS. THAT SEEMS TO LET THE DEMON POSSESS US.
OH, YOU'LL LIKE BEING EYGHON. NO MORE PAIN. NO MORE CONFUSION.
NOTHING BUT EYGHON!
DAPHNE, DEFEND YOURSELF!
I--I DON'T WANT TO HURT HER--
NO!
YES.
KNK
OH YES.
HELL!

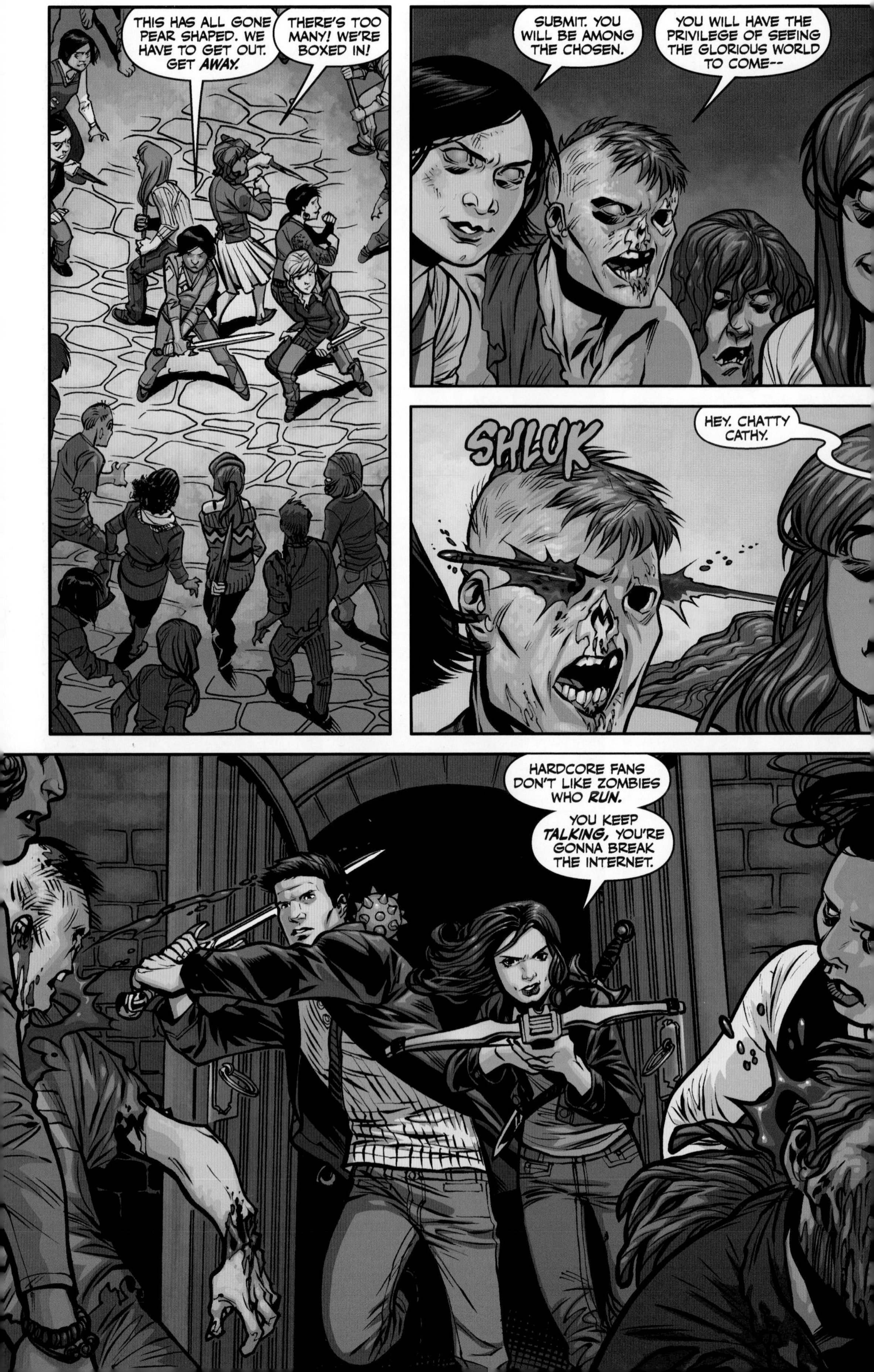
THIS HAS ALL GONE PEAR SHAPED. WE HAVE TO GET OUT. GET AWAY.
THERE'S TOO MANY! WE'RE BOXED IN!
SUBMIT. YOU WILL BE AMONG THE CHOSEN.
YOU WILL HAVE THE PRIVILEGE OF SEEING THE GLORIOUS WORLD TO COME--
SHLUK
HEY. CHATTY CATHY.
HARDCORE FANS DON'T LIKE ZOMBIES WHO RUN.
YOU KEEP TALKING, YOU'RE GONNA BREAK THE INTERNET.

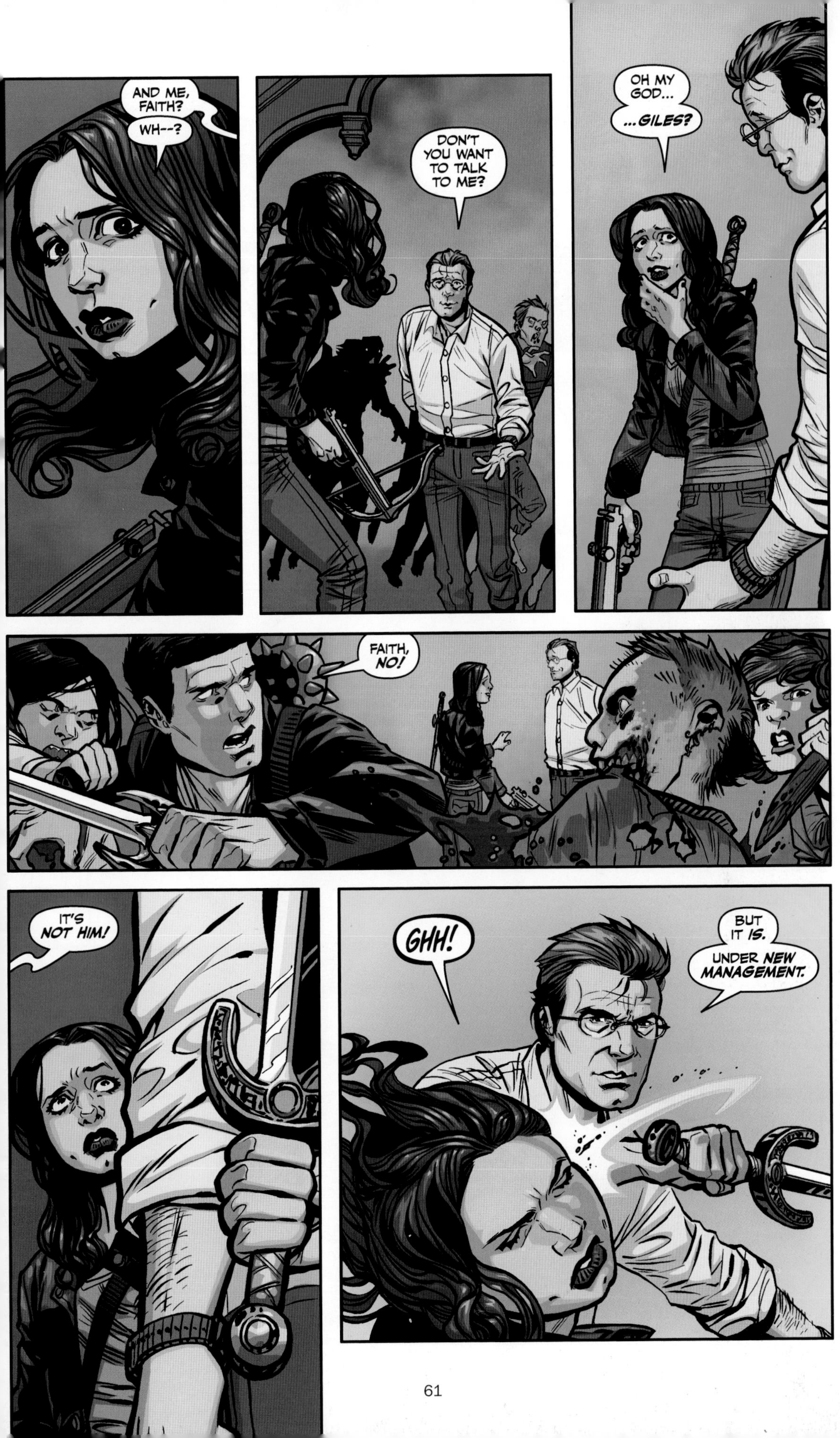
AND ME, FAITH?
WH--?
DON'T YOU WANT TO TALK TO ME?
OH MY GOD...
...GILES?
FAITH, NO!
IT'S NOT HIM!
GHH!
BUT IT IS.
UNDER NEW MANAGEMENT.

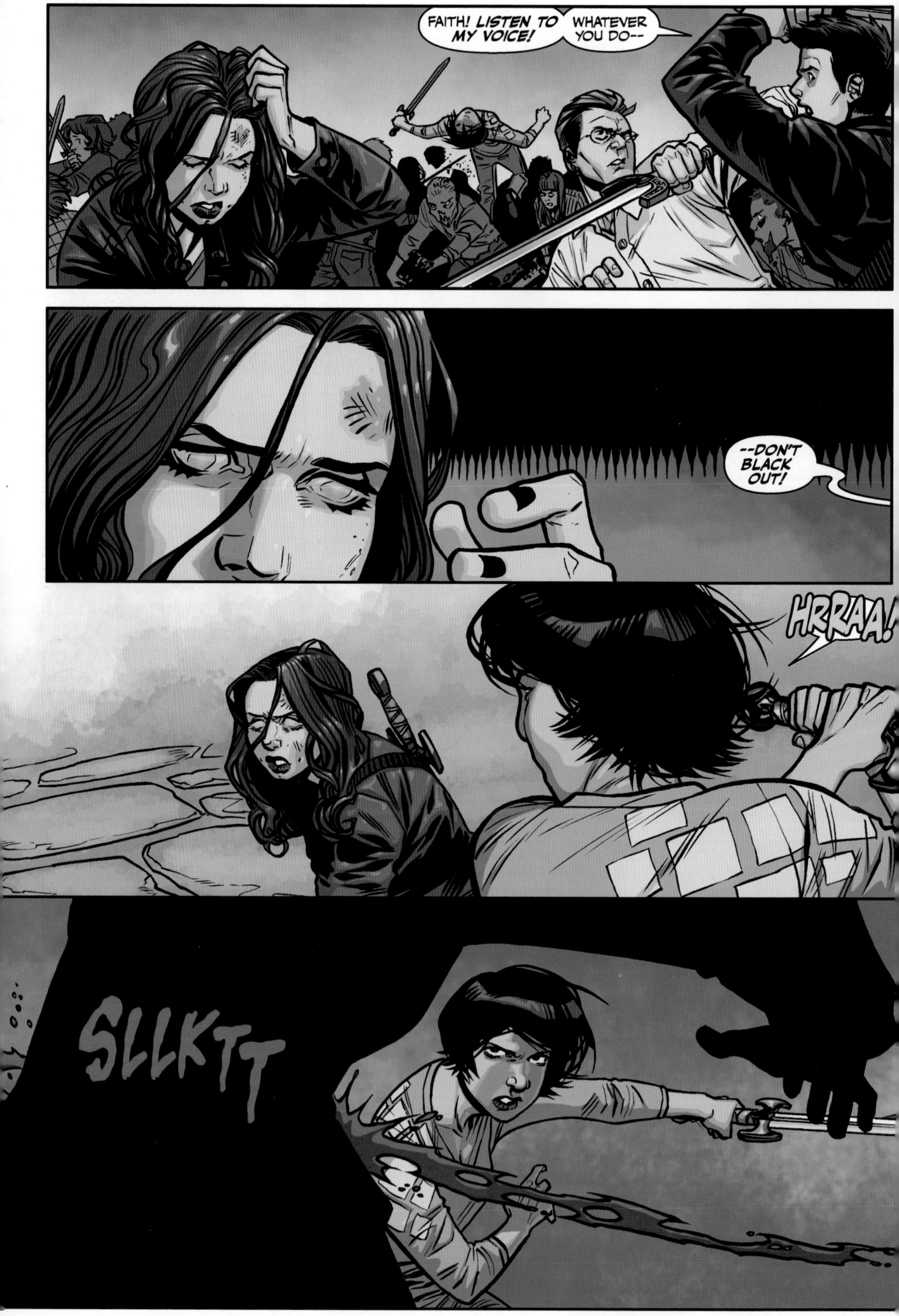
FAITH! LISTEN TO MY VOICE!
WHATEVER YOU DO--
--DON'T BLACK OUT!
HRRAA!
SLLKTT

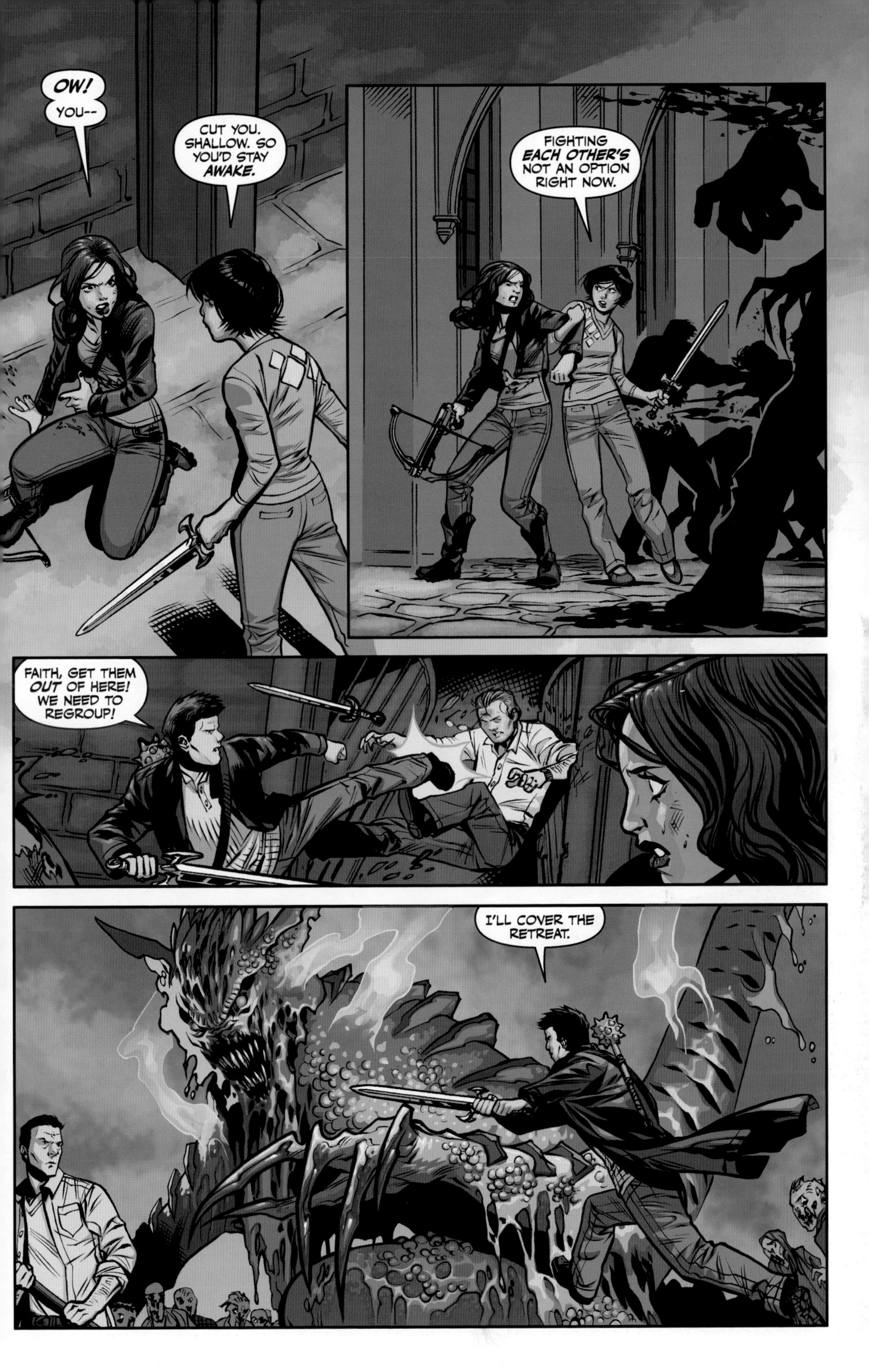
OW!
YOU--
CUT YOU. SHALLOW. SO YOU'D STAY AWAKE.
FIGHTING EACH OTHER'S NOT AN OPTION RIGHT NOW.
FAITH, GET THEM OUT OF HERE! WE NEED TO REGROUP!
I'LL COVER THE RETREAT.

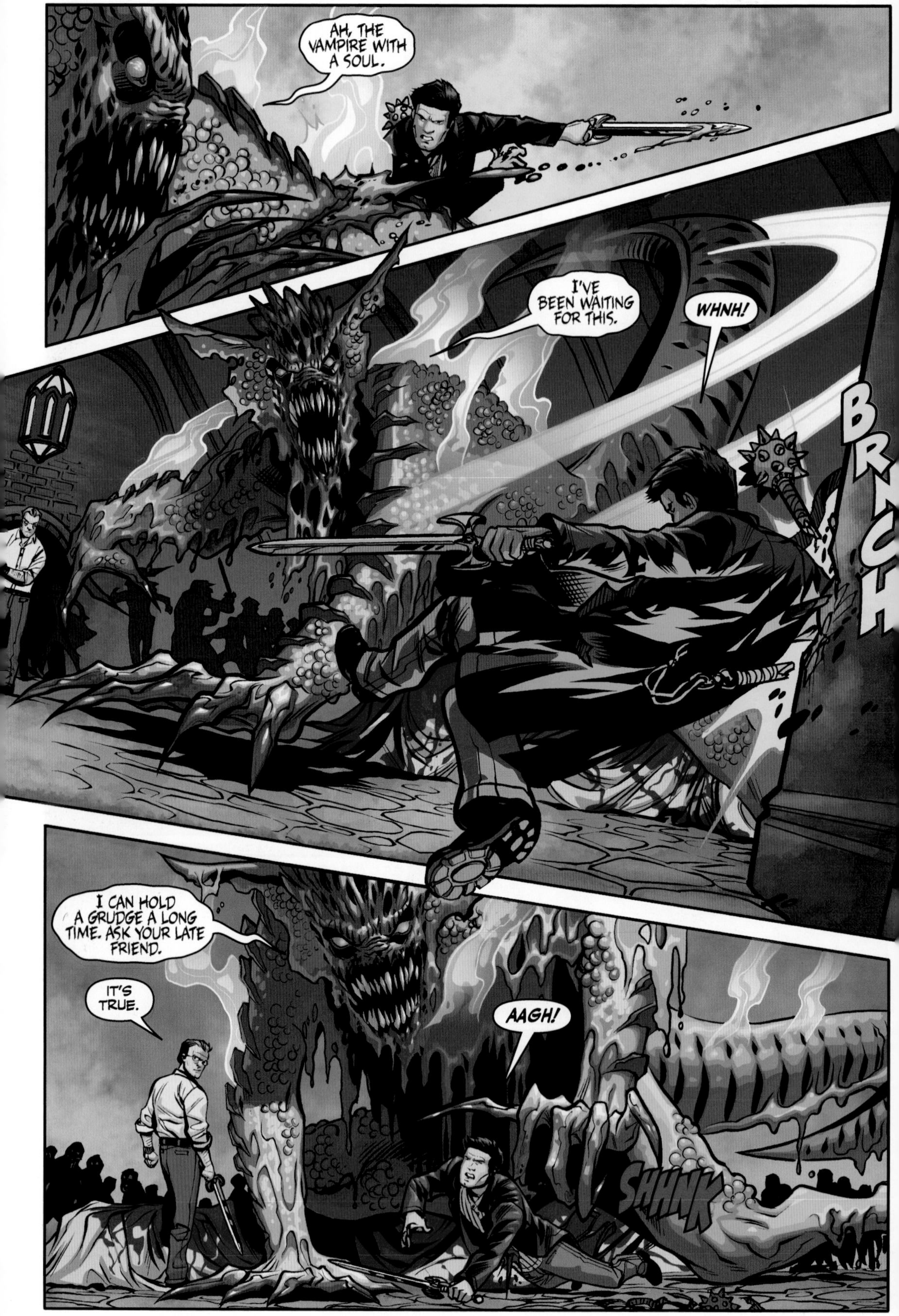
AH, THE VAMPIRE WITH A SOUL.
I'VE BEEN WAITING FOR THIS.
WHNH!
BRNCH
I CAN HOLD A GRUDGE A LONG TIME. ASK YOUR LATE FRIEND.
IT'S TRUE.
AAGH!
SHHNK

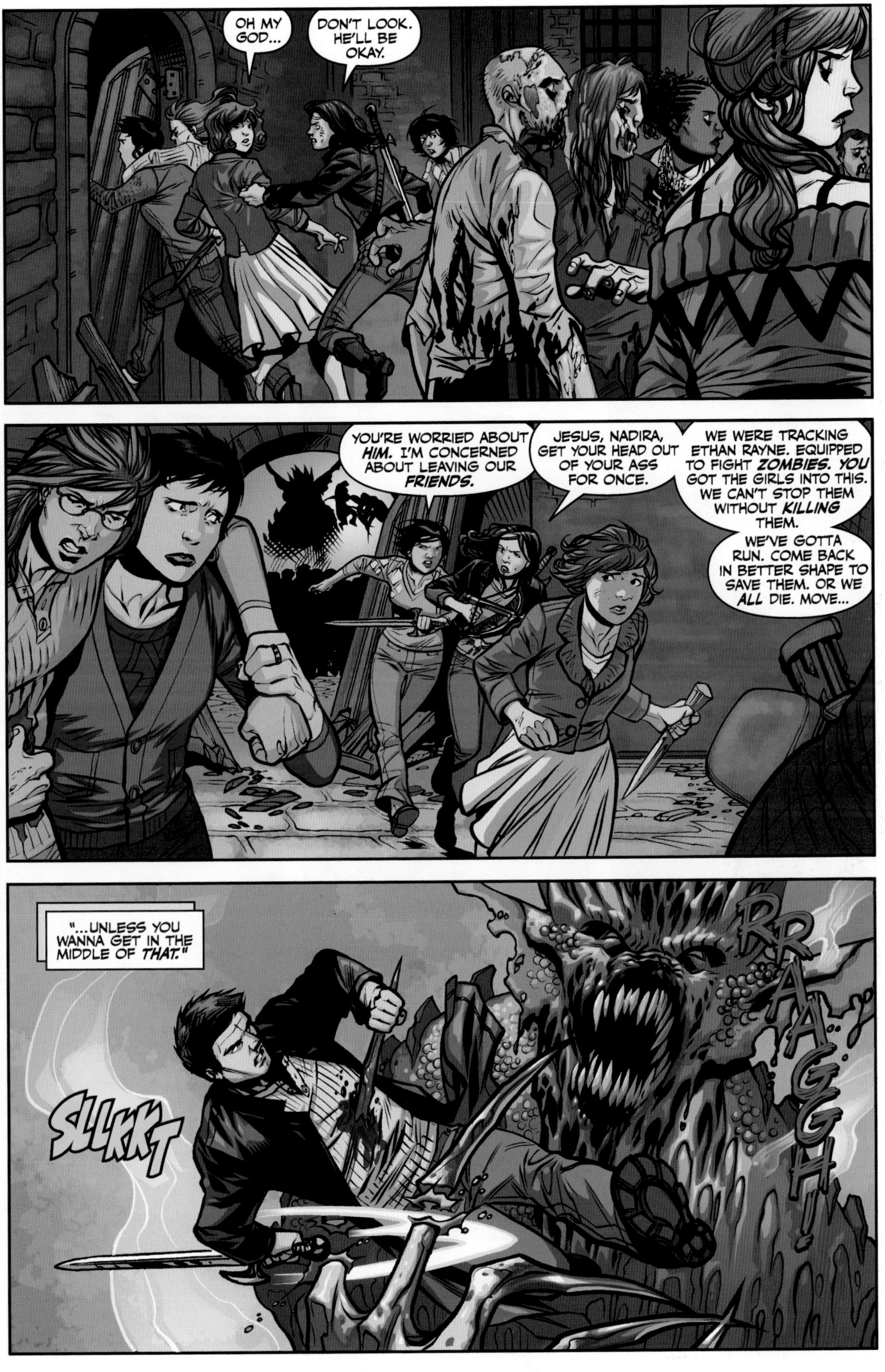
OH MY GOD...
DON'T LOOK. HE'LL BE OKAY.
YOU'RE WORRIED ABOUT *HIM.* I'M CONCERNED ABOUT LEAVING OUR *FRIENDS.*
JESUS, NADIRA, GET YOUR HEAD OUT OF YOUR ASS FOR ONCE.
WE WERE TRACKING ETHAN RAYNE. EQUIPPED TO FIGHT *ZOMBIES. YOU* GOT THE GIRLS INTO THIS. WE CAN'T STOP THEM WITHOUT *KILLING* THEM.
WE'VE GOTTA RUN. COME BACK IN BETTER SHAPE TO SAVE THEM. OR WE *ALL* DIE. MOVE...
"...UNLESS YOU WANNA GET IN THE MIDDLE OF *THAT.*"
RRAAGGH!
SLLKKT

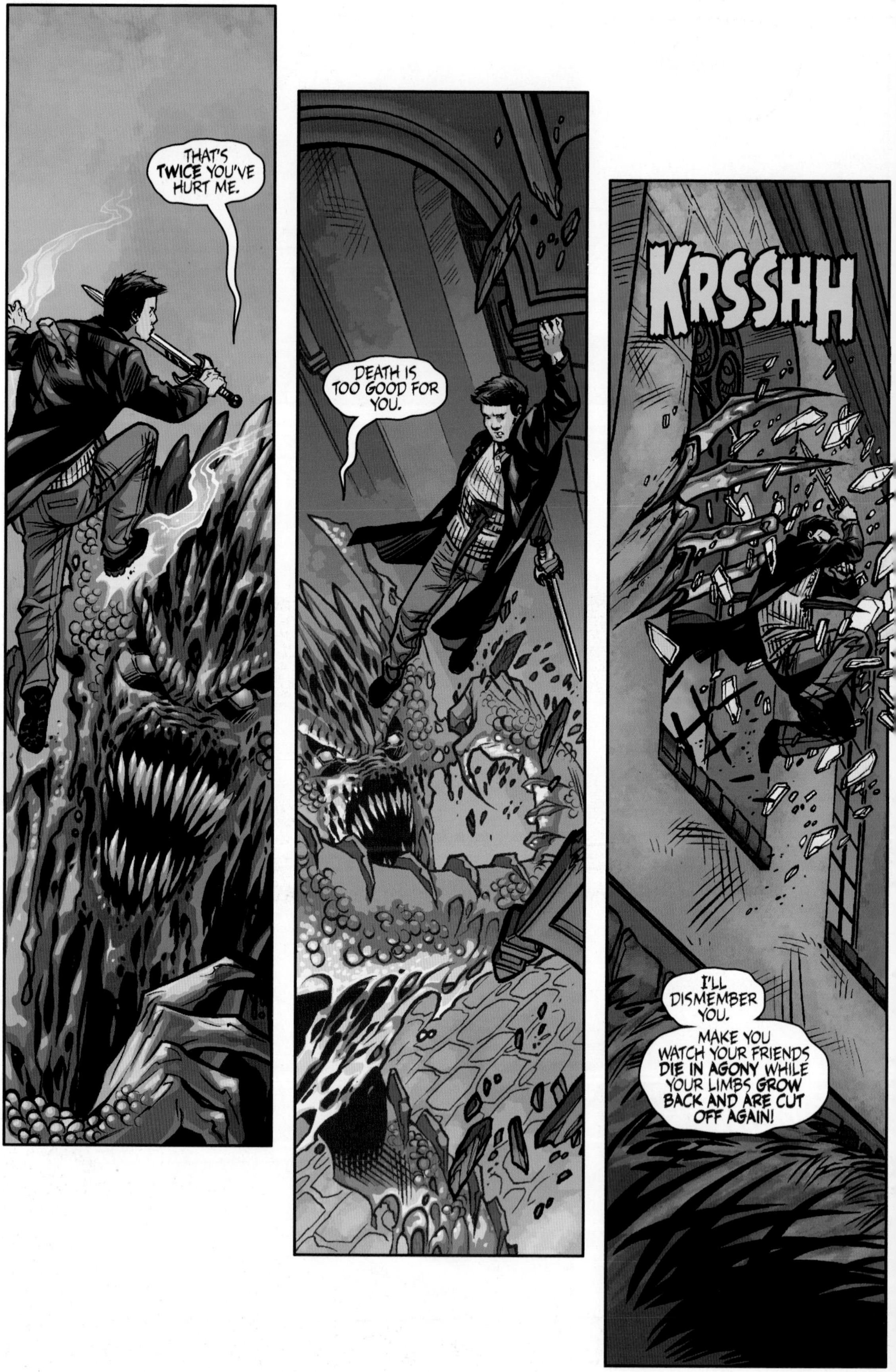
THAT'S TWICE YOU'VE HURT ME.
DEATH IS TOO GOOD FOR YOU.
KRSSHH
I'LL DISMEMBER YOU.
MAKE YOU WATCH YOUR FRIENDS DIE IN AGONY WHILE YOUR LIMBS GROW BACK AND ARE CUT OFF AGAIN!

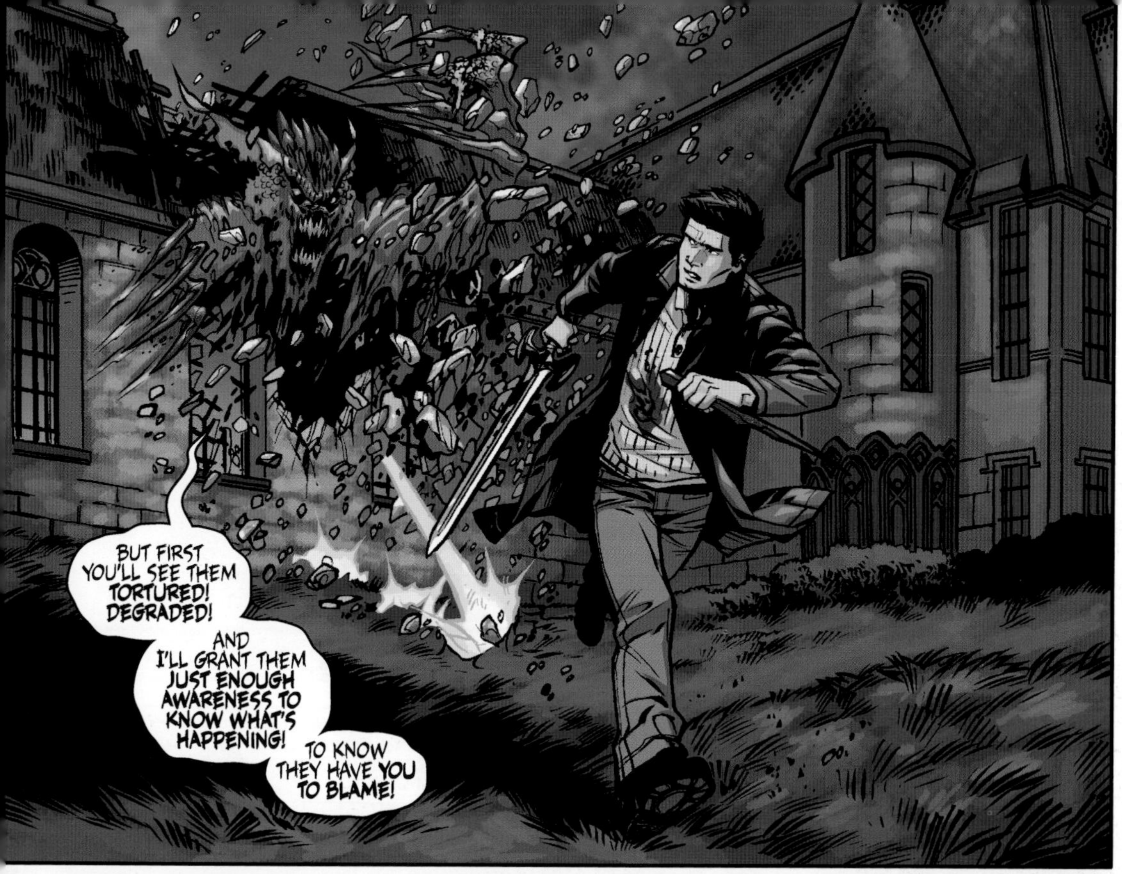
BUT FIRST YOU'LL SEE THEM TORTURED! DEGRADED!
AND I'LL GRANT THEM JUST ENOUGH AWARENESS TO KNOW WHAT'S HAPPENING!
TO KNOW THEY HAVE YOU TO BLAME!

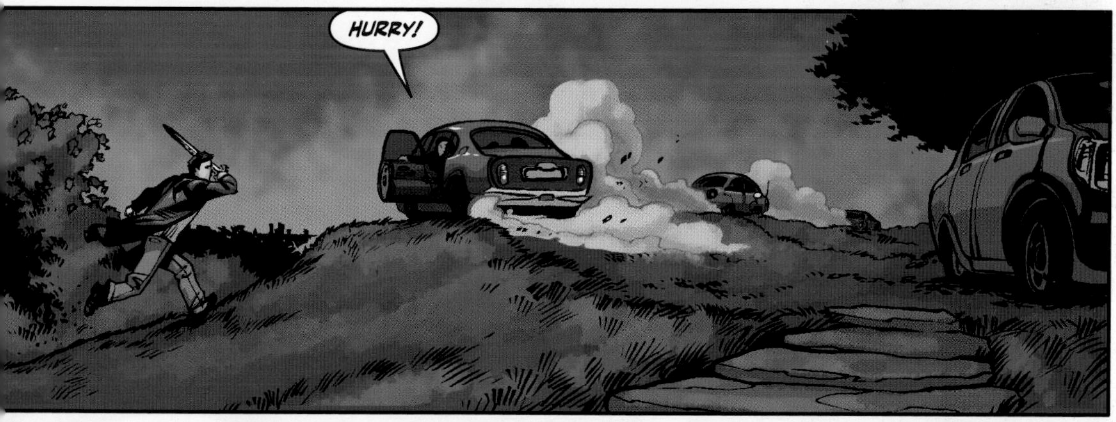
HURRY!

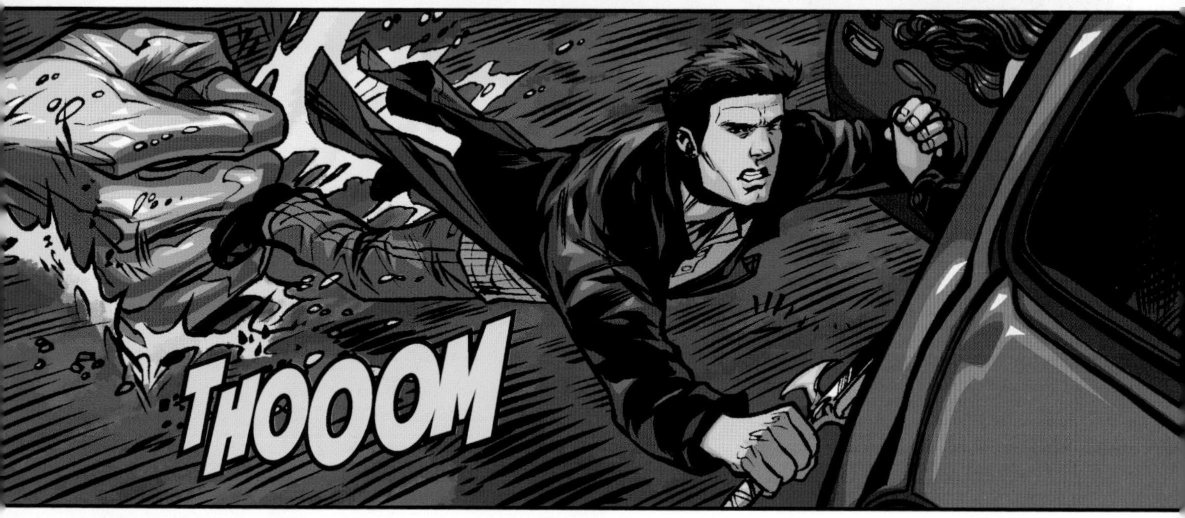
THOOOM

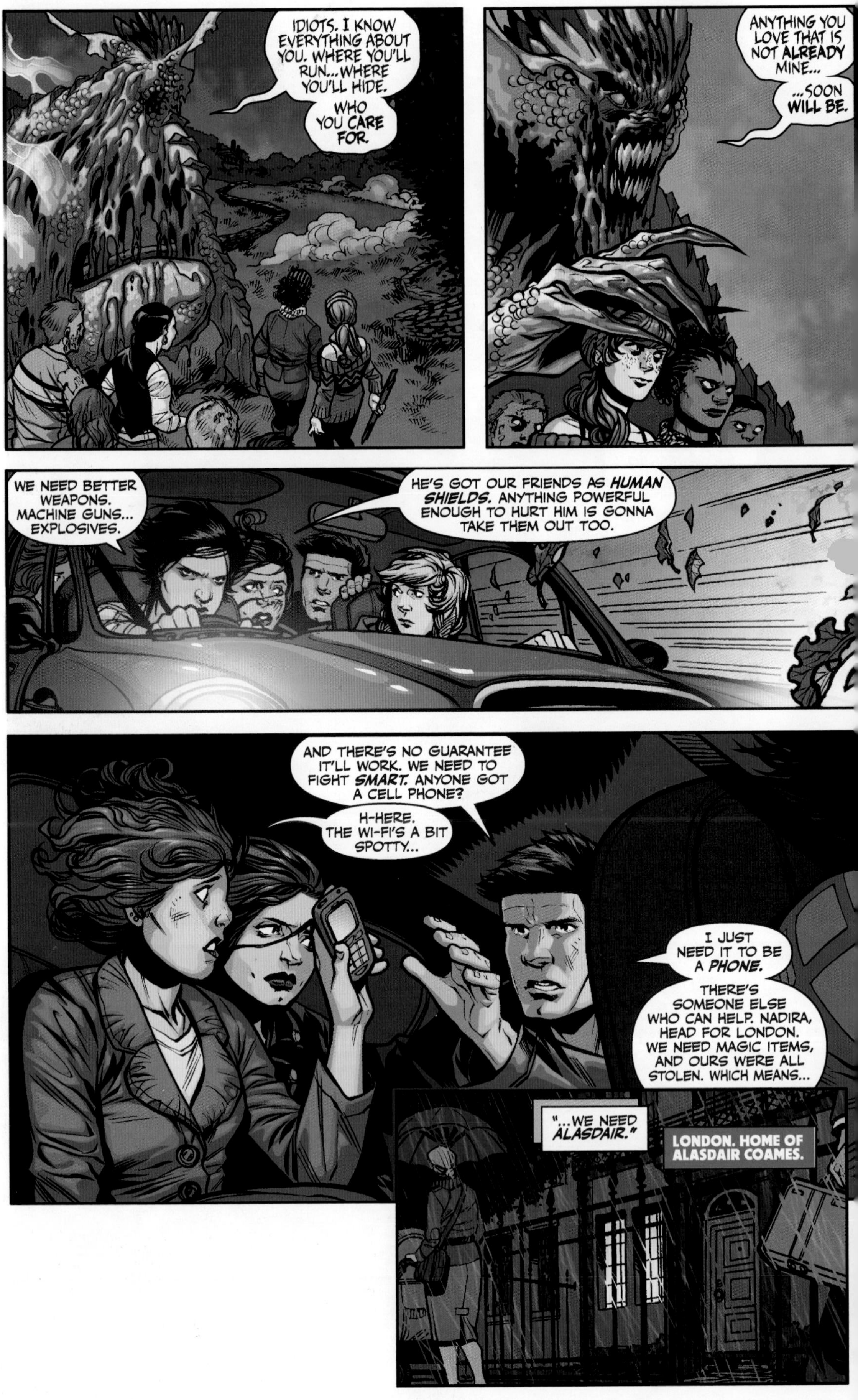
IDIOTS. I KNOW EVERYTHING ABOUT YOU. WHERE YOU'LL RUN...WHERE YOU'LL HIDE.
WHO YOU CARE FOR.
ANYTHING YOU LOVE THAT IS NOT ALREADY MINE...
...SOON WILL BE.
WE NEED BETTER WEAPONS. MACHINE GUNS... EXPLOSIVES.
HE'S GOT OUR FRIENDS AS HUMAN SHIELDS. ANYTHING POWERFUL ENOUGH TO HURT HIM IS GONNA TAKE THEM OUT TOO.
AND THERE'S NO GUARANTEE IT'LL WORK. WE NEED TO FIGHT SMART. ANYONE GOT A CELL PHONE?
H-HERE. THE WI-FI'S A BIT SPOTTY...
I JUST NEED IT TO BE A PHONE.
THERE'S SOMEONE ELSE WHO CAN HELP. NADIRA, HEAD FOR LONDON. WE NEED MAGIC ITEMS, AND OURS WERE ALL STOLEN. WHICH MEANS...
"...WE NEED ALASDAIR."
LONDON. HOME OF ALASDAIR COAMES.

IS THERE ANY WAY TO BREAK EYGHON'S HOLD ON PEOPLE?

ONLY BY KILLING HIM.

BONUS. WE WERE GONNA DO THAT ANYWAY.

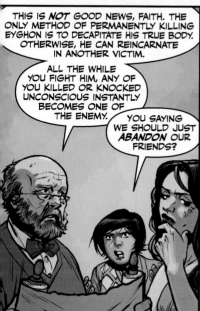

THIS IS *NOT* GOOD NEWS, FAITH. THE ONLY METHOD OF PERMANENTLY KILLING EYGHON IS TO DECAPITATE HIS TRUE BODY. OTHERWISE, HE CAN REINCARNATE IN ANOTHER VICTIM.

ALL THE WHILE YOU FIGHT HIM, ANY OF YOU KILLED OR KNOCKED UNCONSCIOUS INSTANTLY BECOMES ONE OF THE ENEMY.

YOU SAYING WE SHOULD JUST *ABANDON* OUR FRIENDS?

NOT AT ALL. SIMPLY THAT YOU MUST FIGHT *INTELLIGENTLY*, WITH *MAGICAL* WEAPONS, LIKE THESE.

BUT YOU SMOKED THIS GUY ONCE ALREADY, RIGHT, ANGEL?

I THOUGHT I HAD. BUT I SHOULD'VE KNOWN IT WOULDN'T BE THAT EASY.

"I FOUND THIS OUT WHEN I WAS *TWILIGHT*, GATHERING INTEL ON SUPERNATURAL POWER PLAYERS. ONE OF THEM TURNED OUT TO BE EYGHON.

"I THOUGHT HE'D BEEN DESTROYED-- OR AT LEAST BANISHED-- WHEN HE TRIED TO JUMP INTO *ME*, AND THE DEMON ALREADY IN THERE THREW HIM OUT.

"THERE WEREN'T ANY DEAD OR UNCONSCIOUS BODIES AROUND FOR HIM TO ESCAPE INTO.

"NO *HUMAN* ONES.

"HE JUMPED INTO A *DEAD RAT.*

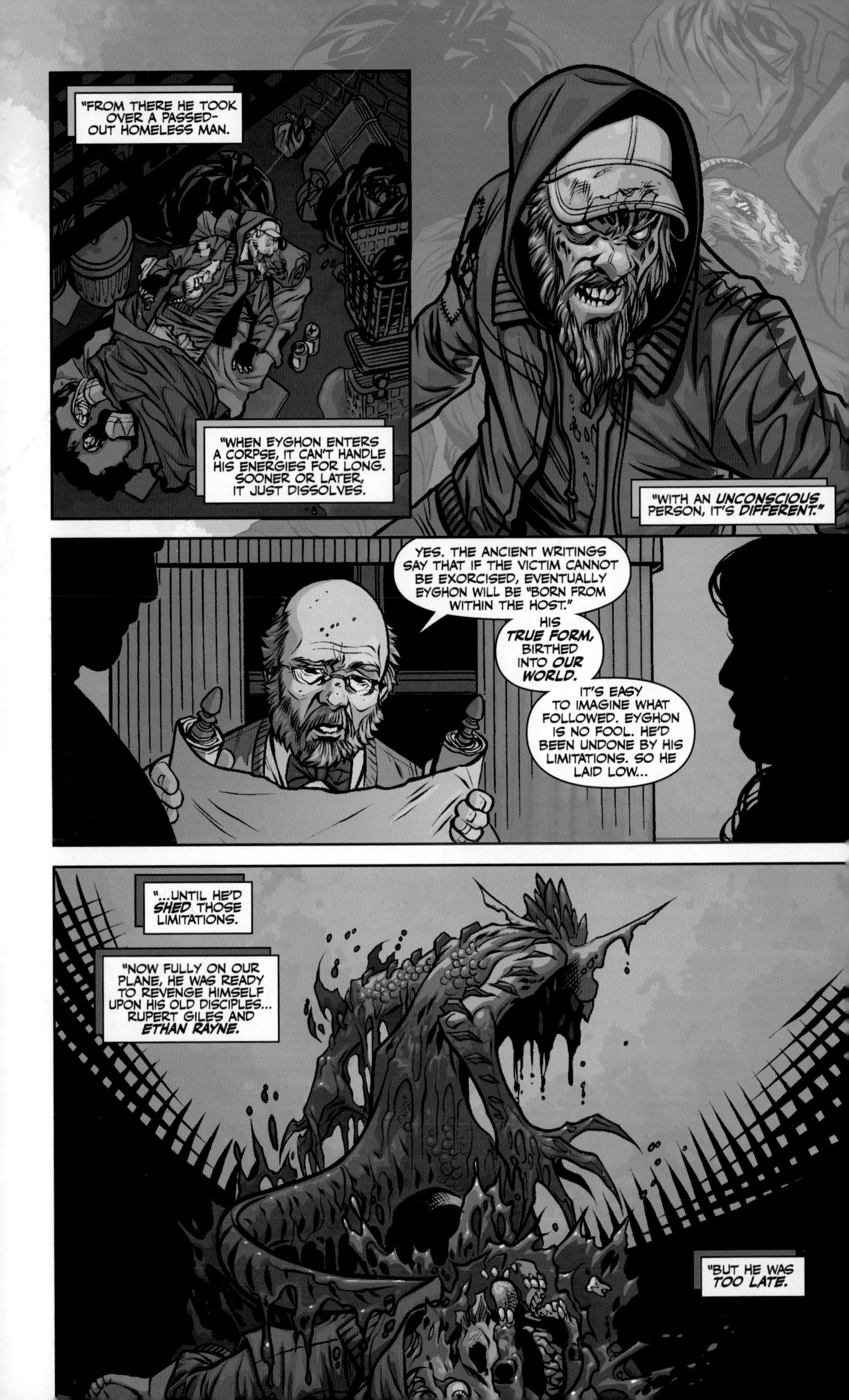
"FROM THERE HE TOOK OVER A PASSED-OUT HOMELESS MAN.
"WHEN EYGHON ENTERS A CORPSE, IT CAN'T HANDLE HIS ENERGIES FOR LONG. SOONER OR LATER, IT JUST DISSOLVES.
"WITH AN UNCONSCIOUS PERSON, IT'S DIFFERENT."
YES. THE ANCIENT WRITINGS SAY THAT IF THE VICTIM CANNOT BE EXORCISED, EVENTUALLY EYGHON WILL BE "BORN FROM WITHIN THE HOST."
HIS TRUE FORM, BIRTHED INTO OUR WORLD.
IT'S EASY TO IMAGINE WHAT FOLLOWED. EYGHON IS NO FOOL. HE'D BEEN UNDONE BY HIS LIMITATIONS. SO HE LAID LOW...
"...UNTIL HE'D SHED THOSE LIMITATIONS.
"NOW FULLY ON OUR PLANE, HE WAS READY TO REVENGE HIMSELF UPON HIS OLD DISCIPLES... RUPERT GILES AND ETHAN RAYNE.
"BUT HE WAS TOO LATE.

"ETHAN WAS KILLED...

"...THEN RUPERT.

"EYGHON WAS DENIED THE PLEASURE OF MURDERING THEM. BUT HE STILL GOT WHAT HE HAD COMING."

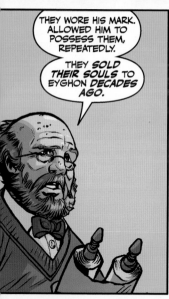

THEY WORE HIS MARK. ALLOWED HIM TO POSSESS THEM, REPEATEDLY.

THEY *SOLD THEIR SOULS* TO EYGHON *DECADES AGO.*

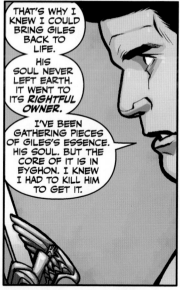

THAT'S WHY I KNEW I COULD BRING GILES BACK TO LIFE.

HIS SOUL NEVER LEFT EARTH. IT WENT TO ITS *RIGHTFUL OWNER.*

I'VE BEEN GATHERING PIECES OF GILES'S ESSENCE. HIS SOUL. BUT THE CORE OF IT IS IN EYGHON. I KNEW I HAD TO KILL HIM TO GET IT.

IN HIS PURE FORM, THAT WILL BE EASIER SAID THAN DONE. STILL, IF ANYTHING CAN ACCOMPLISH THE TASK, IT IS THE WEAPONS IN MY ARMORY.

BUT SUPPOSE HE DOESN'T WANT TO TAKE THE CHANCE? WHAT IF HE CHOOSES TO TAKE THE CAPTIVES HE HAS AND GO INTO HIDING AGAIN?

HE WON'T.

BEFORE NADIRA CUT ME, I WAS *PART* OF HIM. JUST FOR A SECOND...BUT I SAW IT.

I KNOW WHAT HE *WANTS.*

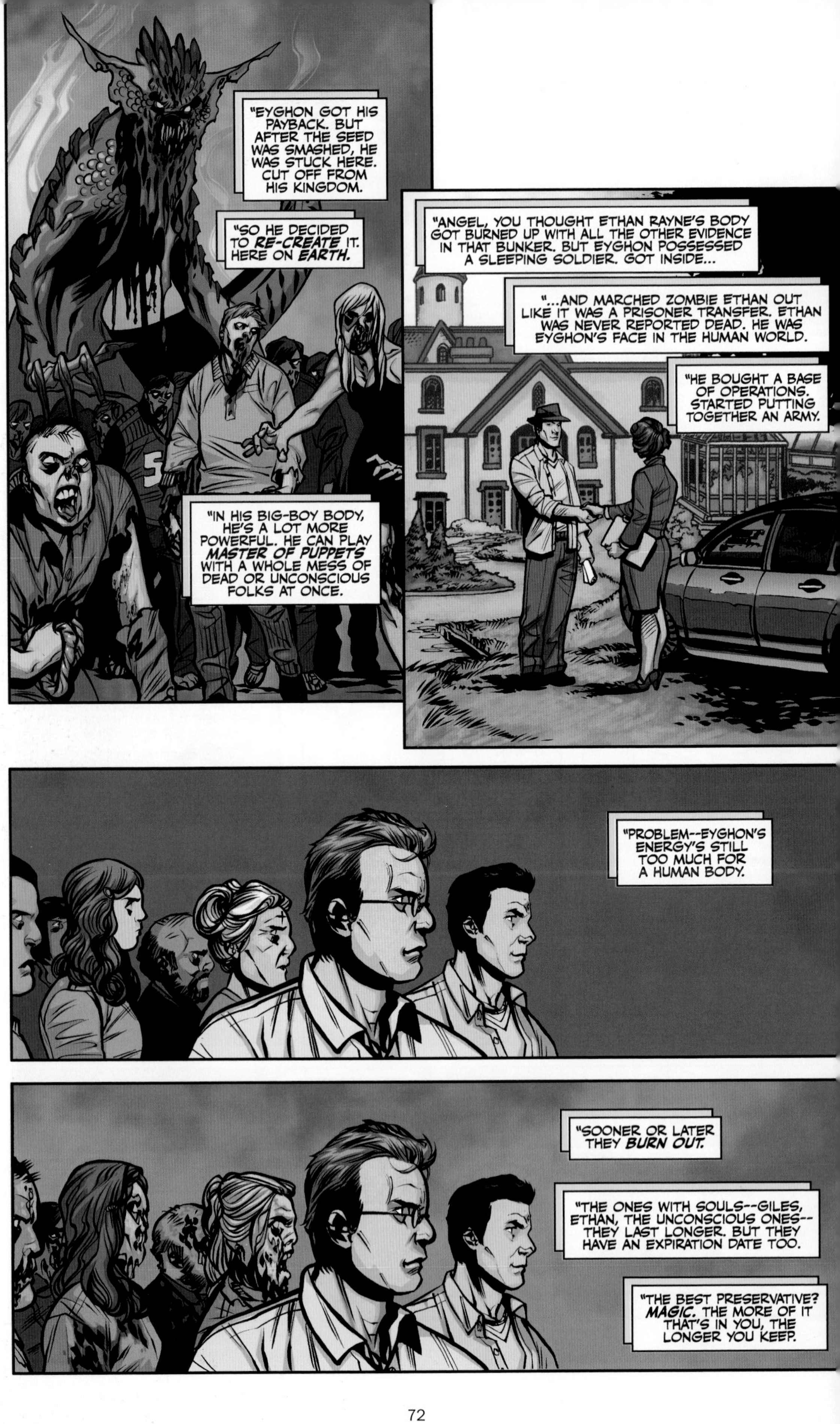
"EYGHON GOT HIS PAYBACK. BUT AFTER THE SEED WAS SMASHED, HE WAS STUCK HERE. CUT OFF FROM HIS KINGDOM.
"SO HE DECIDED TO RE-CREATE IT. HERE ON EARTH.
"IN HIS BIG-BOY BODY, HE'S A LOT MORE POWERFUL. HE CAN PLAY MASTER OF PUPPETS WITH A WHOLE MESS OF DEAD OR UNCONSCIOUS FOLKS AT ONCE.
"ANGEL, YOU THOUGHT ETHAN RAYNE'S BODY GOT BURNED UP WITH ALL THE OTHER EVIDENCE IN THAT BUNKER. BUT EYGHON POSSESSED A SLEEPING SOLDIER. GOT INSIDE...
"...AND MARCHED ZOMBIE ETHAN OUT LIKE IT WAS A PRISONER TRANSFER. ETHAN WAS NEVER REPORTED DEAD. HE WAS EYGHON'S FACE IN THE HUMAN WORLD.
"HE BOUGHT A BASE OF OPERATIONS. STARTED PUTTING TOGETHER AN ARMY.
"PROBLEM--EYGHON'S ENERGY'S STILL TOO MUCH FOR A HUMAN BODY.
"SOONER OR LATER THEY BURN OUT.
"THE ONES WITH SOULS--GILES, ETHAN, THE UNCONSCIOUS ONES--THEY LAST LONGER. BUT THEY HAVE AN EXPIRATION DATE TOO.
"THE BEST PRESERVATIVE? MAGIC. THE MORE OF IT THAT'S IN YOU, THE LONGER YOU KEEP.

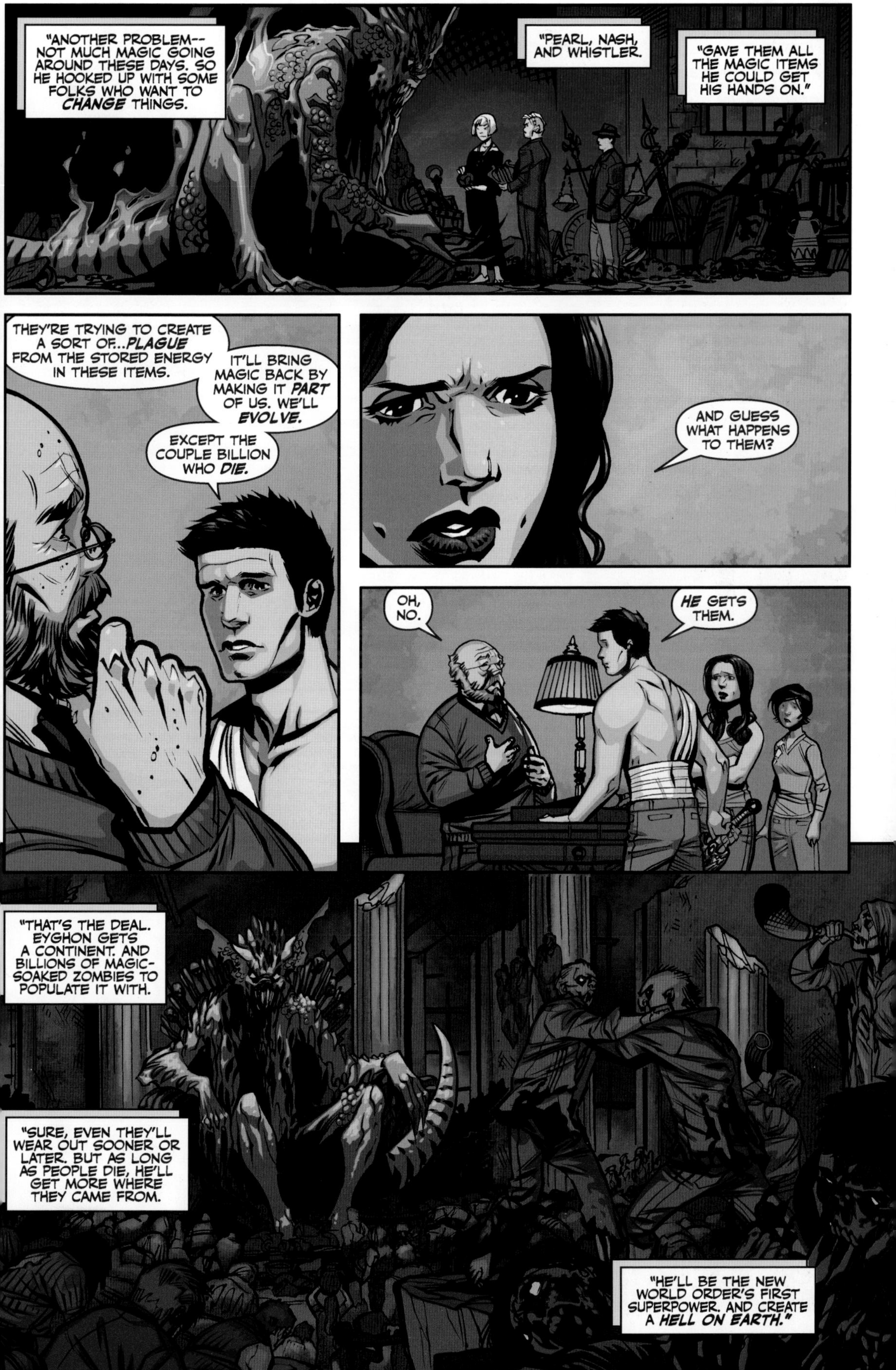
"ANOTHER PROBLEM-- NOT MUCH MAGIC GOING AROUND THESE DAYS. SO HE HOOKED UP WITH SOME FOLKS WHO WANT TO CHANGE THINGS.
"PEARL, NASH, AND WHISTLER.
"GAVE THEM ALL THE MAGIC ITEMS HE COULD GET HIS HANDS ON."
THEY'RE TRYING TO CREATE A SORT OF...PLAGUE FROM THE STORED ENERGY IN THESE ITEMS.
IT'LL BRING MAGIC BACK BY MAKING IT PART OF US. WE'LL EVOLVE.
EXCEPT THE COUPLE BILLION WHO DIE.
AND GUESS WHAT HAPPENS TO THEM?
OH, NO.
HE GETS THEM.
"THAT'S THE DEAL. EYGHON GETS A CONTINENT. AND BILLIONS OF MAGIC-SOAKED ZOMBIES TO POPULATE IT WITH.
"SURE, EVEN THEY'LL WEAR OUT SOONER OR LATER. BUT AS LONG AS PEOPLE DIE, HE'LL GET MORE WHERE THEY CAME FROM.
"HE'LL BE THE NEW WORLD ORDER'S FIRST SUPERPOWER. AND CREATE A HELL ON EARTH."

THEN WHY DOES HE WANT *US*? OUR *FRIENDS*?

I GOT THE FEELING HE LURED US THERE *SPECIFICALLY.* IF HE JUST WANTS BODIES FOR HIS ARMY, THERE'S EASIER PREY.

HE DOESN'T WANT EASY PREY. HE WANTS *SLAYERS.*

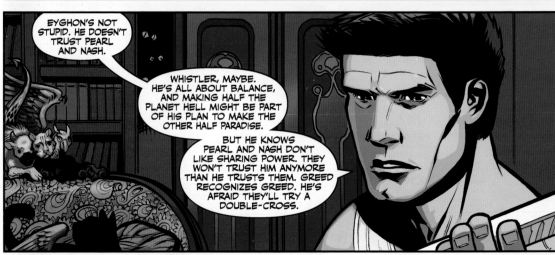

EYGHON'S NOT STUPID. HE DOESN'T TRUST PEARL AND NASH.

WHISTLER, MAYBE. HE'S ALL ABOUT BALANCE, AND MAKING HALF THE PLANET HELL MIGHT BE PART OF HIS PLAN TO MAKE THE OTHER HALF PARADISE.

BUT HE KNOWS PEARL AND NASH DON'T LIKE SHARING POWER. THEY WON'T TRUST HIM ANYMORE THAN HE TRUSTS THEM. GREED RECOGNIZES GREED. HE'S AFRAID THEY'LL TRY A DOUBLE-CROSS.

HE WANTS AN ARMY OF SUPERHUMAN WARRIORS WHOSE BODIES ARE INFUSED WITH MAGIC. SO THEY'LL *LAST.*

HE'S ALREADY GOT ENOUGH TO DO A LOT OF DAMAGE. BUT HE NEEDS *MORE.*

WE NEED TO TAKE HIM OUT BEFORE THEIR NUMBERS GROW.

YOU DO REALIZE HE'LL BE TAKING ADVANTAGE OF THE FACT THAT YOU DON'T WANT TO HURT HIS THRALLS. WHILE THEY HAVE NO SUCH RESTRICTIONS.

THAT'S WHY I'M LOOKING FOR WEAPONS WE CAN USE TO DISABLE THEM WITHOUT CAUSING PERMANENT DAMAGE. GOT ANY HANDCUFFS?

THE CABINET TO THE LEFT.

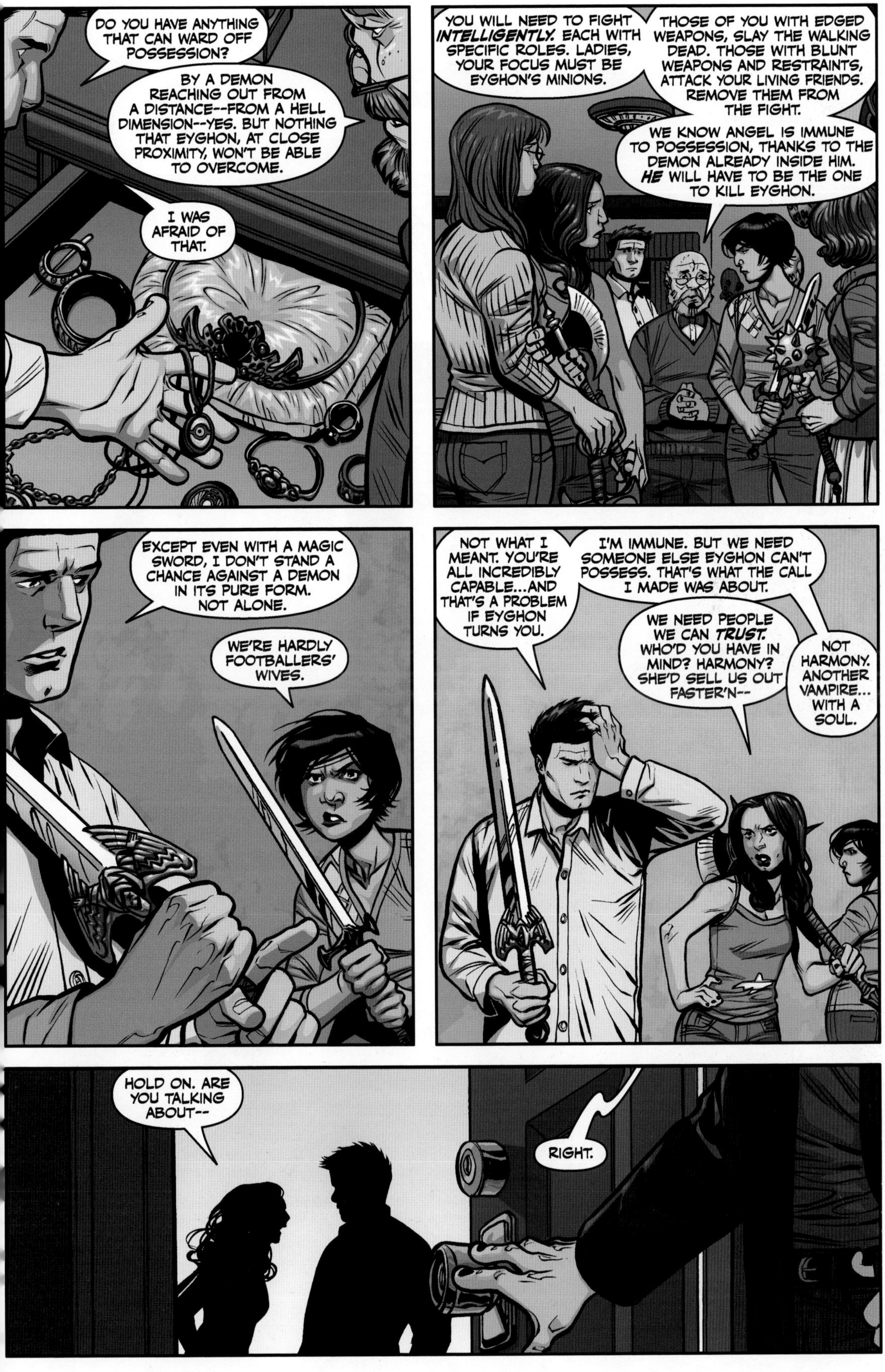
DO YOU HAVE ANYTHING THAT CAN WARD OFF POSSESSION?
BY A DEMON REACHING OUT FROM A DISTANCE--FROM A HELL DIMENSION--YES. BUT NOTHING THAT EYGHON, AT CLOSE PROXIMITY, WON'T BE ABLE TO OVERCOME.
I WAS AFRAID OF THAT.
YOU WILL NEED TO FIGHT *INTELLIGENTLY.* EACH WITH SPECIFIC ROLES. LADIES, YOUR FOCUS MUST BE EYGHON'S MINIONS.
THOSE OF YOU WITH EDGED WEAPONS, SLAY THE WALKING DEAD. THOSE WITH BLUNT WEAPONS AND RESTRAINTS, ATTACK YOUR LIVING FRIENDS. REMOVE THEM FROM THE FIGHT.
WE KNOW ANGEL IS IMMUNE TO POSSESSION, THANKS TO THE DEMON ALREADY INSIDE HIM. *HE* WILL HAVE TO BE THE ONE TO KILL EYGHON.
EXCEPT EVEN WITH A MAGIC SWORD, I DON'T STAND A CHANCE AGAINST A DEMON IN ITS PURE FORM. NOT ALONE.
WE'RE HARDLY FOOTBALLERS' WIVES.
NOT WHAT I MEANT. YOU'RE ALL INCREDIBLY CAPABLE...AND THAT'S A PROBLEM IF EYGHON TURNS YOU.
I'M IMMUNE. BUT WE NEED SOMEONE ELSE EYGHON CAN'T POSSESS. THAT'S WHAT THE CALL I MADE WAS ABOUT.
WE NEED PEOPLE WE CAN *TRUST.* WHO'D YOU HAVE IN MIND? HARMONY? SHE'D SELL US OUT FASTER'N--
NOT HARMONY. ANOTHER VAMPIRE... WITH A SOUL.
HOLD ON. ARE YOU TALKING ABOUT--
RIGHT.

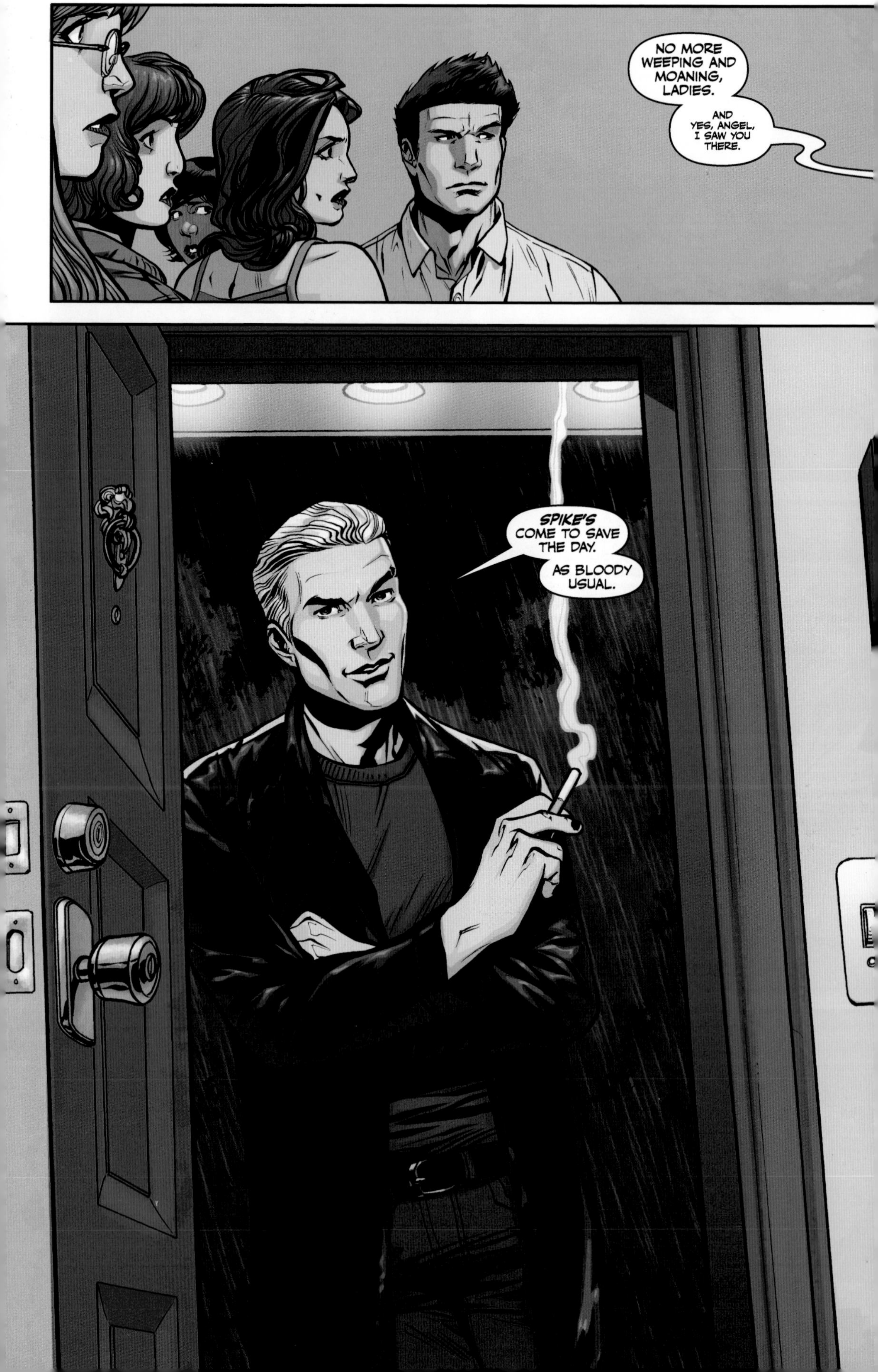
NO MORE WEEPING AND MOANING, LADIES.
AND YES, ANGEL, I SAW YOU THERE.
SPIKE'S COME TO SAVE THE DAY.
AS BLOODY USUAL.

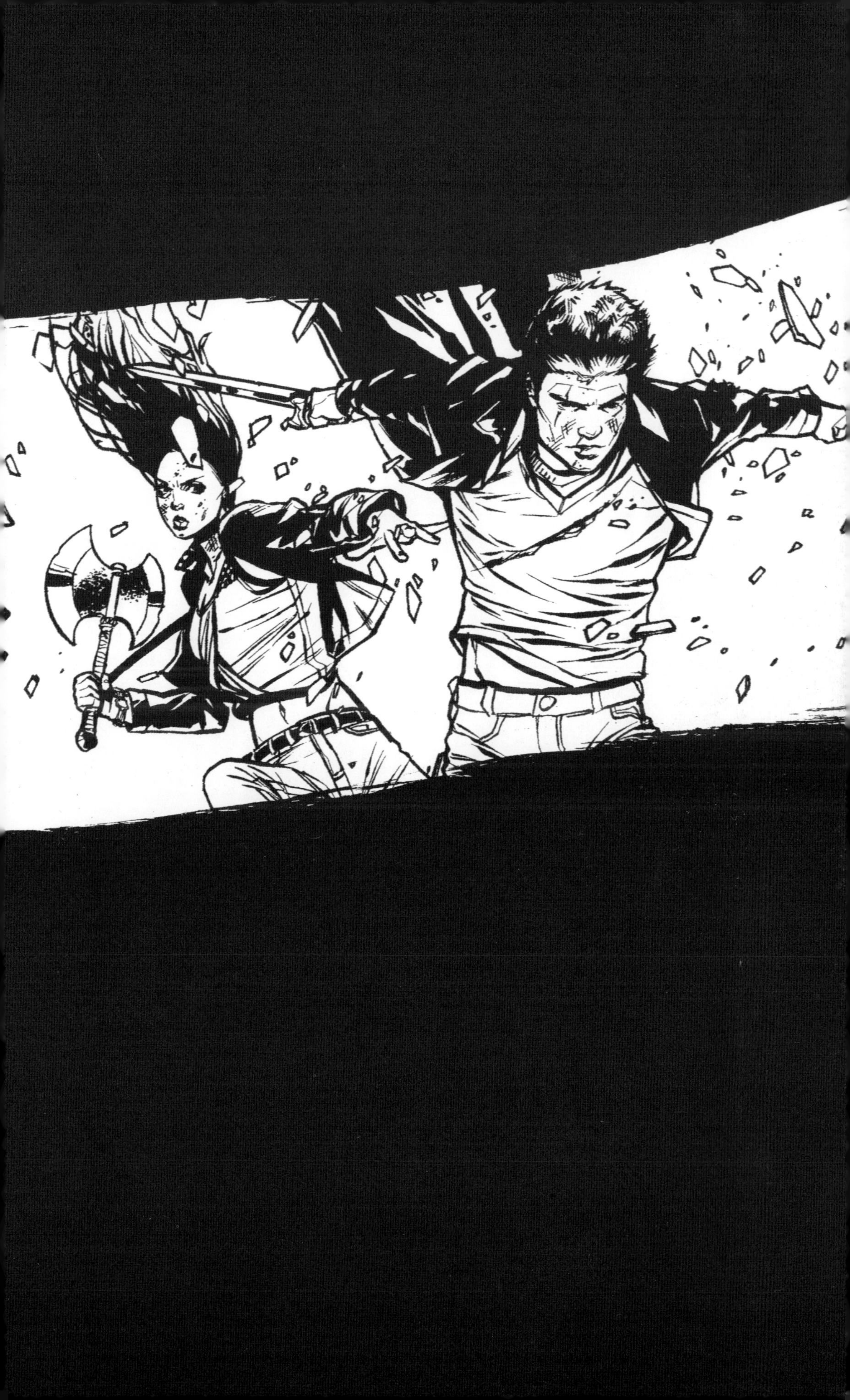

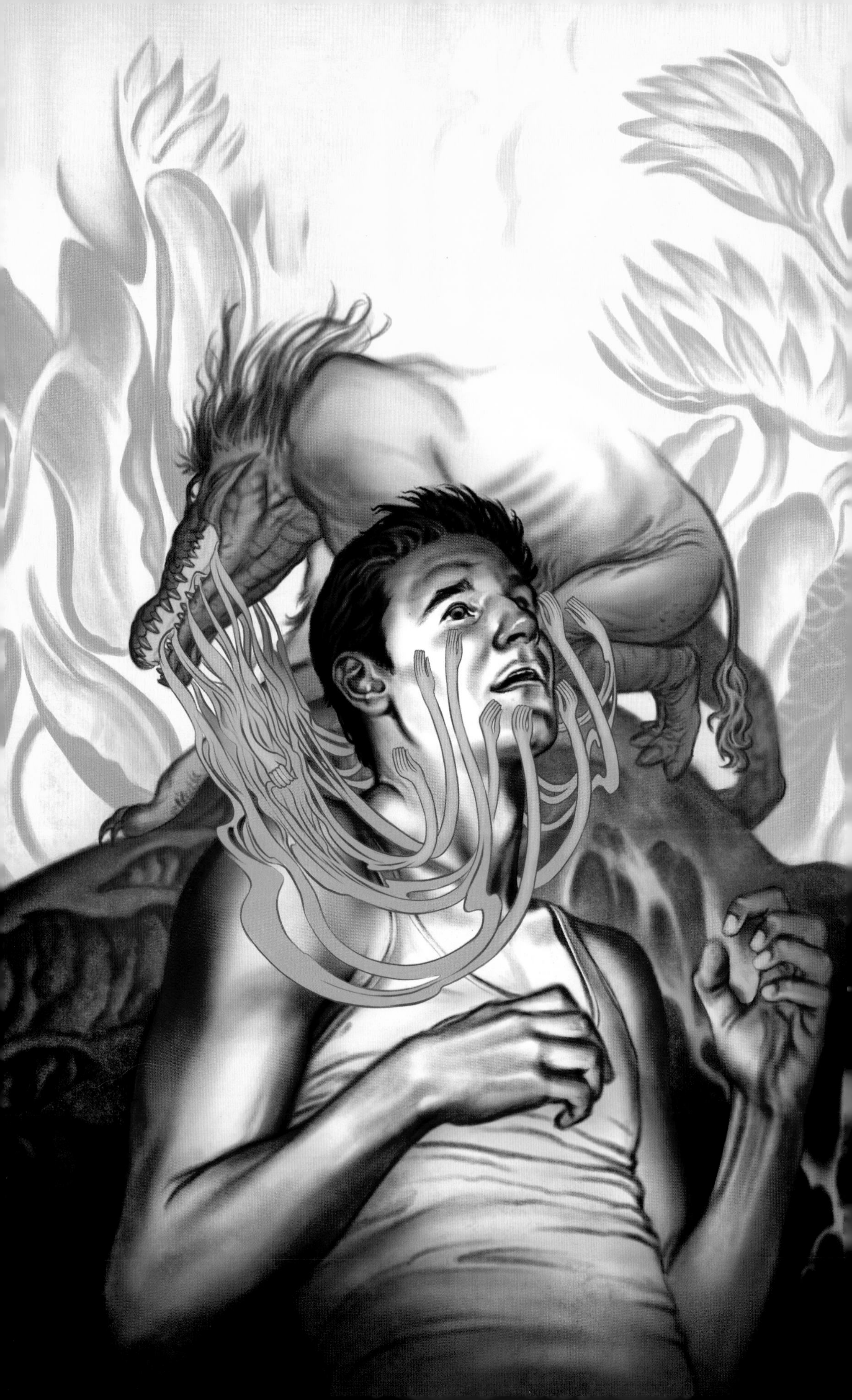

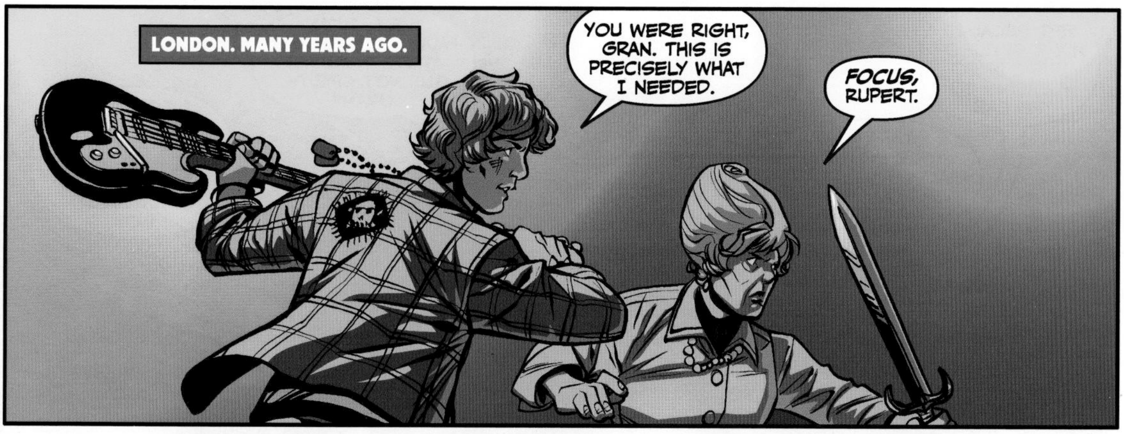
LONDON. MANY YEARS AGO.
YOU WERE RIGHT, GRAN. THIS IS PRECISELY WHAT I NEEDED.
FOCUS, RUPERT.

DEATH AND CONSEQUENCES

PART 4 OF 4

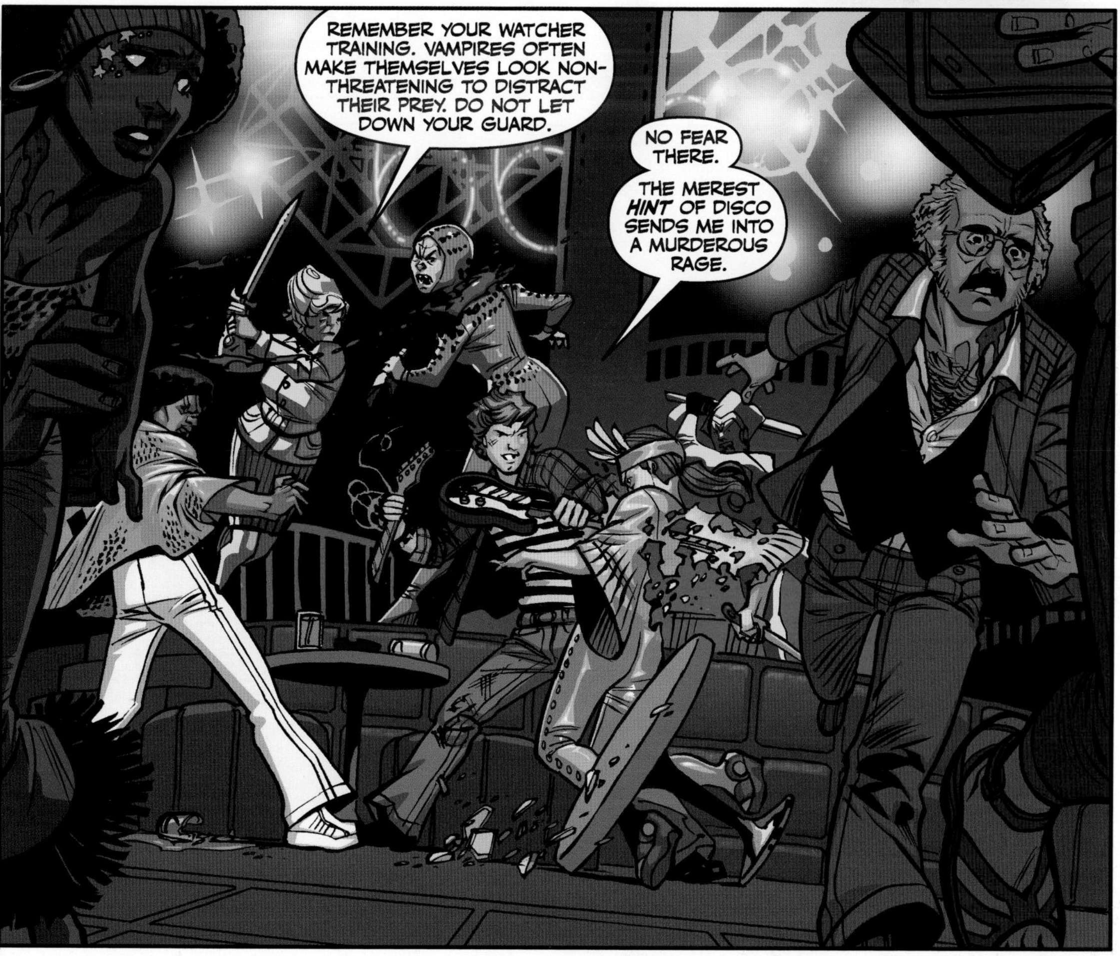
REMEMBER YOUR WATCHER TRAINING. VAMPIRES OFTEN MAKE THEMSELVES LOOK NON-THREATENING TO DISTRACT THEIR PREY. DO NOT LET DOWN YOUR GUARD.
NO FEAR THERE.
THE MEREST HINT OF DISCO SENDS ME INTO A MURDEROUS RAGE.

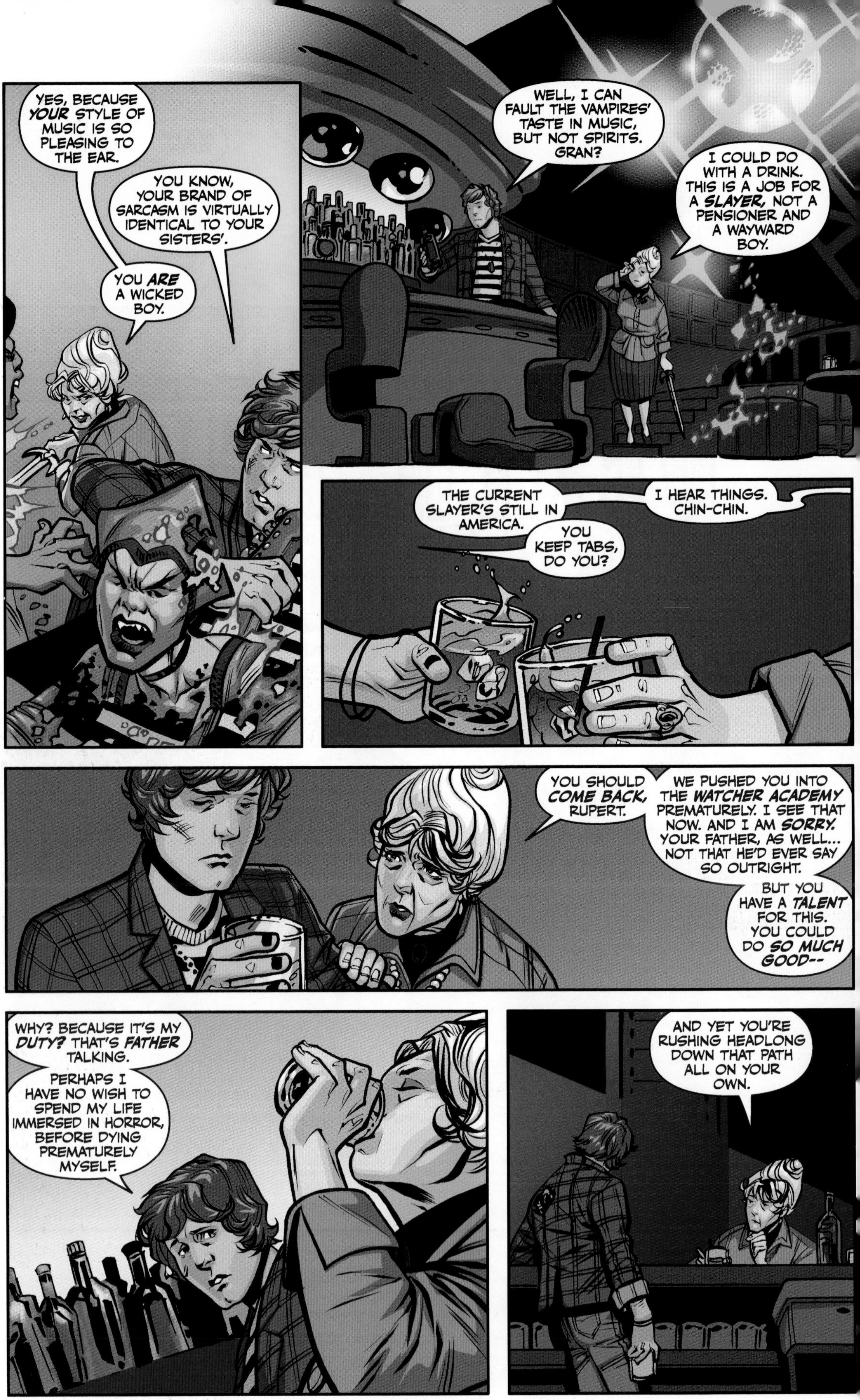
YES, BECAUSE YOUR STYLE OF MUSIC IS SO PLEASING TO THE EAR.
YOU KNOW, YOUR BRAND OF SARCASM IS VIRTUALLY IDENTICAL TO YOUR SISTERS'.
YOU ARE A WICKED BOY.
WELL, I CAN FAULT THE VAMPIRES' TASTE IN MUSIC, BUT NOT SPIRITS. GRAN?
I COULD DO WITH A DRINK. THIS IS A JOB FOR A SLAYER, NOT A PENSIONER AND A WAYWARD BOY.
THE CURRENT SLAYER'S STILL IN AMERICA.
YOU KEEP TABS, DO YOU?
I HEAR THINGS. CHIN-CHIN.
YOU SHOULD COME BACK, RUPERT.
WE PUSHED YOU INTO THE WATCHER ACADEMY PREMATURELY. I SEE THAT NOW. AND I AM SORRY. YOUR FATHER, AS WELL... NOT THAT HE'D EVER SAY SO OUTRIGHT.
BUT YOU HAVE A TALENT FOR THIS. YOU COULD DO SO MUCH GOOD--
WHY? BECAUSE IT'S MY DUTY? THAT'S FATHER TALKING.
PERHAPS I HAVE NO WISH TO SPEND MY LIFE IMMERSED IN HORROR, BEFORE DYING PREMATURELY MYSELF.
AND YET YOU'RE RUSHING HEADLONG DOWN THAT PATH ALL ON YOUR OWN.

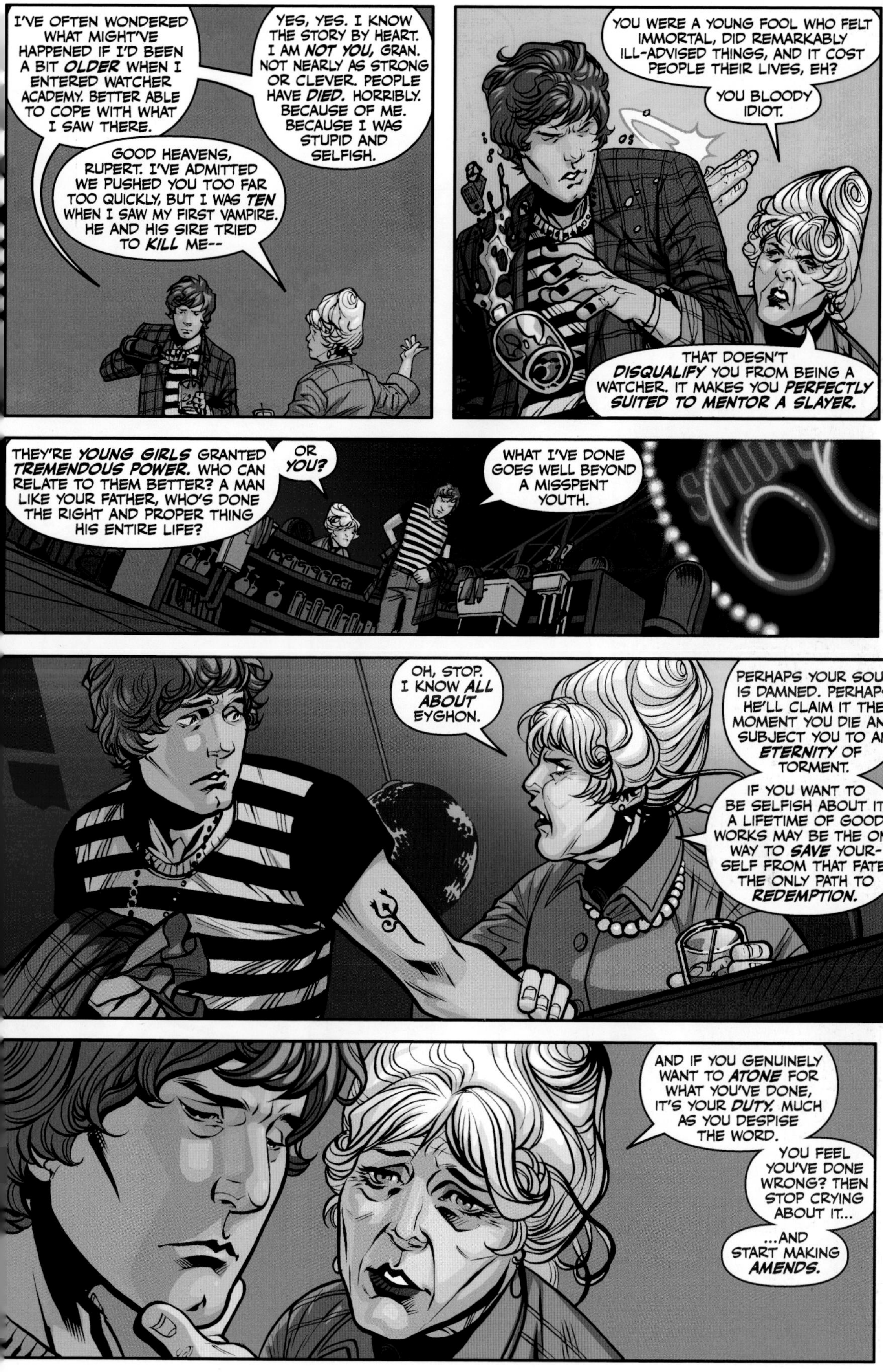
I'VE OFTEN WONDERED WHAT MIGHT'VE HAPPENED IF I'D BEEN A BIT OLDER WHEN I ENTERED WATCHER ACADEMY. BETTER ABLE TO COPE WITH WHAT I SAW THERE.
GOOD HEAVENS, RUPERT. I'VE ADMITTED WE PUSHED YOU TOO FAR TOO QUICKLY, BUT I WAS TEN WHEN I SAW MY FIRST VAMPIRE. HE AND HIS SIRE TRIED TO KILL ME--
YES, YES. I KNOW THE STORY BY HEART. I AM NOT YOU, GRAN. NOT NEARLY AS STRONG OR CLEVER. PEOPLE HAVE DIED. HORRIBLY. BECAUSE OF ME. BECAUSE I WAS STUPID AND SELFISH.
YOU WERE A YOUNG FOOL WHO FELT IMMORTAL, DID REMARKABLY ILL-ADVISED THINGS, AND IT COST PEOPLE THEIR LIVES, EH?
YOU BLOODY IDIOT.
THAT DOESN'T DISQUALIFY YOU FROM BEING A WATCHER. IT MAKES YOU PERFECTLY SUITED TO MENTOR A SLAYER.
THEY'RE YOUNG GIRLS GRANTED TREMENDOUS POWER. WHO CAN RELATE TO THEM BETTER? A MAN LIKE YOUR FATHER, WHO'S DONE THE RIGHT AND PROPER THING HIS ENTIRE LIFE?
OR YOU?
WHAT I'VE DONE GOES WELL BEYOND A MISSPENT YOUTH.
OH, STOP. I KNOW ALL ABOUT EYGHON.
PERHAPS YOUR SOUL IS DAMNED. PERHAPS HE'LL CLAIM IT THE MOMENT YOU DIE AND SUBJECT YOU TO AN ETERNITY OF TORMENT.
IF YOU WANT TO BE SELFISH ABOUT IT, A LIFETIME OF GOOD WORKS MAY BE THE ONE WAY TO SAVE YOURSELF FROM THAT FATE. THE ONLY PATH TO REDEMPTION.
AND IF YOU GENUINELY WANT TO ATONE FOR WHAT YOU'VE DONE, IT'S YOUR DUTY. MUCH AS YOU DESPISE THE WORD.
YOU FEEL YOU'VE DONE WRONG? THEN STOP CRYING ABOUT IT...
...AND START MAKING AMENDS.

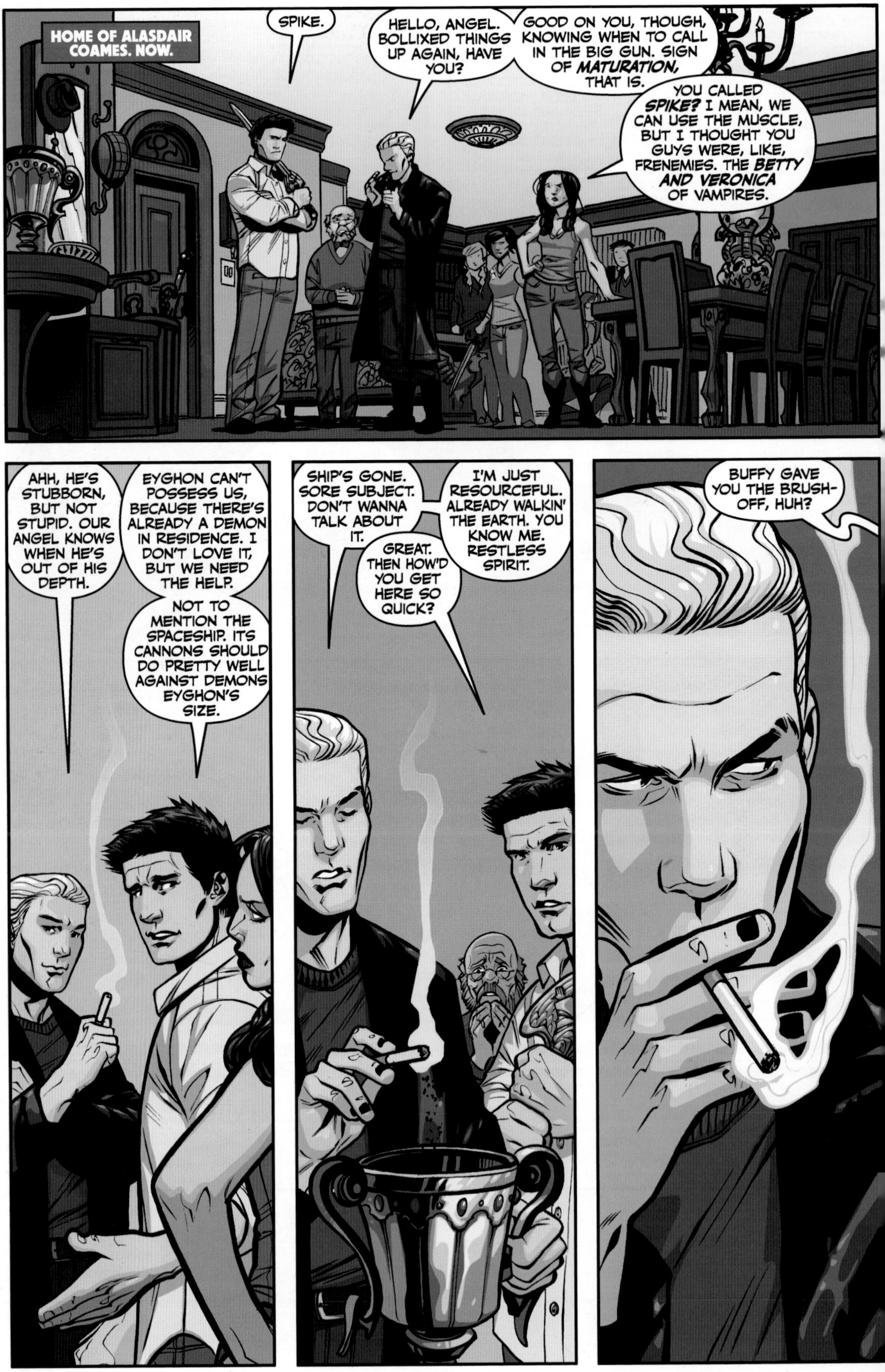

HOME OF ALASDAIR COAMES. NOW.
SPIKE.
HELLO, ANGEL. BOLLIXED THINGS UP AGAIN, HAVE YOU?
GOOD ON YOU, THOUGH, KNOWING WHEN TO CALL IN THE BIG GUN. SIGN OF MATURATION, THAT IS.
YOU CALLED SPIKE? I MEAN, WE CAN USE THE MUSCLE, BUT I THOUGHT YOU GUYS WERE, LIKE, FRENEMIES. THE BETTY AND VERONICA OF VAMPIRES.
AHH, HE'S STUBBORN, BUT NOT STUPID. OUR ANGEL KNOWS WHEN HE'S OUT OF HIS DEPTH.
EYGHON CAN'T POSSESS US, BECAUSE THERE'S ALREADY A DEMON IN RESIDENCE. I DON'T LOVE IT, BUT WE NEED THE HELP.
NOT TO MENTION THE SPACESHIP. ITS CANNONS SHOULD DO PRETTY WELL AGAINST DEMONS EYGHON'S SIZE.
SHIP'S GONE. SORE SUBJECT. DON'T WANNA TALK ABOUT IT.
GREAT. THEN HOW'D YOU GET HERE SO QUICK?
I'M JUST RESOURCEFUL. ALREADY WALKIN' THE EARTH. YOU KNOW ME. RESTLESS SPIRIT.
BUFFY GAVE YOU THE BRUSH-OFF, HUH?

I LEFT OF MY *OWN BLOODY ACCORD!* SHE CAN AT LEAST STAND THE SIGHT OF ME, UNLIKE SOME UNDEAD PEOPLE I COULD MENTION!

ANNND CUE THE SLAP FIGHT.

I'M NOT *YOU*, MOONING ABOUT OUTSIDE HER WINDOW. I KNOW WHEN A BIT OF SPACE IS HEALTHY FOR *ALL* CONCERNED.

SHE'S *WITH* SOMEBODY, HUH? HE A GOOD GUY, AT LEAST?

BEEN GETTING CHUMMY WITH A COPPER. SEEMS A DECENT ENOUGH SORT. DUNNO IF IT'S ANYTHING-- WASN'T ABOUT TO HANG AROUND AND FIND OUT. MORE IMPORTANT THINGS TO DO.

MY THINKING EXACTLY.

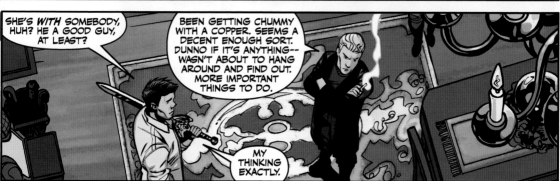

OH, TOO RIGHT. YOU'RE OUT TO RESURRECT THE *LIBRARIAN* IN THE HOPES SHE WON'T *HATE* YOU ANYMORE.

I'M *TAKING RESPONSIBILITY* FOR MY MISTAKES. NOT THAT YOU'D KNOW ANYTHING ABOUT THAT.

WHAT DO *YOU* KNOW ABOUT IT, NEVER BOTHERING TO CHECK IN AFTER YOUR LITTLE COSMIC SHAG? DID YOU HAVE *ANY BLOODY IDEA* SHE THOUGHT SHE WAS--

OI. WHAT'S THIS, THEN?

WILLIAM THE BLOODY. MASS MURDERER. KILLER OF TWO SLAYERS.

I'VE GOT SOMETHING FOR YOU.

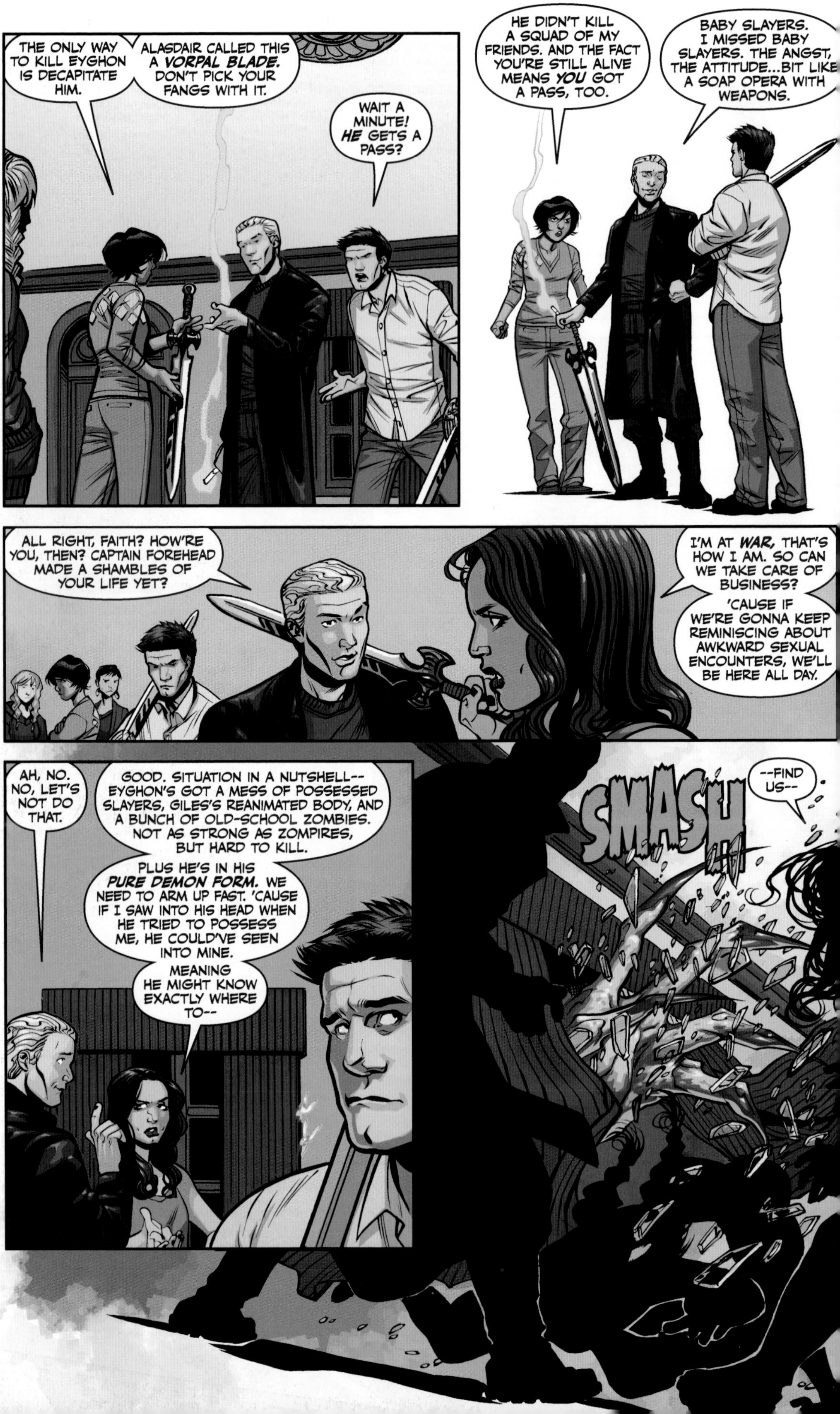
THE ONLY WAY TO KILL EYGHON IS DECAPITATE HIM.
ALASDAIR CALLED THIS A VORPAL BLADE. DON'T PICK YOUR FANGS WITH IT.
WAIT A MINUTE! HE GETS A PASS?
HE DIDN'T KILL A SQUAD OF MY FRIENDS. AND THE FACT YOU'RE STILL ALIVE MEANS YOU GOT A PASS, TOO.
BABY SLAYERS. I MISSED BABY SLAYERS. THE ANGST, THE ATTITUDE...BIT LIKE A SOAP OPERA WITH WEAPONS.
ALL RIGHT, FAITH? HOW'RE YOU, THEN? CAPTAIN FOREHEAD MADE A SHAMBLES OF YOUR LIFE YET?
I'M AT WAR, THAT'S HOW I AM. SO CAN WE TAKE CARE OF BUSINESS?
'CAUSE IF WE'RE GONNA KEEP REMINISCING ABOUT AWKWARD SEXUAL ENCOUNTERS, WE'LL BE HERE ALL DAY.
AH, NO. NO, LET'S NOT DO THAT.
GOOD. SITUATION IN A NUTSHELL--EYGHON'S GOT A MESS OF POSSESSED SLAYERS, GILES'S REANIMATED BODY, AND A BUNCH OF OLD-SCHOOL ZOMBIES. NOT AS STRONG AS ZOMPIRES, BUT HARD TO KILL.
PLUS HE'S IN HIS PURE DEMON FORM. WE NEED TO ARM UP FAST. 'CAUSE IF I SAW INTO HIS HEAD WHEN HE TRIED TO POSSESS ME, HE COULD'VE SEEN INTO MINE.
MEANING HE MIGHT KNOW EXACTLY WHERE TO--
SMASH
--FIND US--

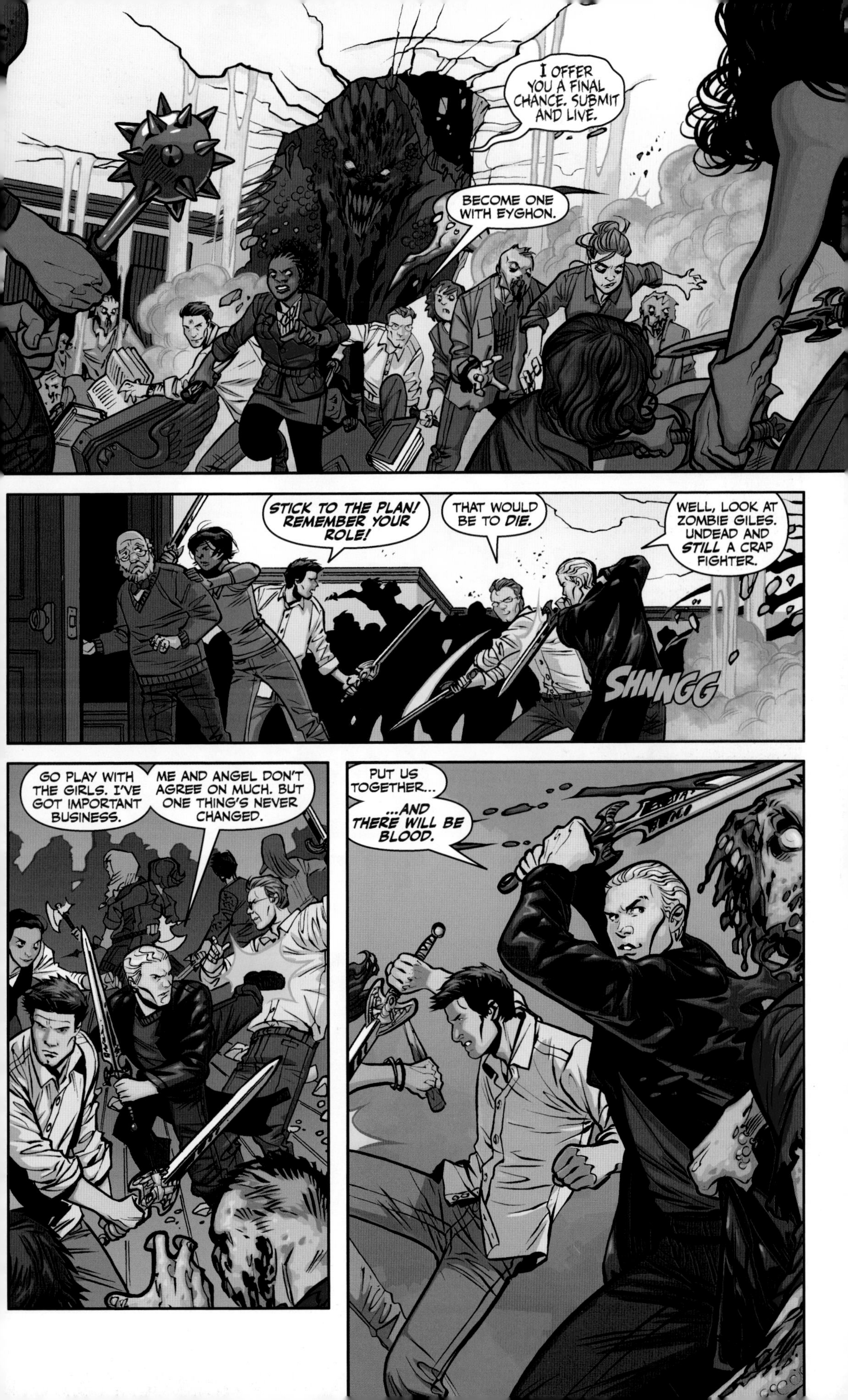

I OFFER YOU A FINAL CHANCE. SUBMIT AND LIVE.
BECOME ONE WITH EYGHON.
STICK TO THE PLAN! REMEMBER YOUR ROLE!
THAT WOULD BE TO DIE.
WELL, LOOK AT ZOMBIE GILES. UNDEAD AND STILL A CRAP FIGHTER.
SHNNGG
GO PLAY WITH THE GIRLS. I'VE GOT IMPORTANT BUSINESS.
ME AND ANGEL DON'T AGREE ON MUCH. BUT ONE THING'S NEVER CHANGED.
PUT US TOGETHER...
...AND THERE WILL BE BLOOD.

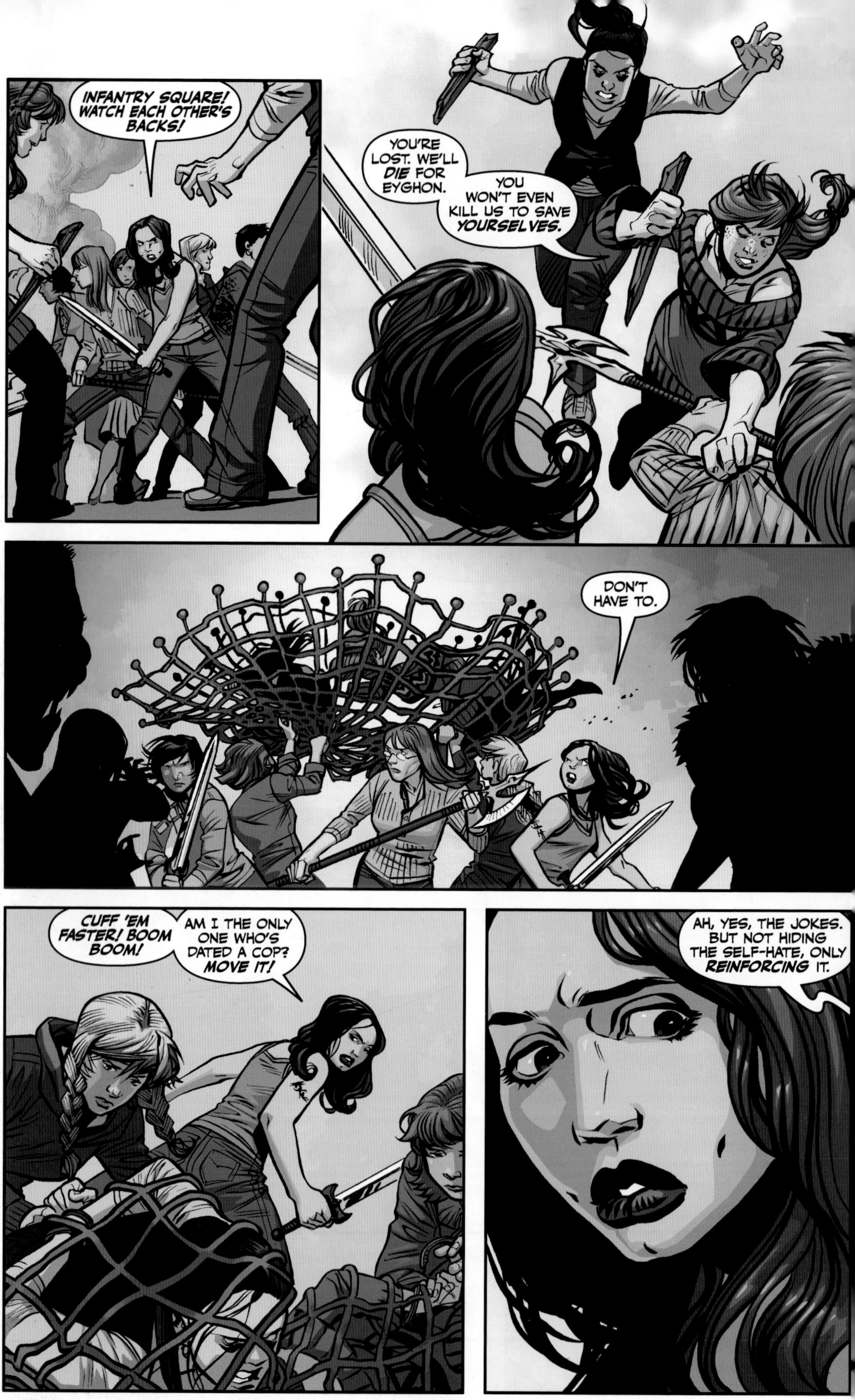
INFANTRY SQUARE! WATCH EACH OTHER'S BACKS!
YOU'RE LOST. WE'LL DIE FOR EYGHON.
YOU WON'T EVEN KILL US TO SAVE YOURSELVES.
DON'T HAVE TO.
CUFF 'EM FASTER! BOOM BOOM!
AM I THE ONLY ONE WHO'S DATED A COP? MOVE IT!
AH, YES, THE JOKES. BUT NOT HIDING THE SELF-HATE, ONLY REINFORCING IT.

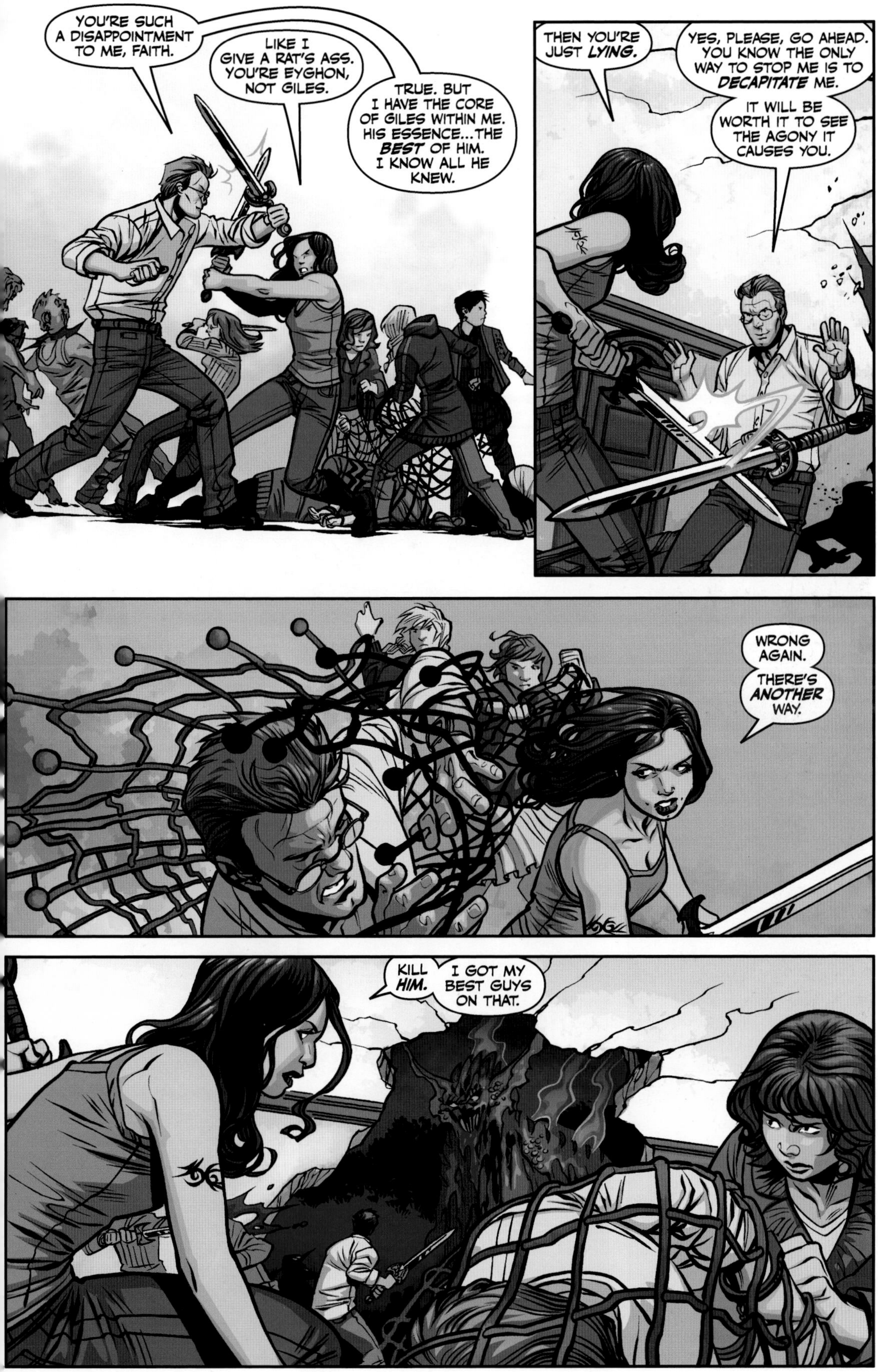
YOU'RE SUCH A DISAPPOINTMENT TO ME, FAITH.
LIKE I GIVE A RAT'S ASS. YOU'RE EYGHON, NOT GILES.
TRUE. BUT I HAVE THE CORE OF GILES WITHIN ME. HIS ESSENCE...THE BEST OF HIM. I KNOW ALL HE KNEW.
THEN YOU'RE JUST LYING.
YES, PLEASE, GO AHEAD. YOU KNOW THE ONLY WAY TO STOP ME IS TO DECAPITATE ME.
IT WILL BE WORTH IT TO SEE THE AGONY IT CAUSES YOU.
WRONG AGAIN.
THERE'S ANOTHER WAY.
KILL HIM.
I GOT MY BEST GUYS ON THAT.

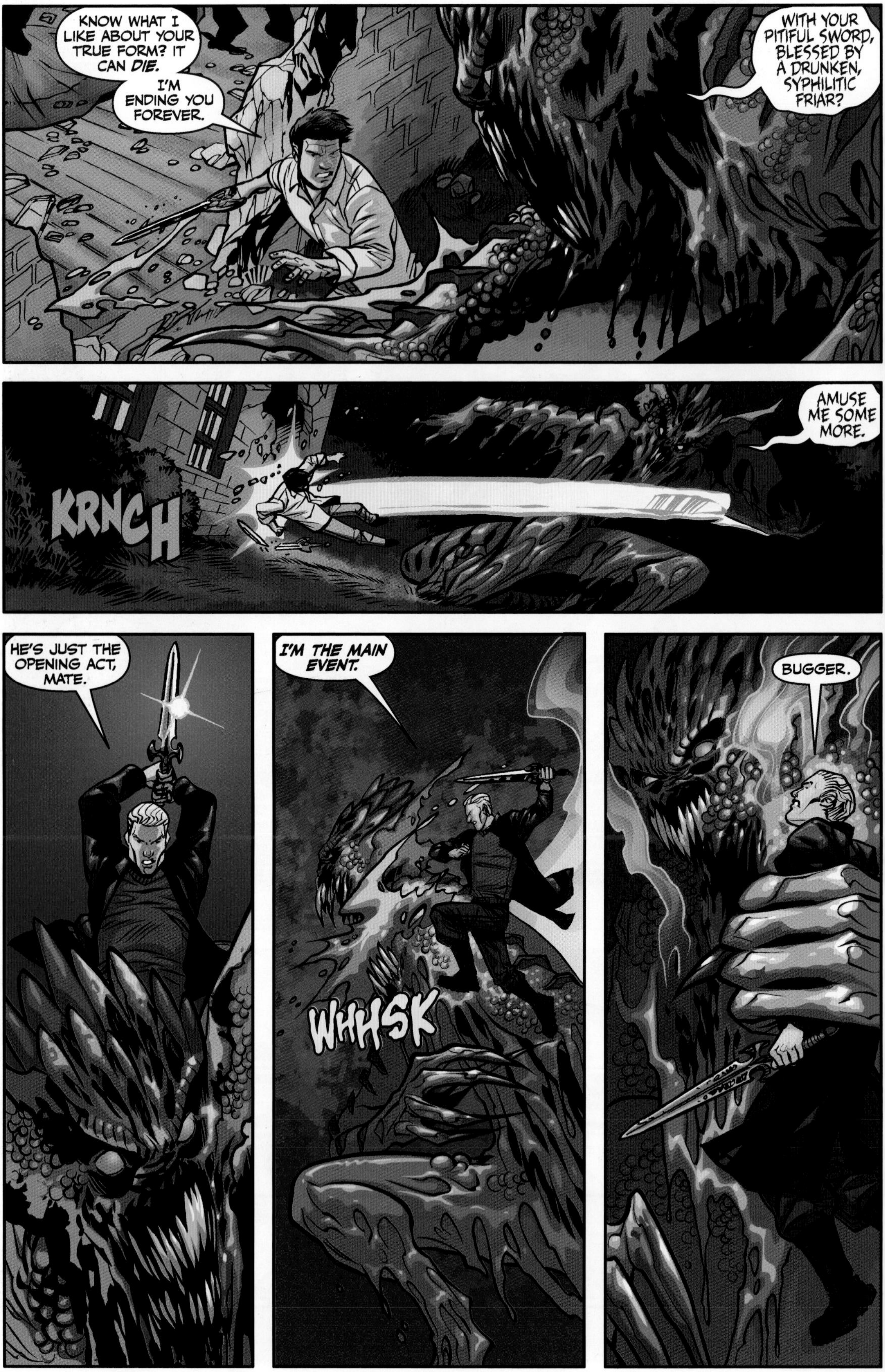
KNOW WHAT I LIKE ABOUT YOUR TRUE FORM? IT CAN *DIE*.
I'M ENDING YOU FOREVER.
WITH YOUR PITIFUL SWORD, BLESSED BY A DRUNKEN, SYPHILITIC FRIAR?
AMUSE ME SOME MORE.
KRNCH
HE'S JUST THE OPENING ACT, MATE.
I'M THE MAIN EVENT.
WHHSK
BUGGER.

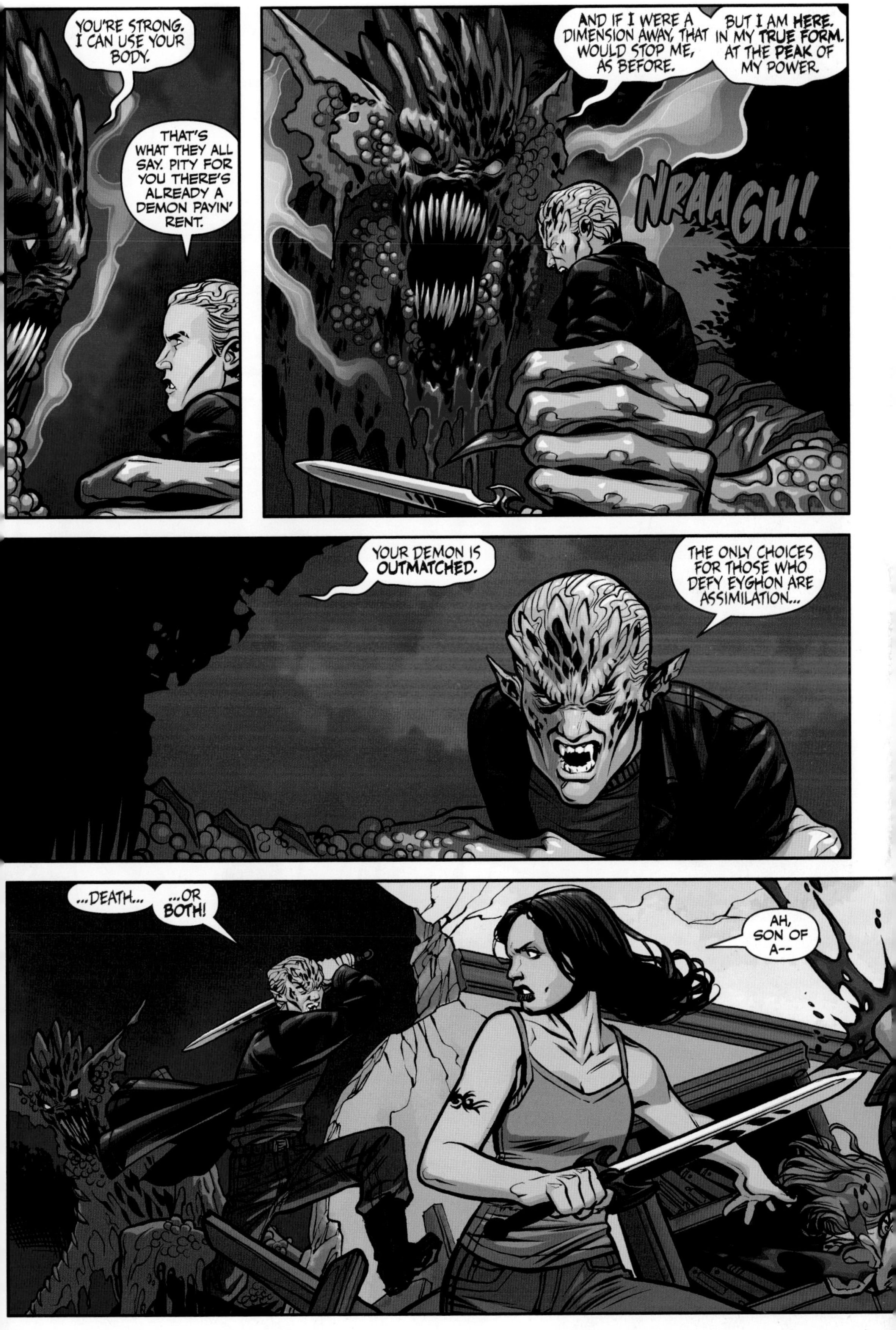

YOU'RE STRONG. I CAN USE YOUR BODY.
THAT'S WHAT THEY ALL SAY. PITY FOR YOU THERE'S ALREADY A DEMON PAYIN' RENT.
AND IF I WERE A DIMENSION AWAY, THAT WOULD STOP ME, AS BEFORE.
BUT I AM HERE. IN MY TRUE FORM. AT THE PEAK OF MY POWER.
NRAAGH!
YOUR DEMON IS OUTMATCHED.
THE ONLY CHOICES FOR THOSE WHO DEFY EYGHON ARE ASSIMILATION...
...DEATH...
...OR BOTH!
AH, SON OF A--

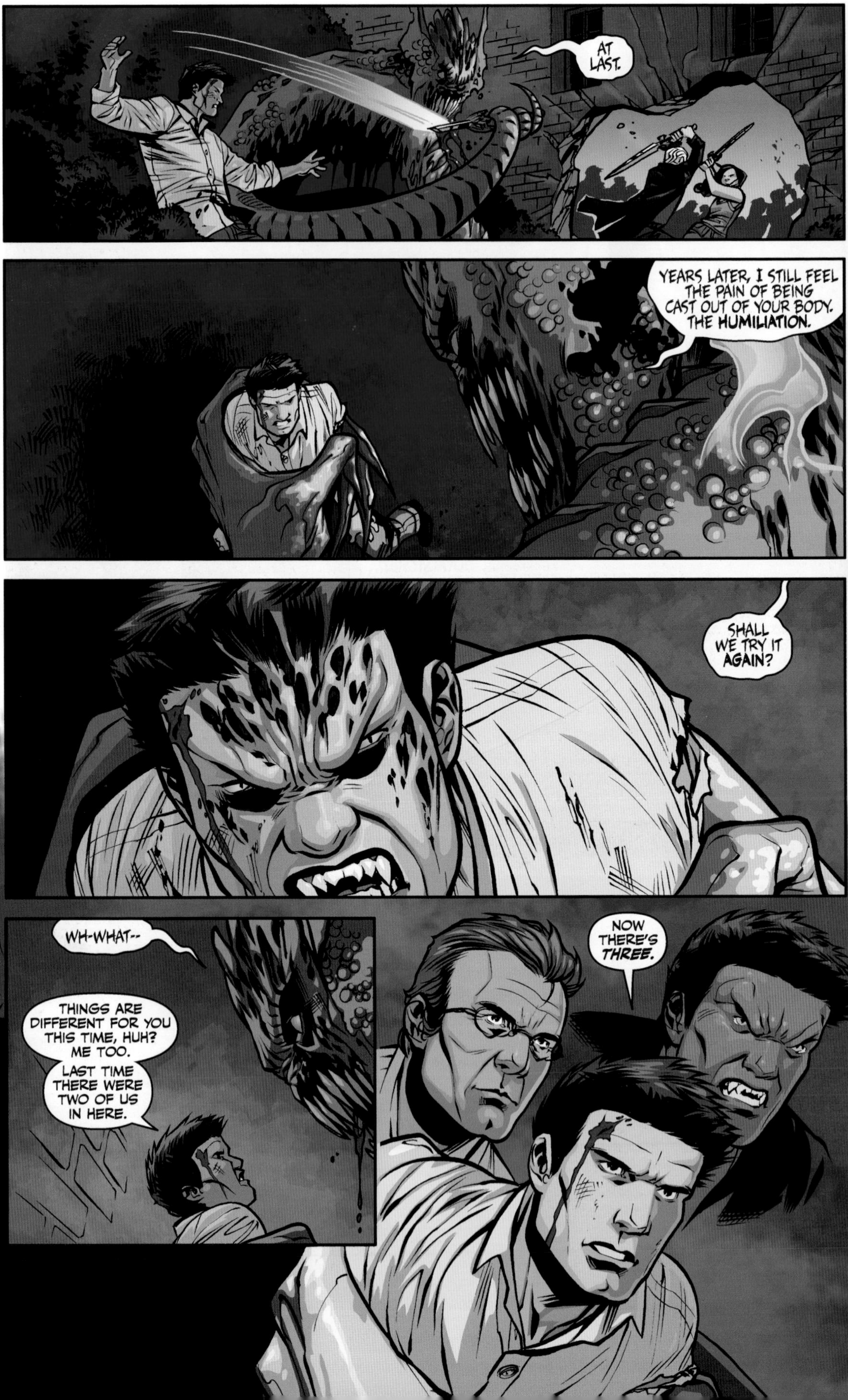
AT LAST.
YEARS LATER, I STILL FEEL THE PAIN OF BEING CAST OUT OF YOUR BODY. THE HUMILIATION.
SHALL WE TRY IT AGAIN?
WH-WHAT--
THINGS ARE DIFFERENT FOR YOU THIS TIME, HUH? ME TOO.
LAST TIME THERE WERE TWO OF US IN HERE.
NOW THERE'S THREE.

THE **TOOTH** OF AMMUT! I BEGIN TO SEE.

BUT THERE IS A FLAW IN YOUR PLAN. ONE OF THE SOULS WITHIN YOU IS ONLY **PARTIALLY** PRESENT...

...AND BELONGS **ENTIRELY** TO ME.

GGAAAHHH!

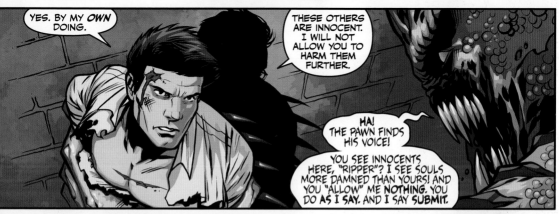

YES. BY MY **OWN** DOING.

THESE OTHERS ARE INNOCENT. I WILL NOT ALLOW YOU TO HARM THEM FURTHER.

HA! THE PAWN FINDS HIS VOICE!

YOU SEE INNOCENTS HERE, "RIPPER"? I SEE SOULS MORE DAMNED THAN YOURS! AND YOU "ALLOW" ME **NOTHING.** YOU DO AS I SAY. AND I SAY SUBMIT.

STOP! THIS IS INTOLERABLE!

YOU ARE MINE! YOU HAVE NO WILL OF YOUR OWN!

WHAT THE DENIZENS OF HELL REFUSE TO ACCEPT IS THAT DAMNATION IS, AT SOME POINT, A *CHOICE.*

AS IS *THIS.*

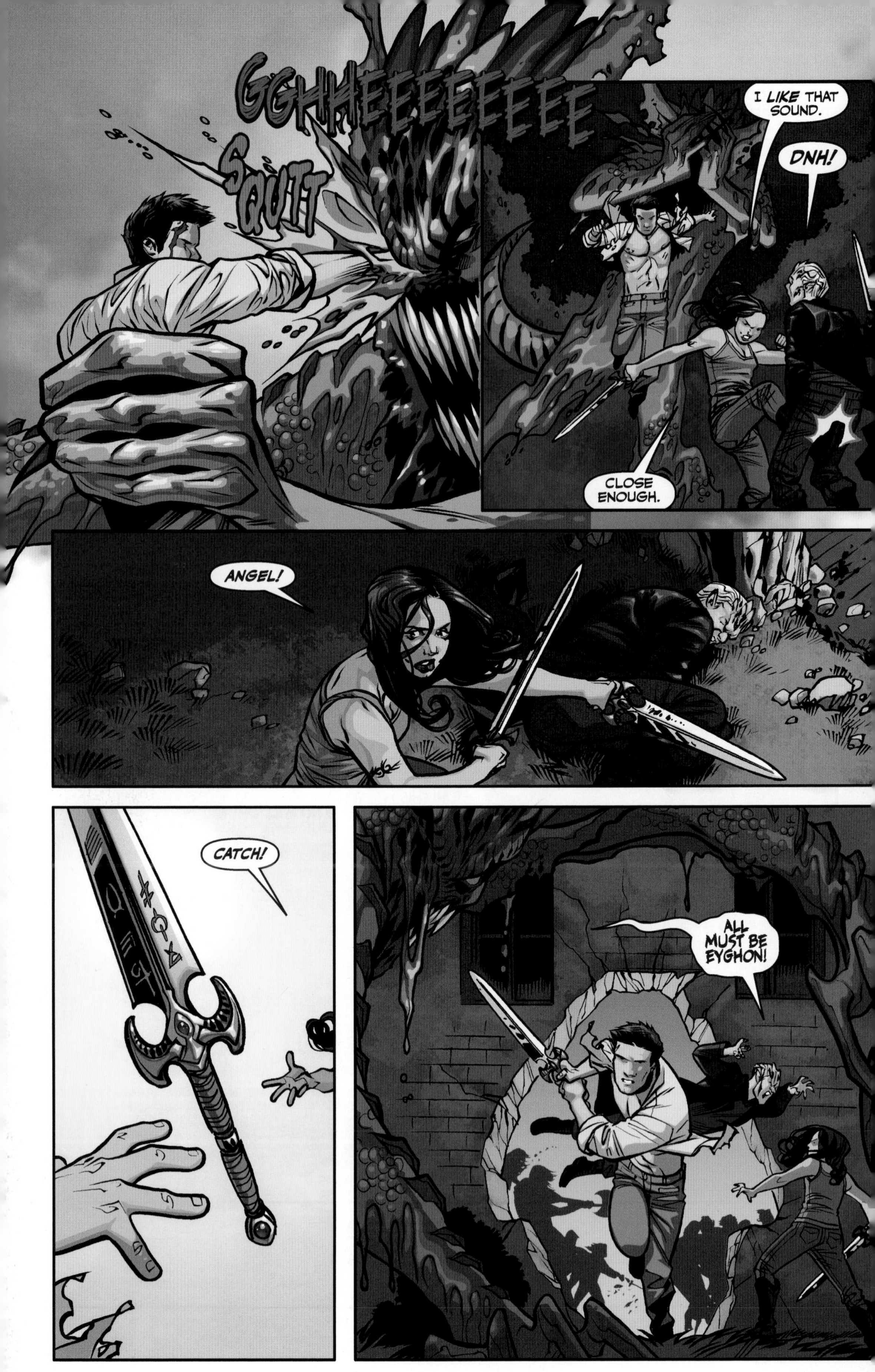
GGHHEEEEEEEEE
SQUIT
I LIKE THAT SOUND.
DNH!
CLOSE ENOUGH.
ANGEL!
CATCH!
ALL MUST BE EYGHON!

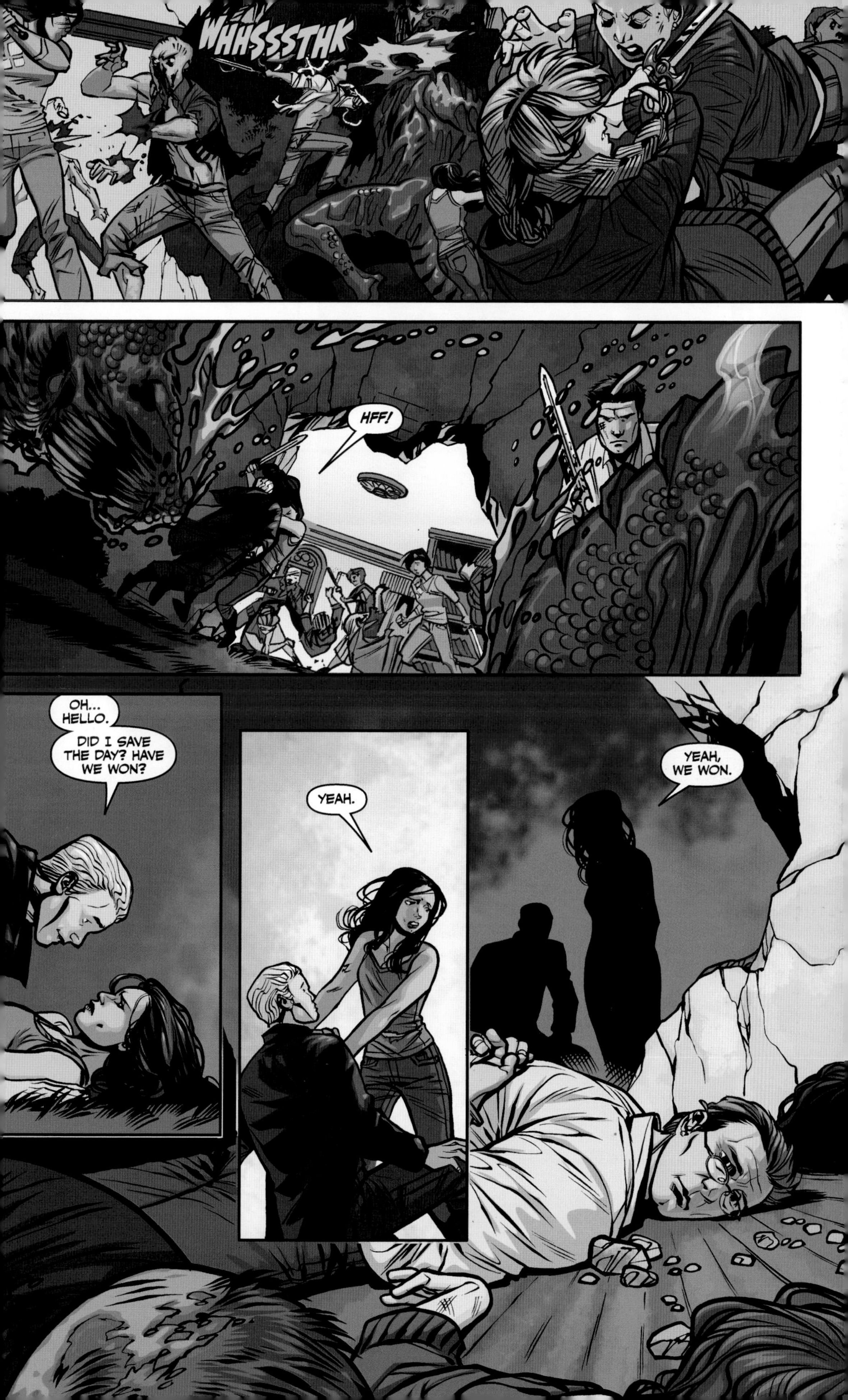
WHHSSSTHK
HFF!
OH... HELLO.
DID I SAVE THE DAY? HAVE WE WON?
YEAH.
YEAH, WE WON.

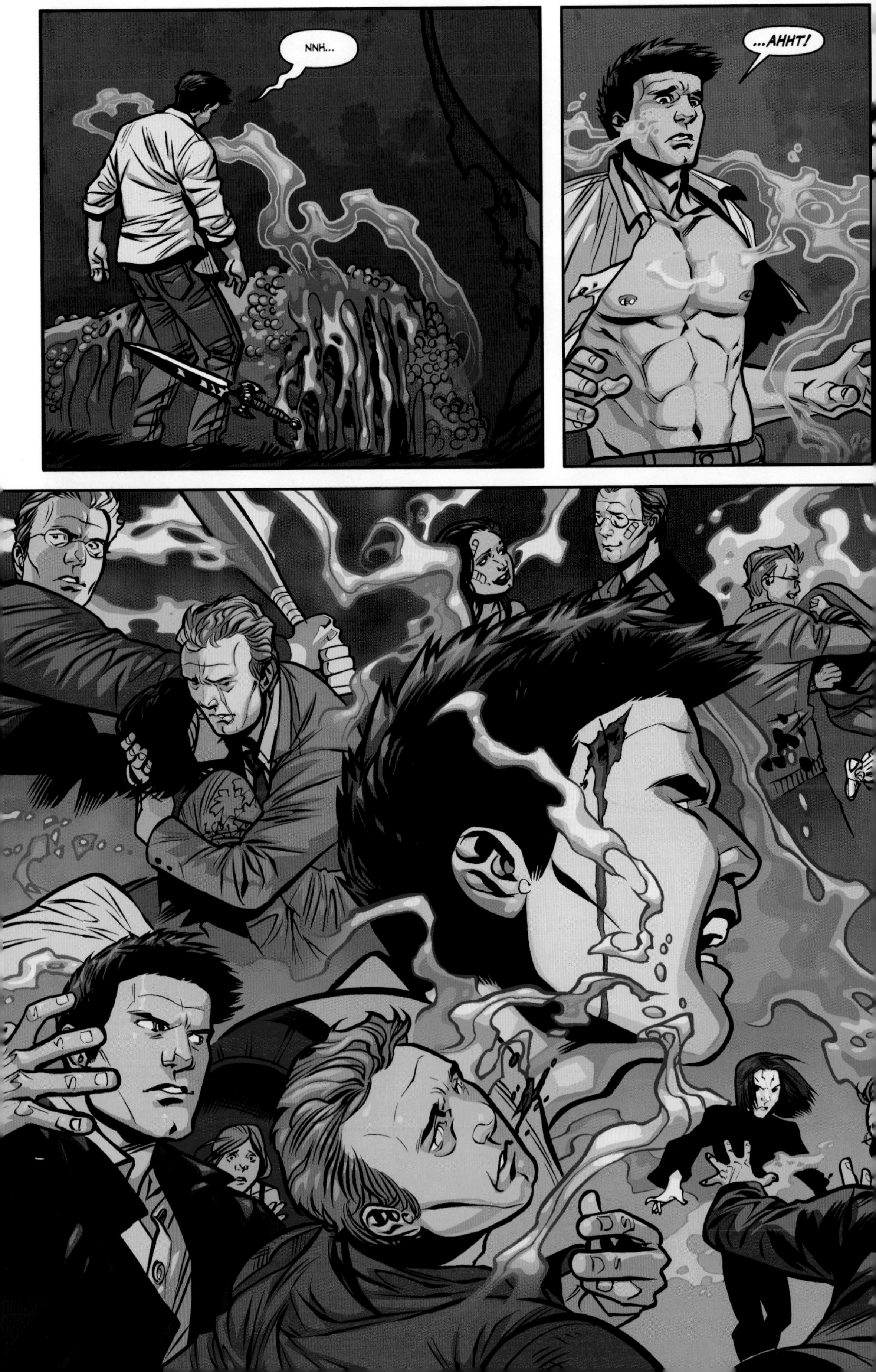
NNH...
...AHHT!

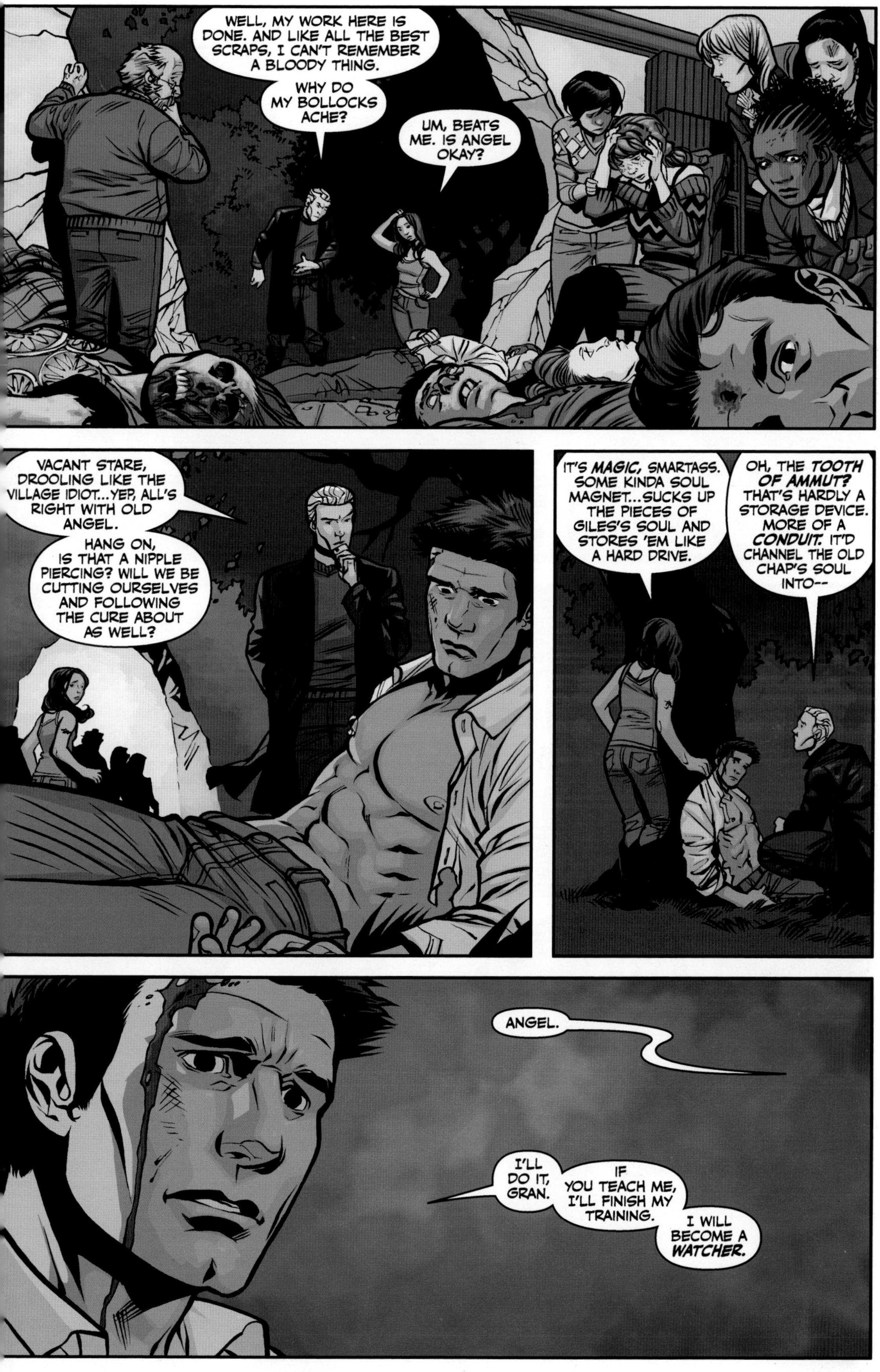

WELL, MY WORK HERE IS DONE. AND LIKE ALL THE BEST SCRAPS, I CAN'T REMEMBER A BLOODY THING.
WHY DO MY BOLLOCKS ACHE?
UM, BEATS ME. IS ANGEL OKAY?
VACANT STARE, DROOLING LIKE THE VILLAGE IDIOT...YEP, ALL'S RIGHT WITH OLD ANGEL.
HANG ON, IS THAT A NIPPLE PIERCING? WILL WE BE CUTTING OURSELVES AND FOLLOWING THE CURE ABOUT AS WELL?
IT'S *MAGIC,* SMARTASS. SOME KINDA SOUL MAGNET...SUCKS UP THE PIECES OF GILES'S SOUL AND STORES 'EM LIKE A HARD DRIVE.
OH, THE *TOOTH OF AMMUT?* THAT'S HARDLY A STORAGE DEVICE. MORE OF A *CONDUIT.* IT'D CHANNEL THE OLD CHAP'S SOUL INTO--
ANGEL.
I'LL DO IT, GRAN.
IF YOU TEACH ME, I'LL FINISH MY TRAINING.
I WILL BECOME A *WATCHER.*

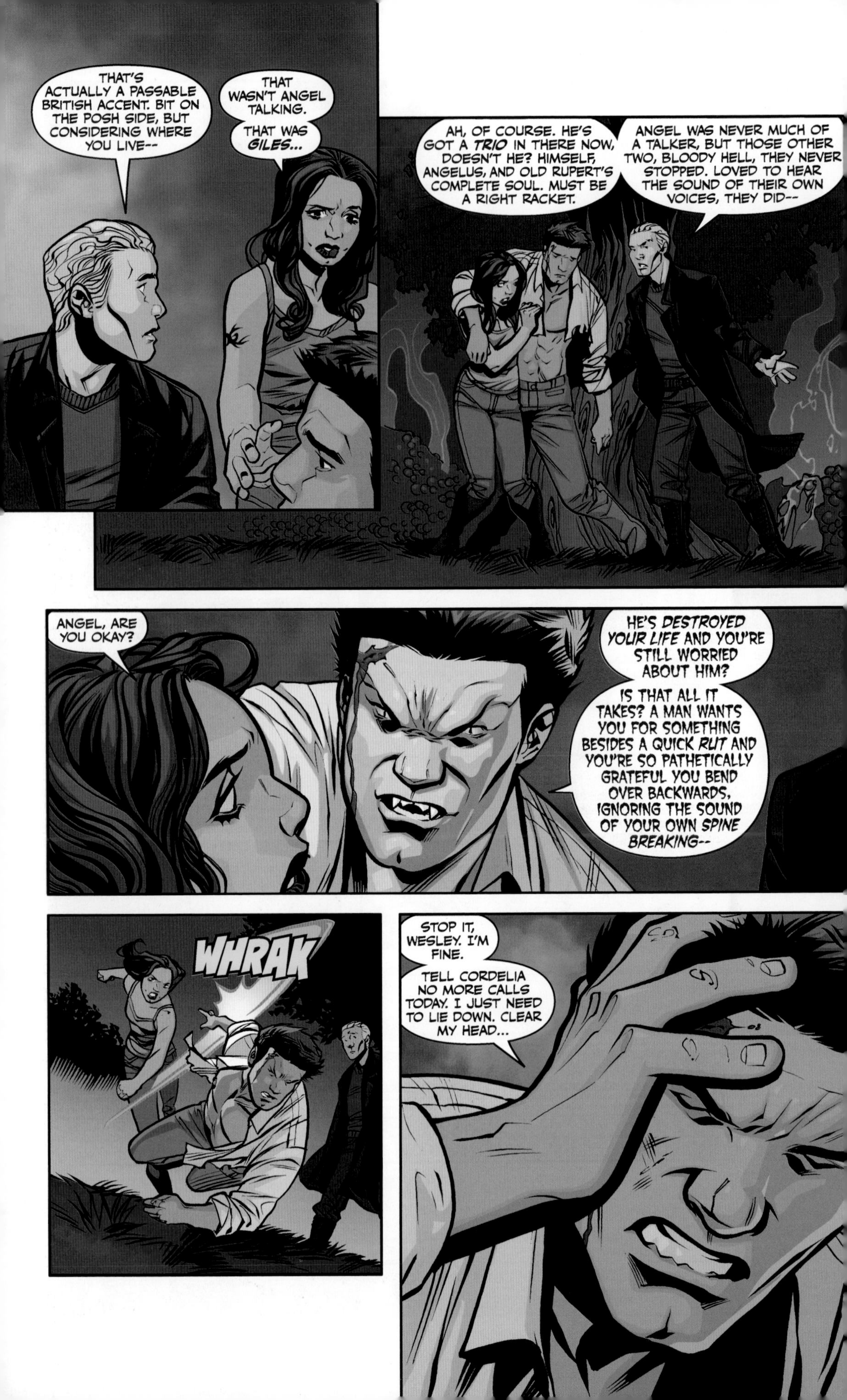
THAT'S ACTUALLY A PASSABLE BRITISH ACCENT. BIT ON THE POSH SIDE, BUT CONSIDERING WHERE YOU LIVE--
THAT WASN'T ANGEL TALKING.
THAT WAS GILES...
AH, OF COURSE. HE'S GOT A TRIO IN THERE NOW, DOESN'T HE? HIMSELF, ANGELUS, AND OLD RUPERT'S COMPLETE SOUL. MUST BE A RIGHT RACKET.
ANGEL WAS NEVER MUCH OF A TALKER, BUT THOSE OTHER TWO, BLOODY HELL, THEY NEVER STOPPED. LOVED TO HEAR THE SOUND OF THEIR OWN VOICES, THEY DID--
ANGEL, ARE YOU OKAY?
HE'S DESTROYED YOUR LIFE AND YOU'RE STILL WORRIED ABOUT HIM?
IS THAT ALL IT TAKES? A MAN WANTS YOU FOR SOMETHING BESIDES A QUICK RUT AND YOU'RE SO PATHETICALLY GRATEFUL YOU BEND OVER BACKWARDS, IGNORING THE SOUND OF YOUR OWN SPINE BREAKING--
WHRAK
STOP IT, WESLEY. I'M FINE.
TELL CORDELIA NO MORE CALLS TODAY. I JUST NEED TO LIE DOWN. CLEAR MY HEAD...

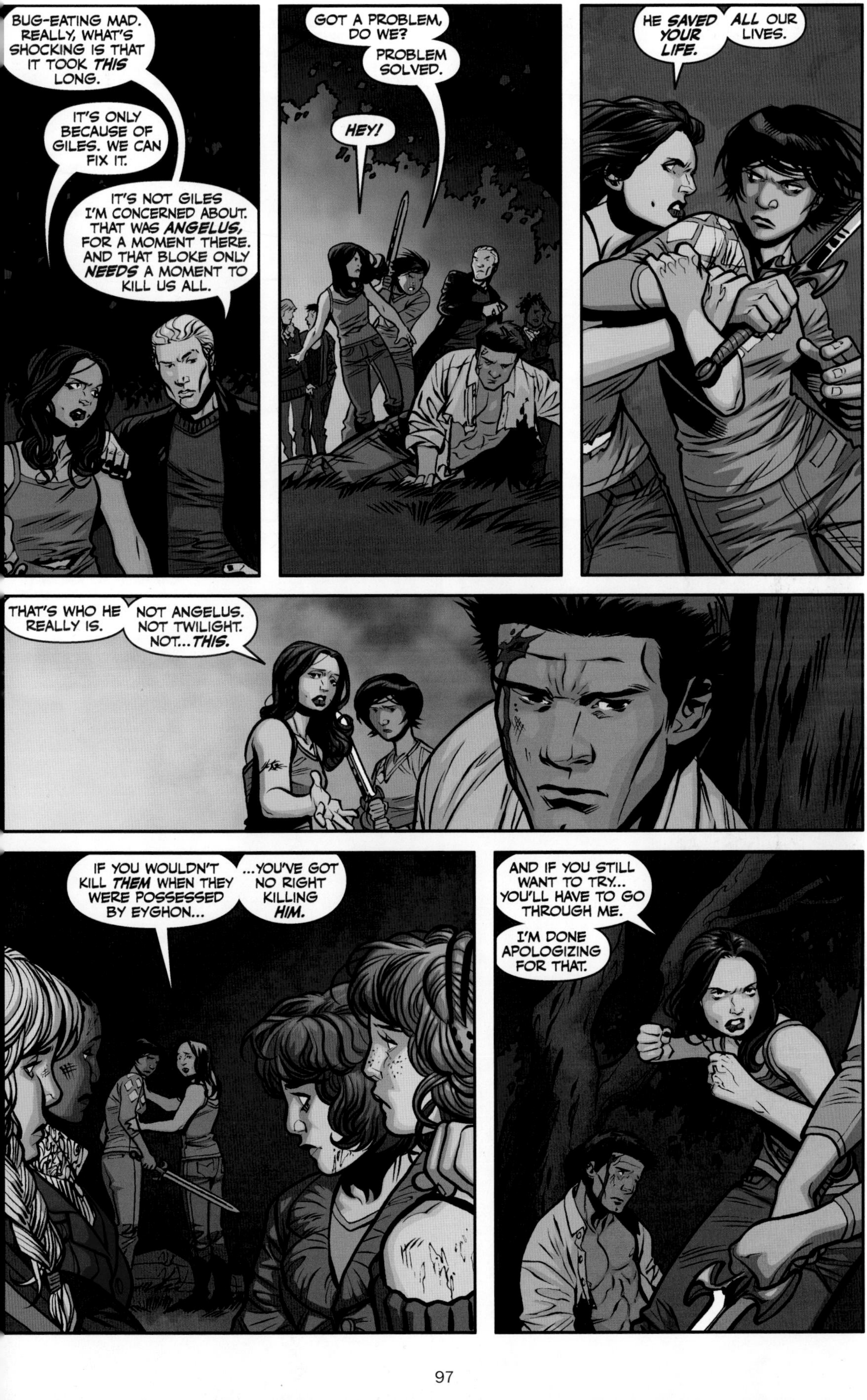
BUG-EATING MAD. REALLY, WHAT'S SHOCKING IS THAT IT TOOK THIS LONG.
IT'S ONLY BECAUSE OF GILES. WE CAN FIX IT.
IT'S NOT GILES I'M CONCERNED ABOUT. THAT WAS ANGELUS, FOR A MOMENT THERE. AND THAT BLOKE ONLY NEEDS A MOMENT TO KILL US ALL.
GOT A PROBLEM, DO WE?
PROBLEM SOLVED.
HEY!
HE SAVED YOUR LIFE.
ALL OUR LIVES.
THAT'S WHO HE REALLY IS.
NOT ANGELUS. NOT TWILIGHT. NOT...THIS.
IF YOU WOULDN'T KILL THEM WHEN THEY WERE POSSESSED BY EYGHON...
...YOU'VE GOT NO RIGHT KILLING HIM.
AND IF YOU STILL WANT TO TRY... YOU'LL HAVE TO GO THROUGH ME.
I'M DONE APOLOGIZING FOR THAT.

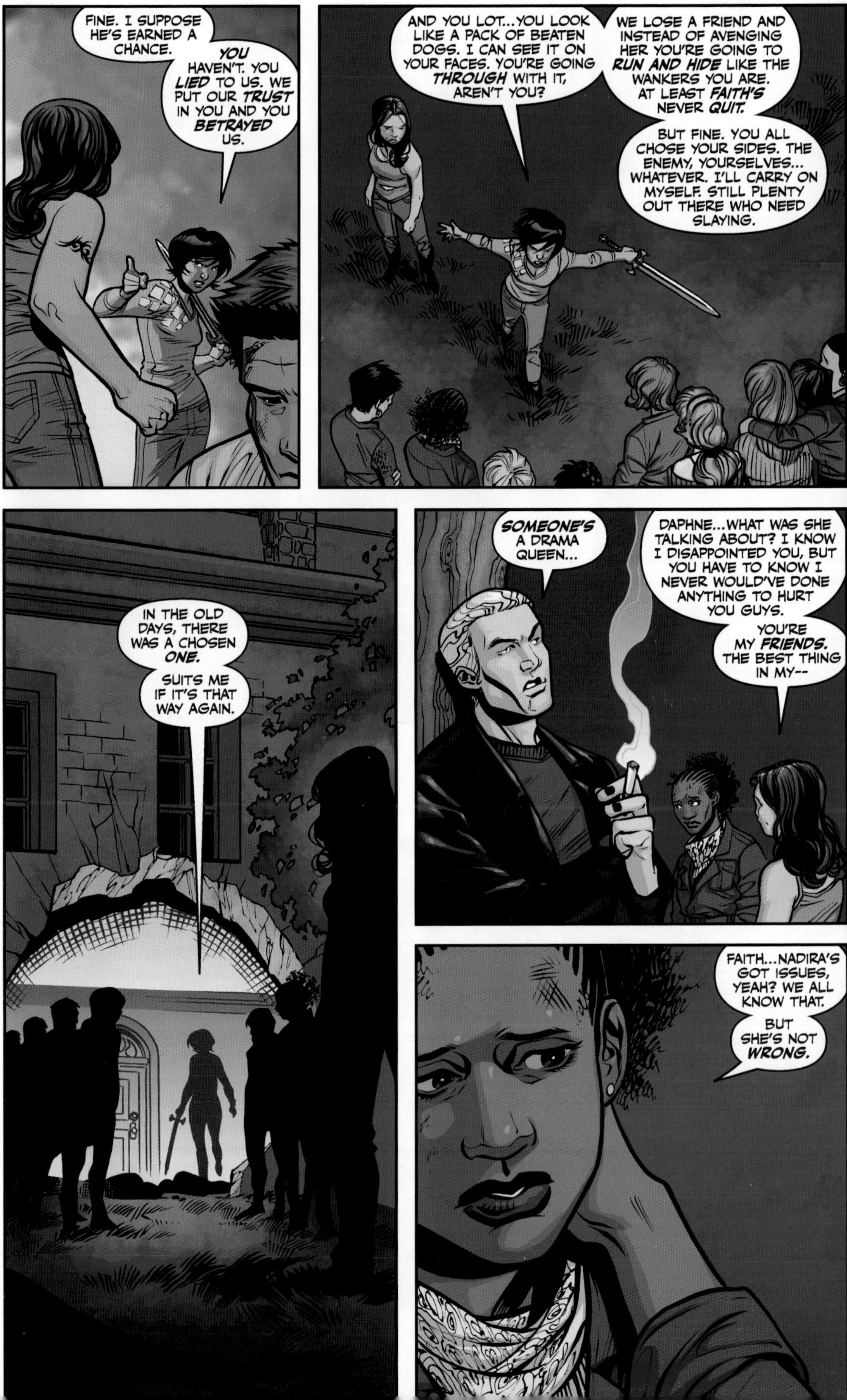
FINE. I SUPPOSE HE'S EARNED A CHANCE.
YOU HAVEN'T. YOU LIED TO US. WE PUT OUR TRUST IN YOU AND YOU BETRAYED US.
AND YOU LOT...YOU LOOK LIKE A PACK OF BEATEN DOGS. I CAN SEE IT ON YOUR FACES. YOU'RE GOING THROUGH WITH IT, AREN'T YOU?
WE LOSE A FRIEND AND INSTEAD OF AVENGING HER YOU'RE GOING TO RUN AND HIDE LIKE THE WANKERS YOU ARE. AT LEAST FAITH'S NEVER QUIT.
BUT FINE. YOU ALL CHOSE YOUR SIDES. THE ENEMY, YOURSELVES... WHATEVER. I'LL CARRY ON MYSELF. STILL PLENTY OUT THERE WHO NEED SLAYING.
IN THE OLD DAYS, THERE WAS A CHOSEN ONE.
SUITS ME IF IT'S THAT WAY AGAIN.
SOMEONE'S A DRAMA QUEEN...
DAPHNE...WHAT WAS SHE TALKING ABOUT? I KNOW I DISAPPOINTED YOU, BUT YOU HAVE TO KNOW I NEVER WOULD'VE DONE ANYTHING TO HURT YOU GUYS.
YOU'RE MY FRIENDS. THE BEST THING IN MY--
FAITH...NADIRA'S GOT ISSUES, YEAH? WE ALL KNOW THAT.
BUT SHE'S NOT WRONG.

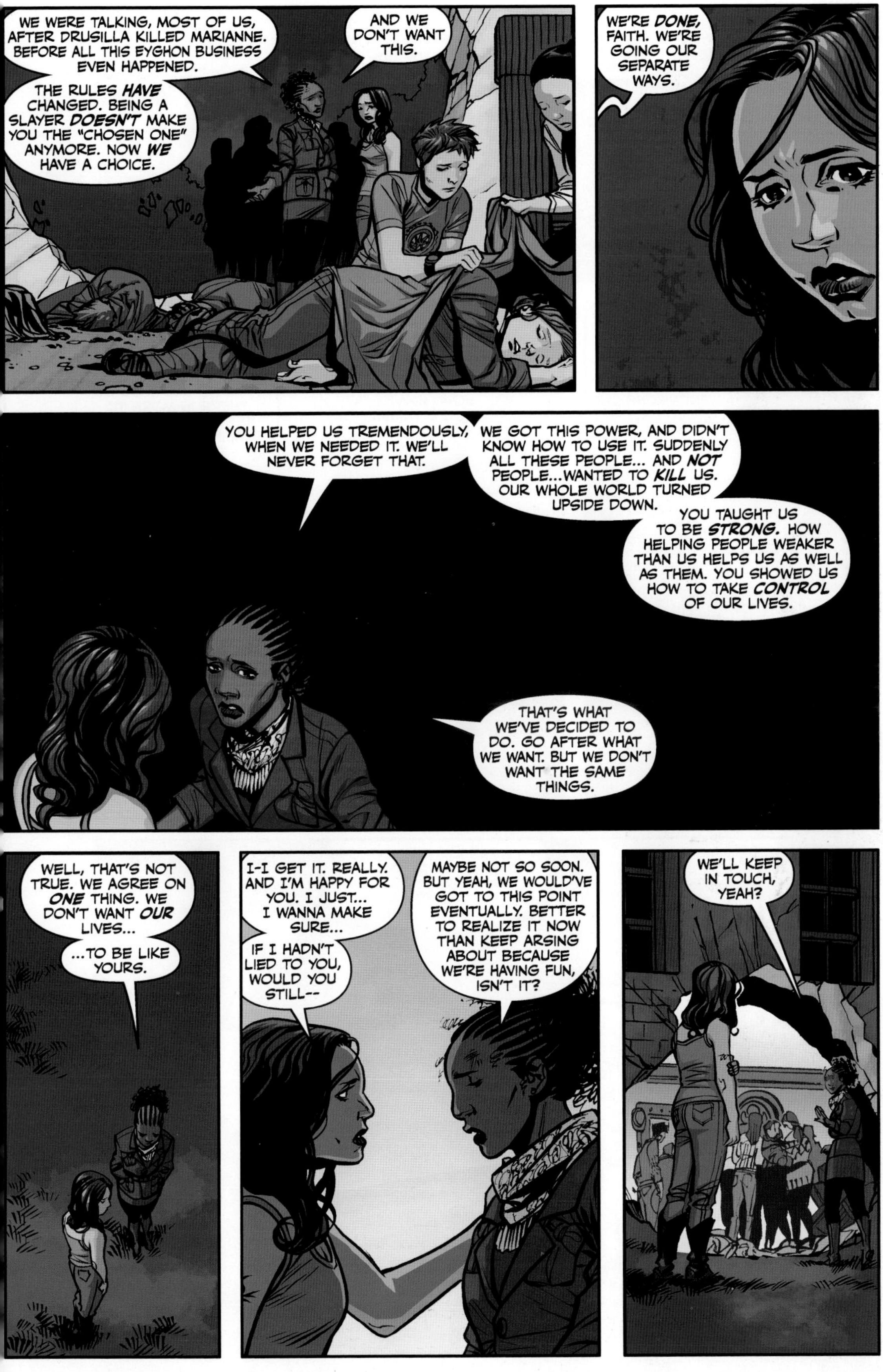
WE WERE TALKING, MOST OF US, AFTER DRUSILLA KILLED MARIANNE. BEFORE ALL THIS EYGHON BUSINESS EVEN HAPPENED.
AND WE DON'T WANT THIS.
THE RULES HAVE CHANGED. BEING A SLAYER DOESN'T MAKE YOU THE "CHOSEN ONE" ANYMORE. NOW WE HAVE A CHOICE.
WE'RE DONE, FAITH. WE'RE GOING OUR SEPARATE WAYS.
YOU HELPED US TREMENDOUSLY, WHEN WE NEEDED IT. WE'LL NEVER FORGET THAT.
WE GOT THIS POWER, AND DIDN'T KNOW HOW TO USE IT. SUDDENLY ALL THESE PEOPLE... AND NOT PEOPLE...WANTED TO KILL US. OUR WHOLE WORLD TURNED UPSIDE DOWN.
YOU TAUGHT US TO BE STRONG. HOW HELPING PEOPLE WEAKER THAN US HELPS US AS WELL AS THEM. YOU SHOWED US HOW TO TAKE CONTROL OF OUR LIVES.
THAT'S WHAT WE'VE DECIDED TO DO. GO AFTER WHAT WE WANT. BUT WE DON'T WANT THE SAME THINGS.
WELL, THAT'S NOT TRUE. WE AGREE ON ONE THING. WE DON'T WANT OUR LIVES...
...TO BE LIKE YOURS.
I-I GET IT. REALLY. AND I'M HAPPY FOR YOU. I JUST... I WANNA MAKE SURE...
IF I HADN'T LIED TO YOU, WOULD YOU STILL--
MAYBE NOT SO SOON. BUT YEAH, WE WOULD'VE GOT TO THIS POINT EVENTUALLY. BETTER TO REALIZE IT NOW THAN KEEP ARSING ABOUT BECAUSE WE'RE HAVING FUN, ISN'T IT?
WE'LL KEEP IN TOUCH, YEAH?

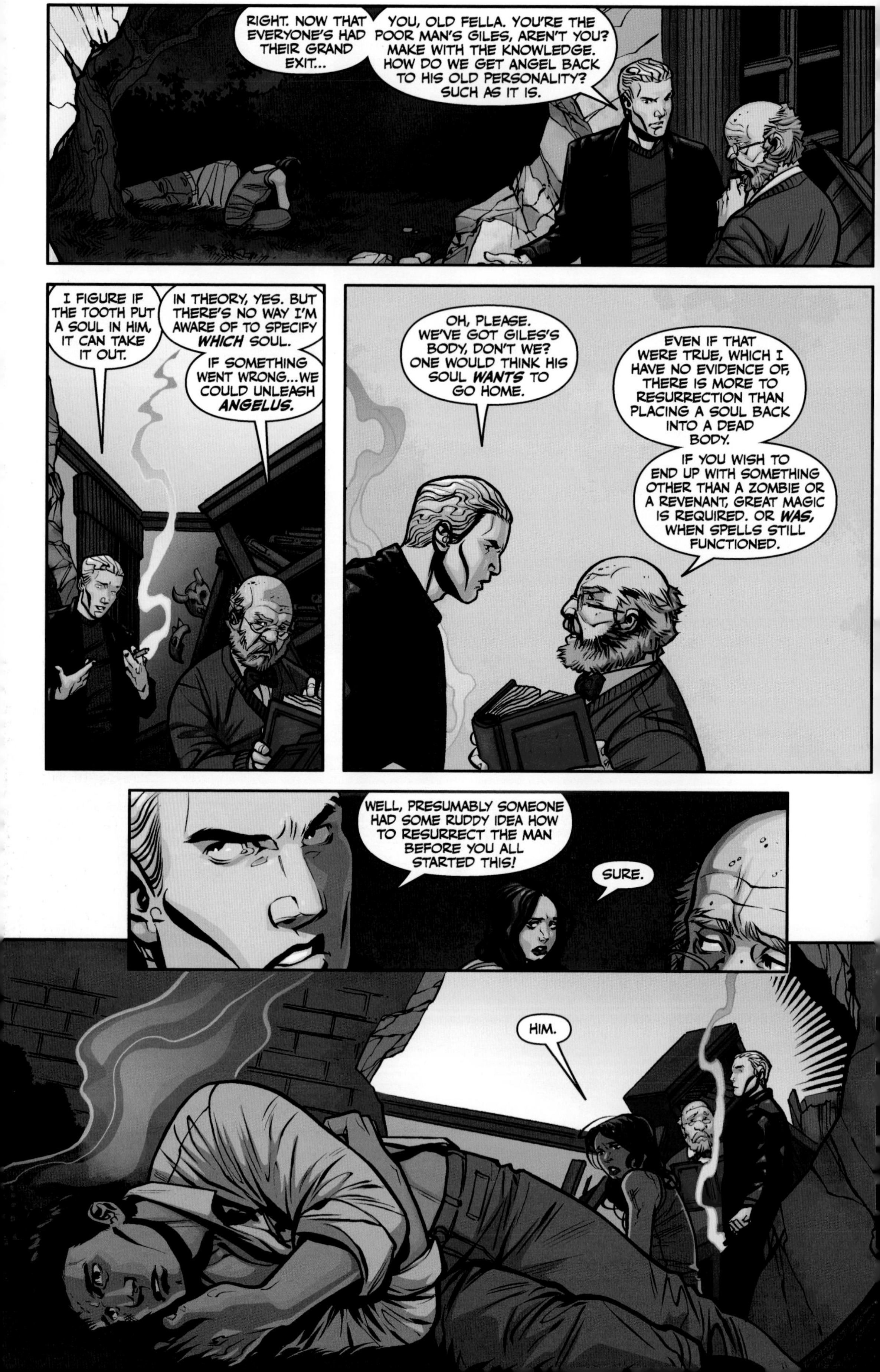
RIGHT. NOW THAT EVERYONE'S HAD THEIR GRAND EXIT...
YOU, OLD FELLA. YOU'RE THE POOR MAN'S GILES, AREN'T YOU? MAKE WITH THE KNOWLEDGE. HOW DO WE GET ANGEL BACK TO HIS OLD PERSONALITY? SUCH AS IT IS.
I FIGURE IF THE TOOTH PUT A SOUL IN HIM, IT CAN TAKE IT OUT.
IN THEORY, YES. BUT THERE'S NO WAY I'M AWARE OF TO SPECIFY *WHICH* SOUL.
IF SOMETHING WENT WRONG...WE COULD UNLEASH *ANGELUS.*
OH, PLEASE. WE'VE GOT GILES'S BODY, DON'T WE? ONE WOULD THINK HIS SOUL *WANTS* TO GO HOME.
EVEN IF THAT WERE TRUE, WHICH I HAVE NO EVIDENCE OF, THERE IS MORE TO RESURRECTION THAN PLACING A SOUL BACK INTO A DEAD BODY.
IF YOU WISH TO END UP WITH SOMETHING OTHER THAN A ZOMBIE OR A REVENANT, GREAT MAGIC IS REQUIRED. OR *WAS,* WHEN SPELLS STILL FUNCTIONED.
WELL, PRESUMABLY SOMEONE HAD SOME RUDDY IDEA HOW TO RESURRECT THE MAN BEFORE YOU ALL STARTED THIS!
SURE.
HIM.

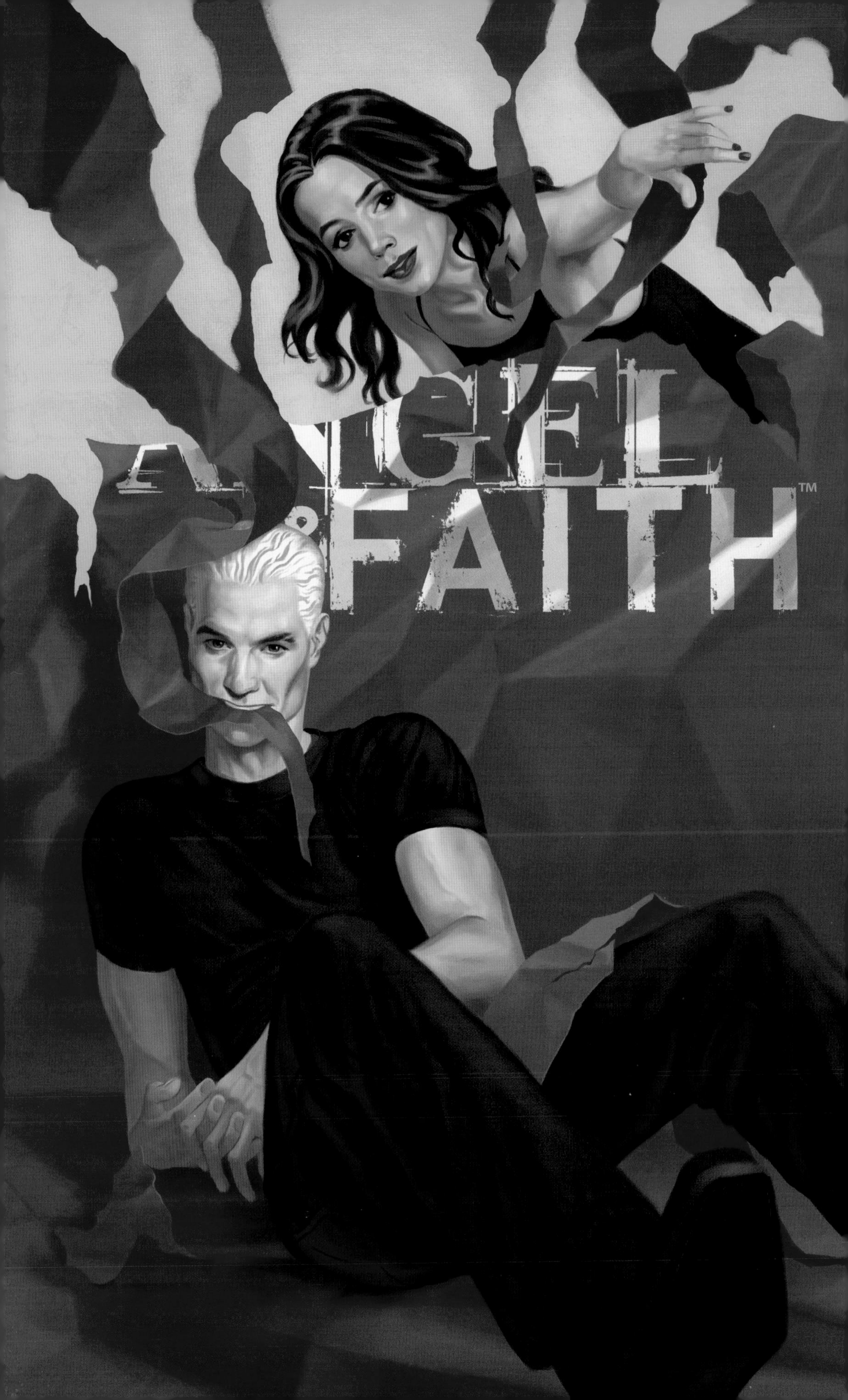
ANGEL & FAITH™

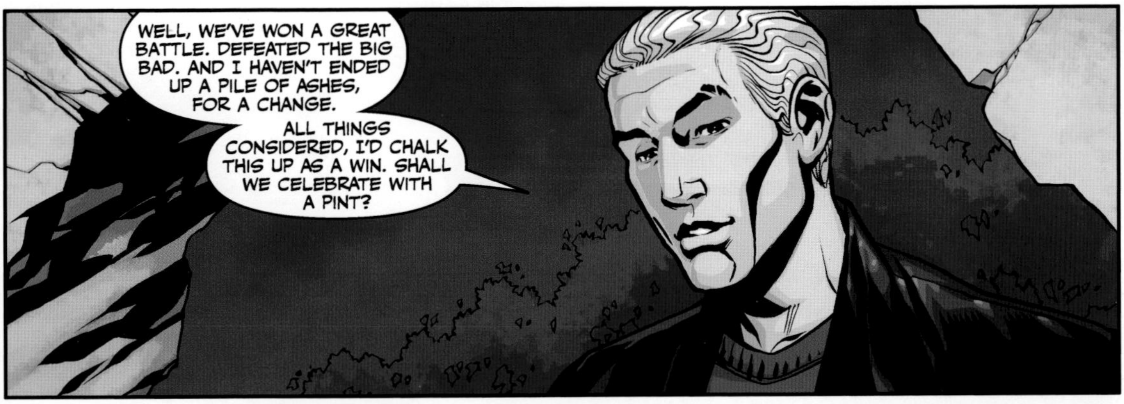
WELL, WE'VE WON A GREAT BATTLE. DEFEATED THE BIG BAD. AND I HAVEN'T ENDED UP A PILE OF ASHES, FOR A CHANGE.
ALL THINGS CONSIDERED, I'D CHALK THIS UP AS A WIN. SHALL WE CELEBRATE WITH A PINT?

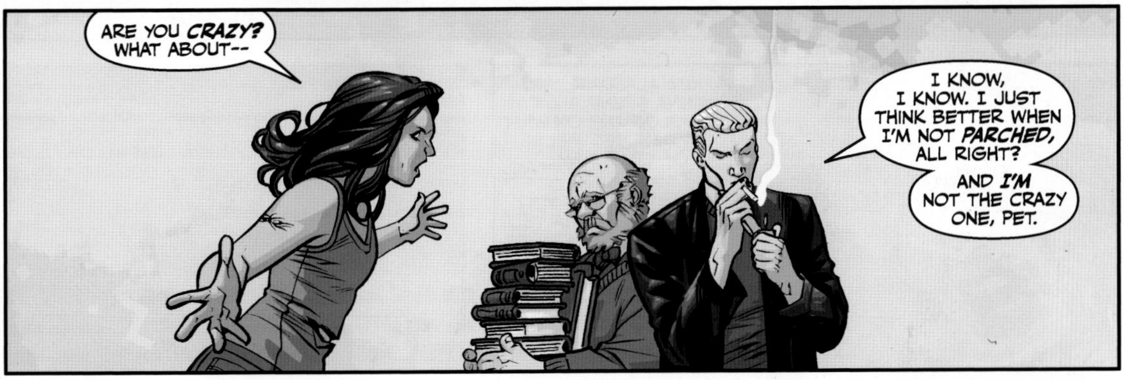
ARE YOU CRAZY? WHAT ABOUT--
I KNOW, I KNOW. I JUST THINK BETTER WHEN I'M NOT PARCHED, ALL RIGHT?
AND I'M NOT THE CRAZY ONE, PET.

SPIKE AND FAITH

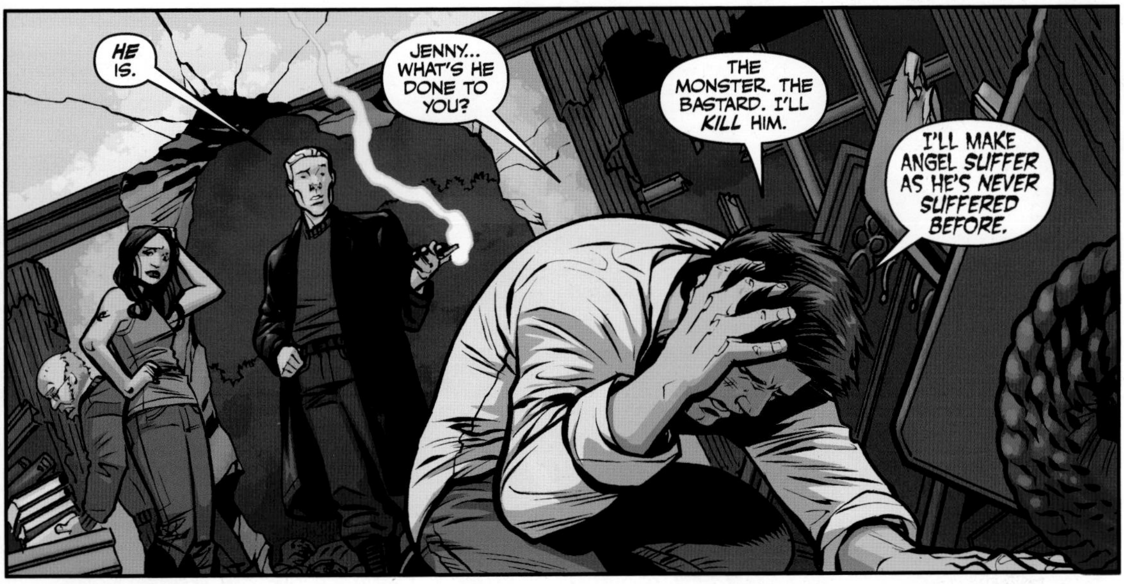
HE IS.
JENNY... WHAT'S HE DONE TO YOU?
THE MONSTER. THE BASTARD. I'LL KILL HIM.
I'LL MAKE ANGEL SUFFER AS HE'S NEVER SUFFERED BEFORE.

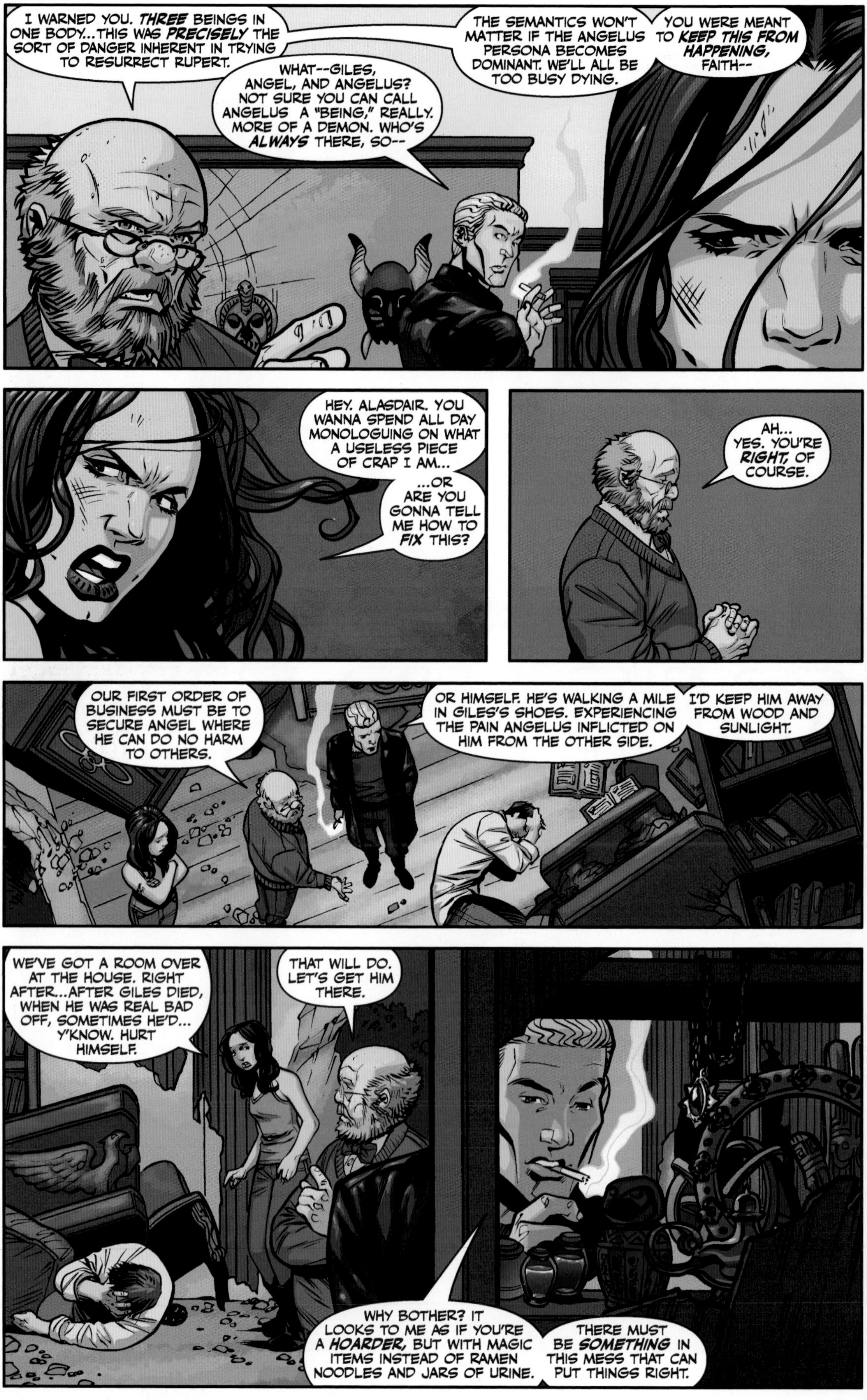
I WARNED YOU. THREE BEINGS IN ONE BODY...THIS WAS PRECISELY THE SORT OF DANGER INHERENT IN TRYING TO RESURRECT RUPERT.
WHAT--GILES, ANGEL, AND ANGELUS? NOT SURE YOU CAN CALL ANGELUS A "BEING," REALLY. MORE OF A DEMON. WHO'S ALWAYS THERE, SO--
THE SEMANTICS WON'T MATTER IF THE ANGELUS PERSONA BECOMES DOMINANT. WE'LL ALL BE TOO BUSY DYING.
YOU WERE MEANT TO KEEP THIS FROM HAPPENING, FAITH--
HEY. ALASDAIR. YOU WANNA SPEND ALL DAY MONOLOGUING ON WHAT A USELESS PIECE OF CRAP I AM...
...OR ARE YOU GONNA TELL ME HOW TO FIX THIS?
AH... YES. YOU'RE RIGHT, OF COURSE.
OUR FIRST ORDER OF BUSINESS MUST BE TO SECURE ANGEL WHERE HE CAN DO NO HARM TO OTHERS.
OR HIMSELF. HE'S WALKING A MILE IN GILES'S SHOES. EXPERIENCING THE PAIN ANGELUS INFLICTED ON HIM FROM THE OTHER SIDE.
I'D KEEP HIM AWAY FROM WOOD AND SUNLIGHT.
WE'VE GOT A ROOM OVER AT THE HOUSE. RIGHT AFTER...AFTER GILES DIED, WHEN HE WAS REAL BAD OFF, SOMETIMES HE'D... Y'KNOW. HURT HIMSELF.
THAT WILL DO. LET'S GET HIM THERE.
WHY BOTHER? IT LOOKS TO ME AS IF YOU'RE A HOARDER, BUT WITH MAGIC ITEMS INSTEAD OF RAMEN NOODLES AND JARS OF URINE.
THERE MUST BE SOMETHING IN THIS MESS THAT CAN PUT THINGS RIGHT.

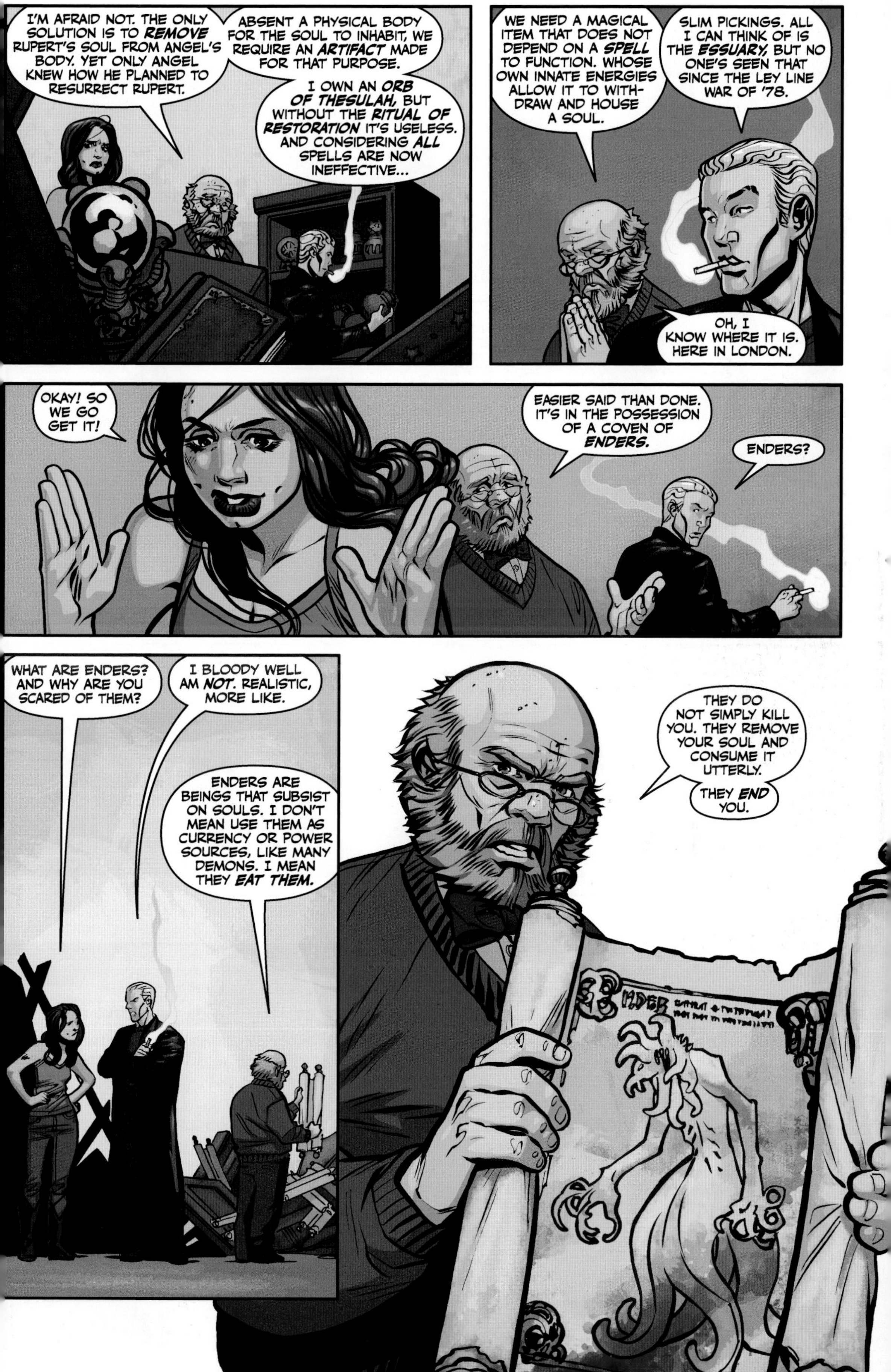
I'M AFRAID NOT. THE ONLY SOLUTION IS TO *REMOVE* RUPERT'S SOUL FROM ANGEL'S BODY. YET ONLY ANGEL KNEW HOW HE PLANNED TO RESURRECT RUPERT.
ABSENT A PHYSICAL BODY FOR THE SOUL TO INHABIT, WE REQUIRE AN *ARTIFACT* MADE FOR THAT PURPOSE.
I OWN AN *ORB OF THESULAH,* BUT WITHOUT THE *RITUAL OF RESTORATION* IT'S USELESS. AND CONSIDERING *ALL* SPELLS ARE NOW INEFFECTIVE...
WE NEED A MAGICAL ITEM THAT DOES NOT DEPEND ON A *SPELL* TO FUNCTION. WHOSE OWN INNATE ENERGIES ALLOW IT TO WITH-DRAW AND HOUSE A SOUL.
SLIM PICKINGS. ALL I CAN THINK OF IS THE *ESSUARY,* BUT NO ONE'S SEEN THAT SINCE THE LEY LINE WAR OF '78.
OH, I KNOW WHERE IT IS. HERE IN LONDON.
OKAY! SO WE GO GET IT!
EASIER SAID THAN DONE. IT'S IN THE POSSESSION OF A COVEN OF *ENDERS.*
ENDERS?
WHAT ARE ENDERS? AND WHY ARE YOU SCARED OF THEM?
I BLOODY WELL AM *NOT*. REALISTIC, MORE LIKE.
ENDERS ARE BEINGS THAT SUBSIST ON SOULS. I DON'T MEAN USE THEM AS CURRENCY OR POWER SOURCES, LIKE MANY DEMONS. I MEAN THEY *EAT THEM.*
THEY DO NOT SIMPLY KILL YOU. THEY REMOVE YOUR SOUL AND CONSUME IT UTTERLY.
THEY *END* YOU.

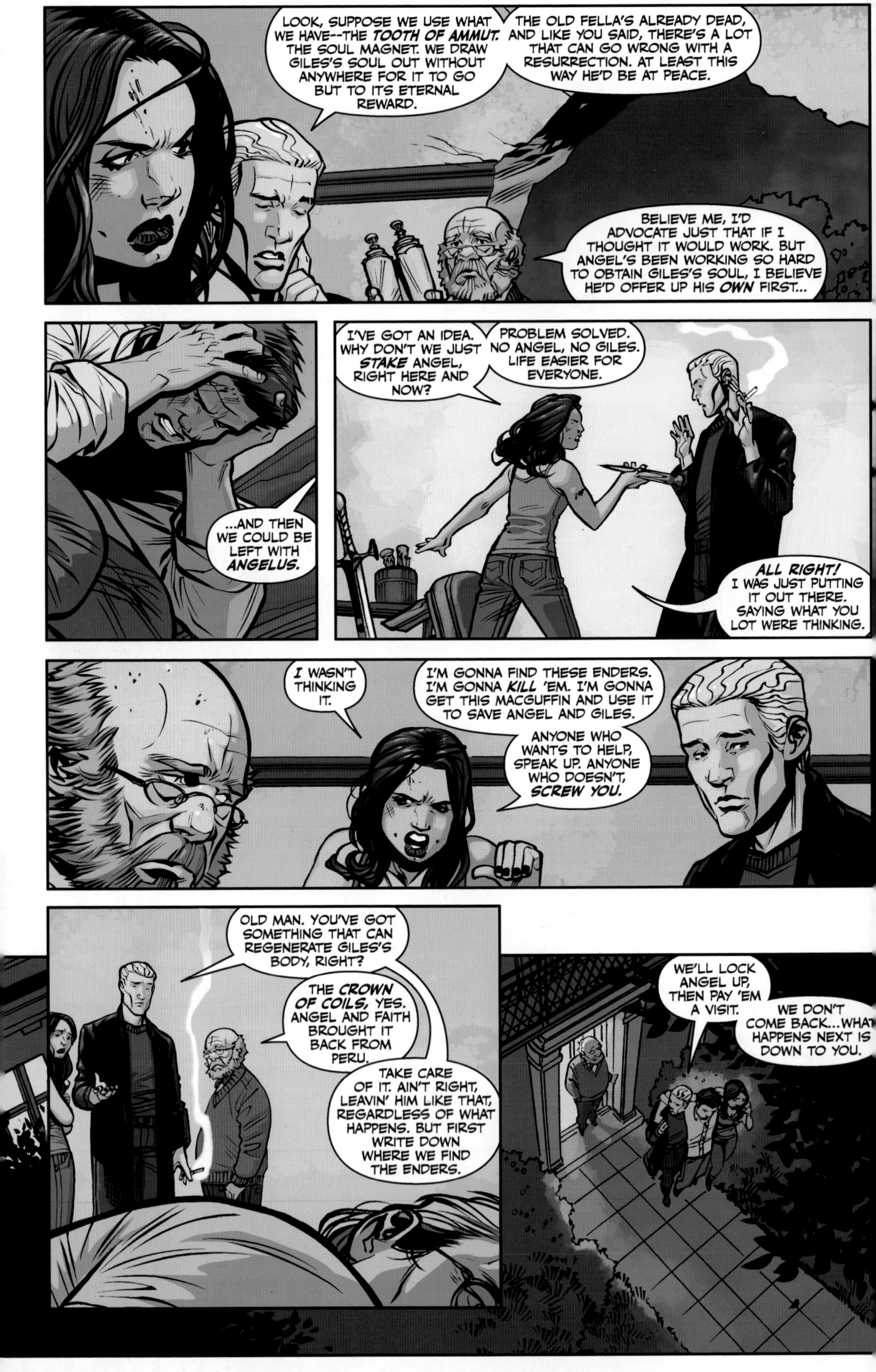
LOOK, SUPPOSE WE USE WHAT WE HAVE--THE TOOTH OF AMMUT. THE SOUL MAGNET. WE DRAW GILES'S SOUL OUT WITHOUT ANYWHERE FOR IT TO GO BUT TO ITS ETERNAL REWARD.
THE OLD FELLA'S ALREADY DEAD, AND LIKE YOU SAID, THERE'S A LOT THAT CAN GO WRONG WITH A RESURRECTION. AT LEAST THIS WAY HE'D BE AT PEACE.
BELIEVE ME, I'D ADVOCATE JUST THAT IF I THOUGHT IT WOULD WORK. BUT ANGEL'S BEEN WORKING SO HARD TO OBTAIN GILES'S SOUL, I BELIEVE HE'D OFFER UP HIS OWN FIRST...
...AND THEN WE COULD BE LEFT WITH ANGELUS.
I'VE GOT AN IDEA. WHY DON'T WE JUST STAKE ANGEL, RIGHT HERE AND NOW?
PROBLEM SOLVED. NO ANGEL, NO GILES. LIFE EASIER FOR EVERYONE.
ALL RIGHT! I WAS JUST PUTTING IT OUT THERE. SAYING WHAT YOU LOT WERE THINKING.
I WASN'T THINKING IT.
I'M GONNA FIND THESE ENDERS. I'M GONNA KILL 'EM. I'M GONNA GET THIS MACGUFFIN AND USE IT TO SAVE ANGEL AND GILES.
ANYONE WHO WANTS TO HELP, SPEAK UP. ANYONE WHO DOESN'T, SCREW YOU.
OLD MAN. YOU'VE GOT SOMETHING THAT CAN REGENERATE GILES'S BODY, RIGHT?
THE CROWN OF COILS, YES. ANGEL AND FAITH BROUGHT IT BACK FROM PERU.
TAKE CARE OF IT. AIN'T RIGHT, LEAVIN' HIM LIKE THAT, REGARDLESS OF WHAT HAPPENS. BUT FIRST WRITE DOWN WHERE WE FIND THE ENDERS.
WE'LL LOCK ANGEL UP, THEN PAY 'EM A VISIT.
WE DON'T COME BACK...WHAT HAPPENS NEXT IS DOWN TO YOU.

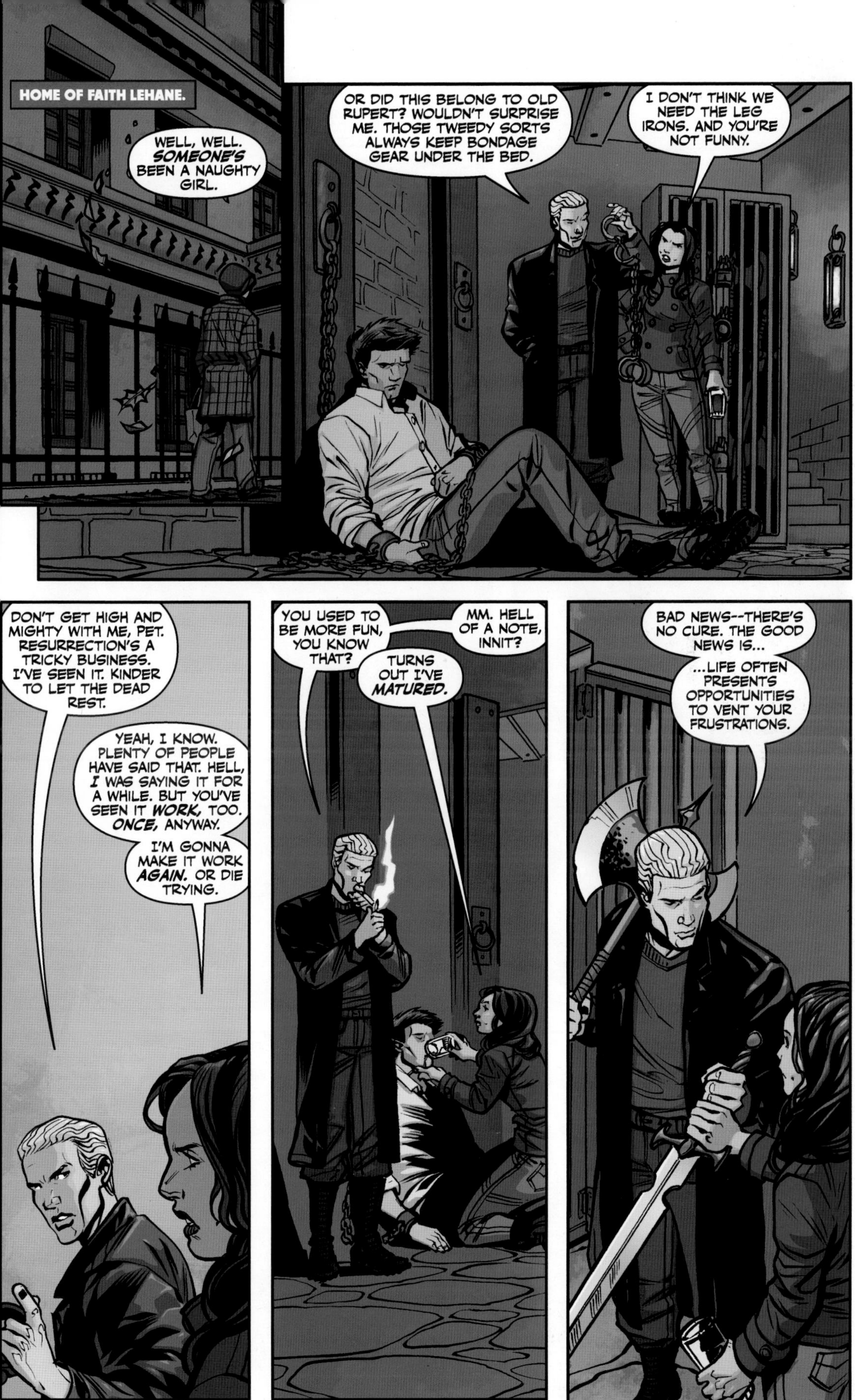

HOME OF FAITH LEHANE.
WELL, WELL. SOMEONE'S BEEN A NAUGHTY GIRL.
OR DID THIS BELONG TO OLD RUPERT? WOULDN'T SURPRISE ME. THOSE TWEEDY SORTS ALWAYS KEEP BONDAGE GEAR UNDER THE BED.
I DON'T THINK WE NEED THE LEG IRONS. AND YOU'RE NOT FUNNY.
DON'T GET HIGH AND MIGHTY WITH ME, PET. RESURRECTION'S A TRICKY BUSINESS. I'VE SEEN IT. KINDER TO LET THE DEAD REST.
YEAH, I KNOW. PLENTY OF PEOPLE HAVE SAID THAT. HELL, I WAS SAYING IT FOR A WHILE. BUT YOU'VE SEEN IT WORK, TOO. ONCE, ANYWAY.
I'M GONNA MAKE IT WORK AGAIN. OR DIE TRYING.
YOU USED TO BE MORE FUN, YOU KNOW THAT?
MM. HELL OF A NOTE, INNIT?
TURNS OUT I'VE MATURED.
BAD NEWS--THERE'S NO CURE. THE GOOD NEWS IS...
...LIFE OFTEN PRESENTS OPPORTUNITIES TO VENT YOUR FRUSTRATIONS.

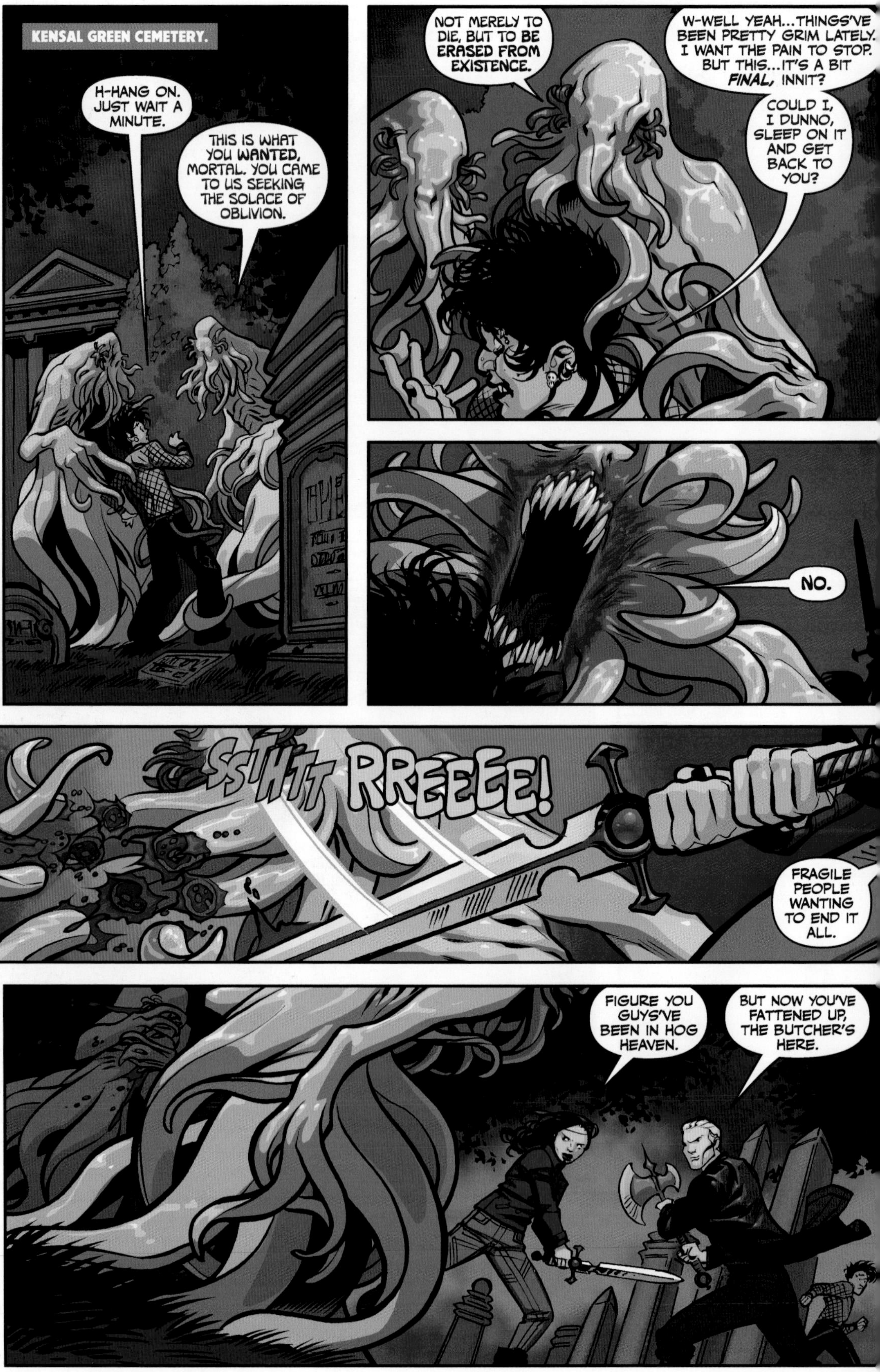
KENSAL GREEN CEMETERY.
H-HANG ON. JUST WAIT A MINUTE.
THIS IS WHAT YOU WANTED, MORTAL. YOU CAME TO US SEEKING THE SOLACE OF OBLIVION.
NOT MERELY TO DIE, BUT TO BE ERASED FROM EXISTENCE.
W-WELL YEAH...THINGS'VE BEEN PRETTY GRIM LATELY. I WANT THE PAIN TO STOP. BUT THIS...IT'S A BIT FINAL, INNIT?
COULD I, I DUNNO, SLEEP ON IT AND GET BACK TO YOU?
NO.
SSHTT RREEEE!
FRAGILE PEOPLE WANTING TO END IT ALL.
FIGURE YOU GUYS'VE BEEN IN HOG HEAVEN.
BUT NOW YOU'VE FATTENED UP, THE BUTCHER'S HERE.

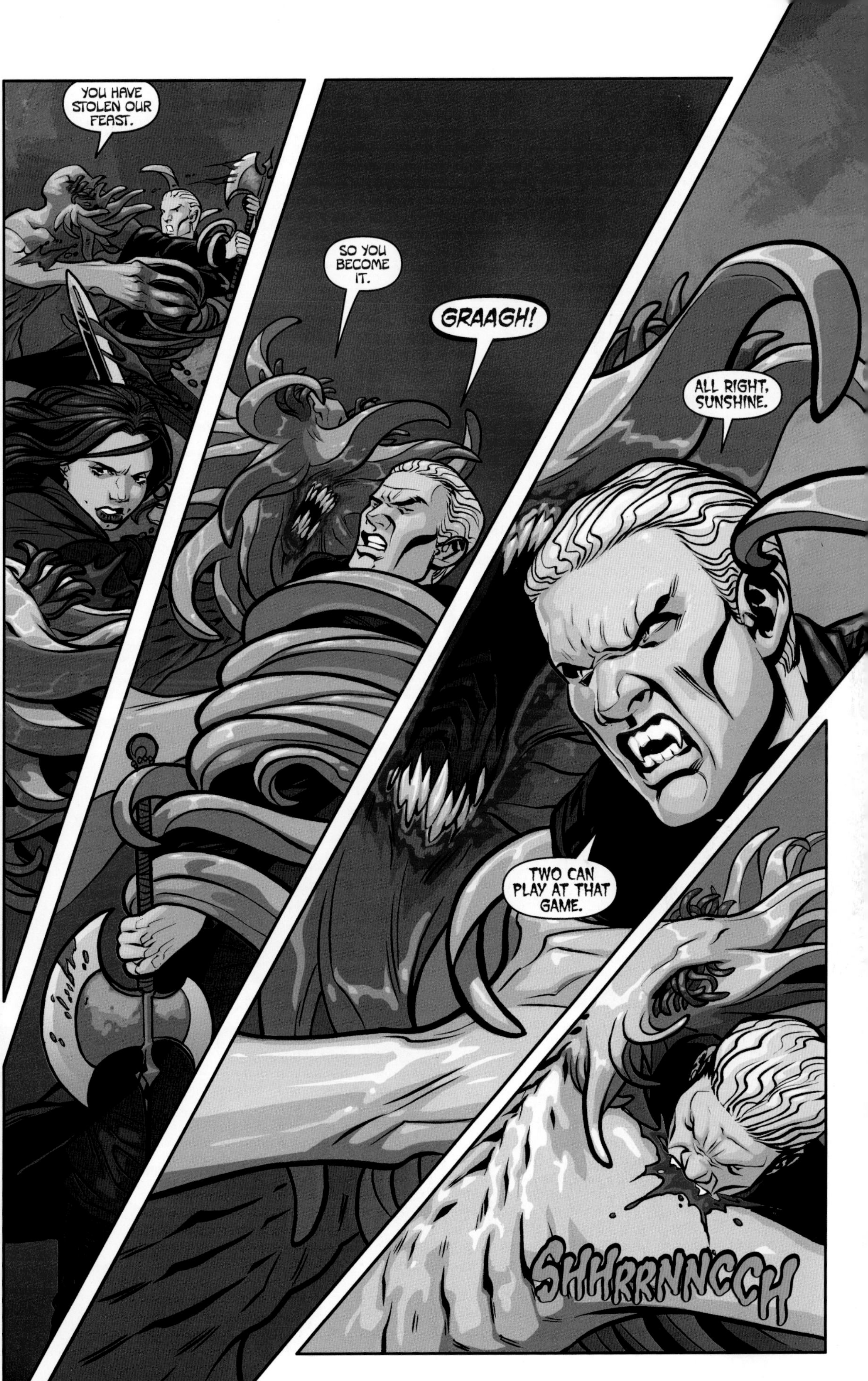
YOU HAVE STOLEN OUR FEAST.
SO YOU BECOME IT.
GRAAGH!
ALL RIGHT, SUNSHINE.
TWO CAN PLAY AT THAT GAME.
SHHRRNNCCH

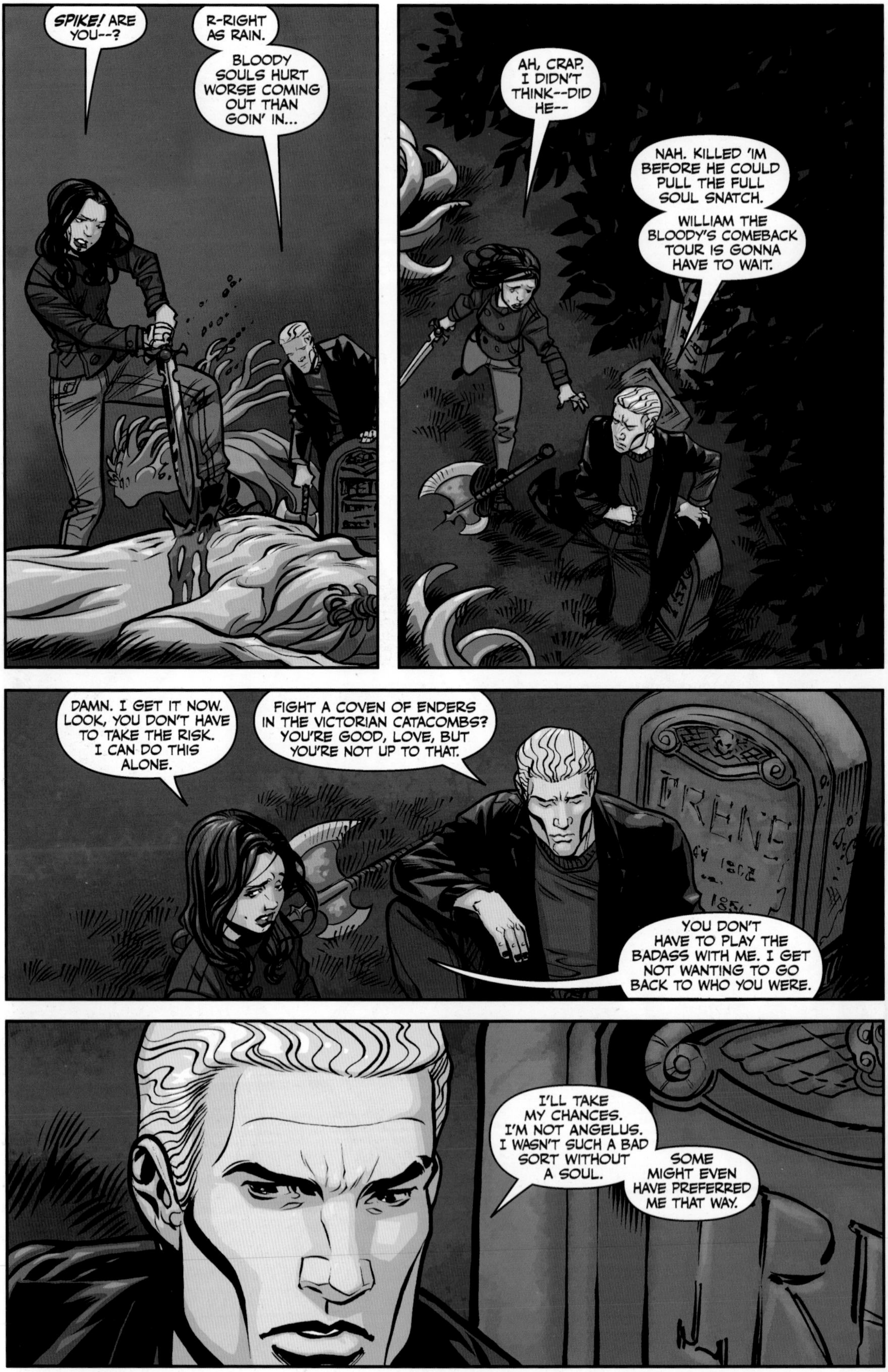

SPIKE! ARE YOU--?
R-RIGHT AS RAIN.
BLOODY SOULS HURT WORSE COMING OUT THAN GOIN' IN...
AH, CRAP. I DIDN'T THINK--DID HE--
NAH. KILLED 'IM BEFORE HE COULD PULL THE FULL SOUL SNATCH.
WILLIAM THE BLOODY'S COMEBACK TOUR IS GONNA HAVE TO WAIT.
DAMN. I GET IT NOW. LOOK, YOU DON'T HAVE TO TAKE THE RISK. I CAN DO THIS ALONE.
FIGHT A COVEN OF ENDERS IN THE VICTORIAN CATACOMBS? YOU'RE GOOD, LOVE, BUT YOU'RE NOT UP TO THAT.
YOU DON'T HAVE TO PLAY THE BADASS WITH ME. I GET NOT WANTING TO GO BACK TO WHO YOU WERE.
I'LL TAKE MY CHANCES. I'M NOT ANGELUS. I WASN'T SUCH A BAD SORT WITHOUT A SOUL.
SOME MIGHT EVEN HAVE PREFERRED ME THAT WAY.

SO, HOW DOES OLD PRINCIPAL WOOD FEEL ABOUT YOU SHACKING UP WITH A VAMPIRE? AS I RECALL, HE'S A BIT PREJUDICED.

YEAH, I'M IN A BIT OF A DRY SPELL MYSELF. CHEERS TO MATURITY, EH?

YOU KIDDING? ME AND ROBIN ARE ANCIENT HISTORY. NOT LIKE HE'D HAVE ANYTHING TO WORRY ABOUT. ALL ANGEL'S DONE FOR MY LOVE LIFE IS KEEP ME TOO BUSY TO HAVE ONE.

PERHAPS I'M BEING A BIT BOLD, BUT I SEEM TO RECALL A CERTAIN CHEMISTRY BETWEEN US.

IF WE LIVE THROUGH THIS, MIGHT BE WE COULD CHANGE EACH OTHER'S LUCK.

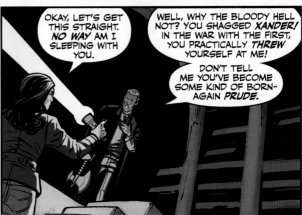

OKAY, LET'S GET THIS STRAIGHT. NO WAY AM I SLEEPING WITH YOU.

WELL, WHY THE BLOODY HELL NOT? YOU SHAGGED XANDER! IN THE WAR WITH THE FIRST, YOU PRACTICALLY THREW YOURSELF AT ME!

DON'T TELL ME YOU'VE BECOME SOME KIND OF BORN-AGAIN PRUDE.

NAH. TO BE HONEST, I COULD USE A ROLL IN THE HAY. IT'S NOT ME. IT'S YOU.

YOU'RE INTO BAD BOYS! I INVENTED THE BAD BOY!

MAYBE. BUT LIKE YOU SAID, YOU'VE MATURED.

THESE DAYS, YOU'RE MORE LIKE ANGEL.

WHAT?

BESIDES. I'M NOBODY'S REBOUND GIRL.

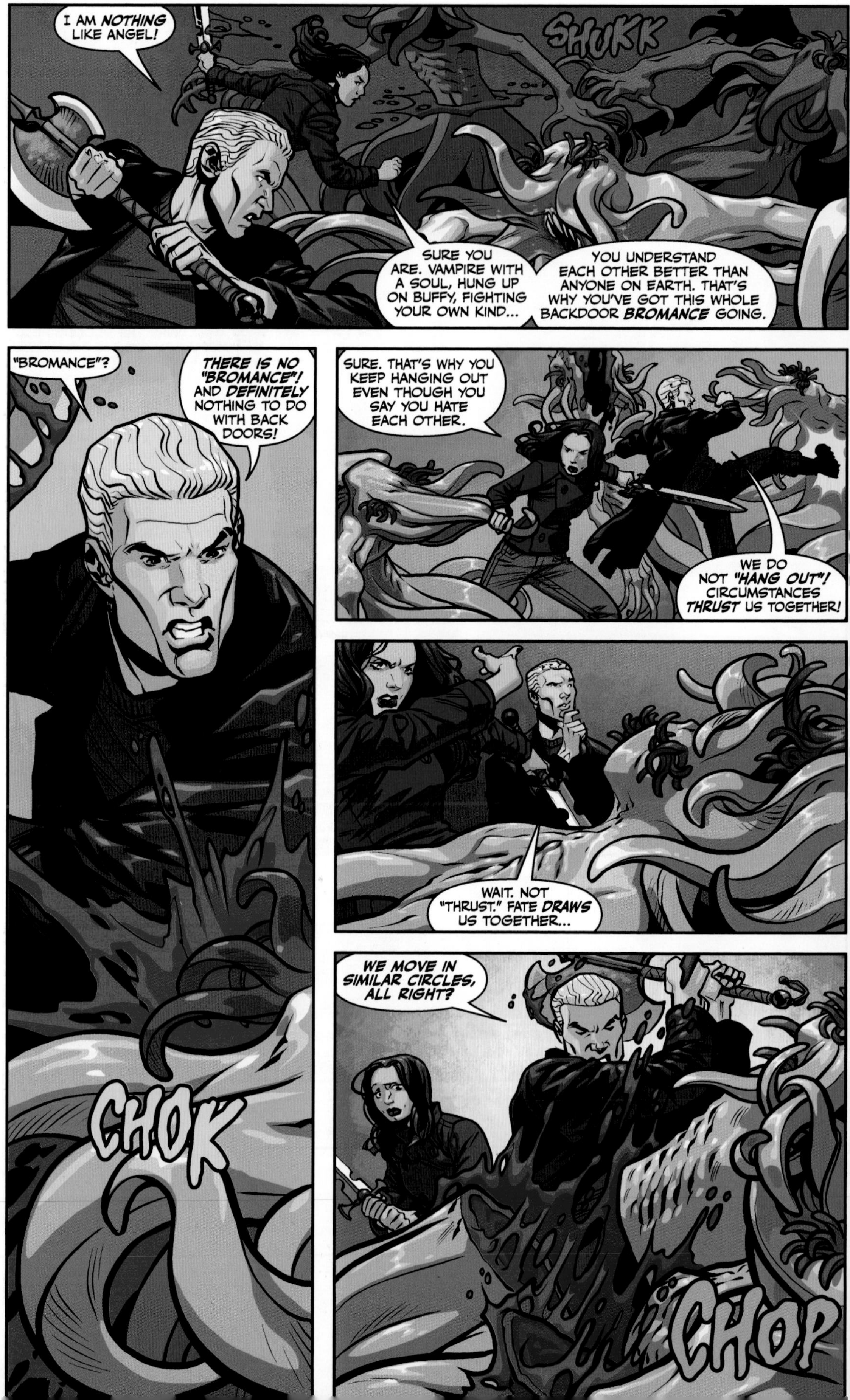
I AM *NOTHING* LIKE ANGEL!
SHUKK
SURE YOU ARE. VAMPIRE WITH A SOUL, HUNG UP ON BUFFY, FIGHTING YOUR OWN KIND...
YOU UNDERSTAND EACH OTHER BETTER THAN ANYONE ON EARTH. THAT'S WHY YOU'VE GOT THIS WHOLE BACKDOOR **BROMANCE** GOING.
"BROMANCE"?
THERE IS NO "BROMANCE"! AND ***DEFINITELY*** NOTHING TO DO WITH BACK DOORS!
CHOK
SURE. THAT'S WHY YOU KEEP HANGING OUT EVEN THOUGH YOU SAY YOU HATE EACH OTHER.
WE DO NOT ***"HANG OUT"!*** CIRCUMSTANCES ***THRUST*** US TOGETHER!
WAIT. NOT "THRUST." FATE ***DRAWS*** US TOGETHER...
WE MOVE IN SIMILAR CIRCLES, ALL RIGHT?
CHOP

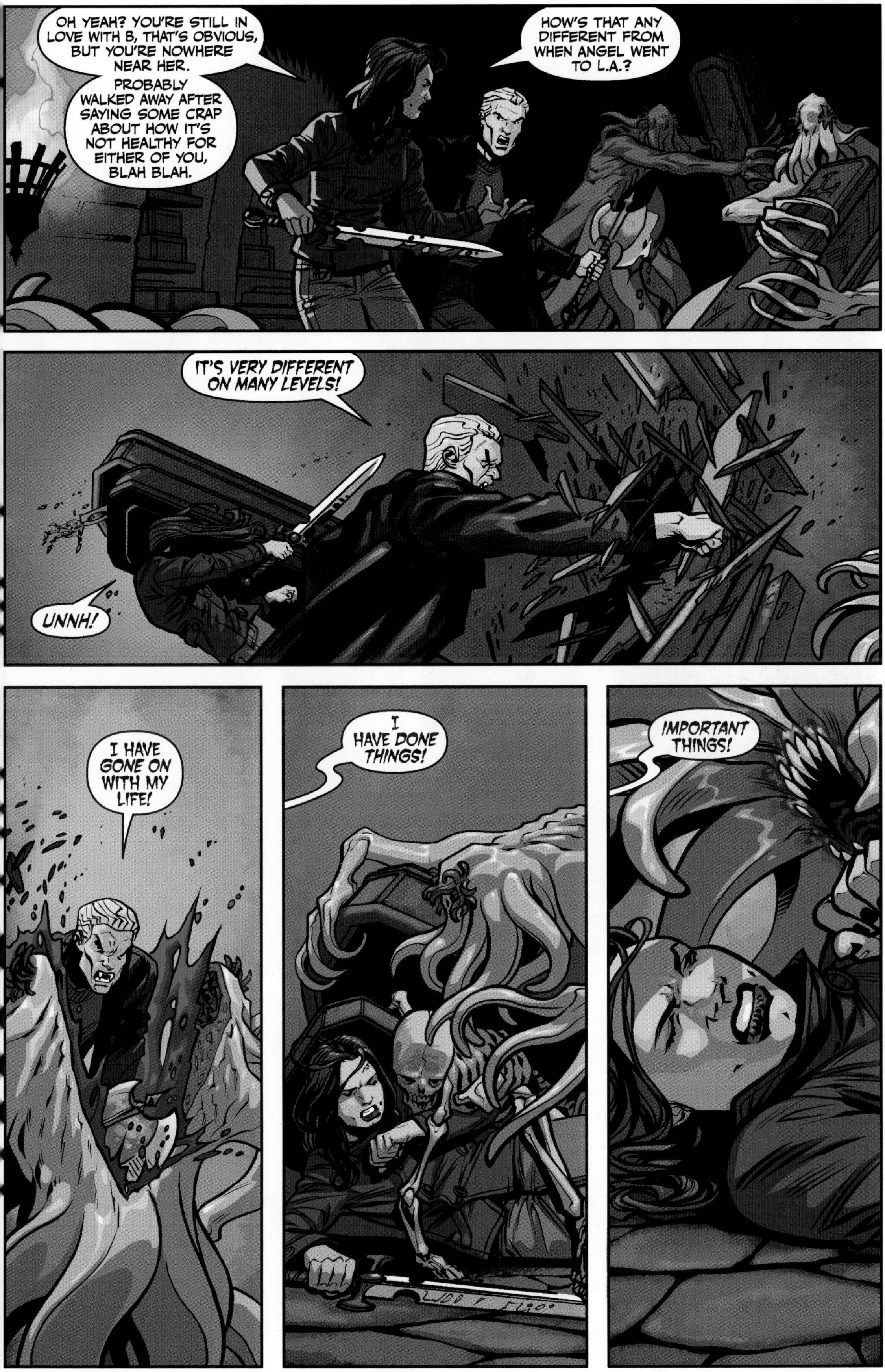
OH YEAH? YOU'RE STILL IN LOVE WITH B, THAT'S OBVIOUS, BUT YOU'RE NOWHERE NEAR HER.
PROBABLY WALKED AWAY AFTER SAYING SOME CRAP ABOUT HOW IT'S NOT HEALTHY FOR EITHER OF YOU, BLAH BLAH.
HOW'S THAT ANY DIFFERENT FROM WHEN ANGEL WENT TO L.A.?
IT'S VERY DIFFERENT ON MANY LEVELS!
UNNH!
I HAVE GONE ON WITH MY LIFE!
I HAVE DONE THINGS!
IMPORTANT THINGS!

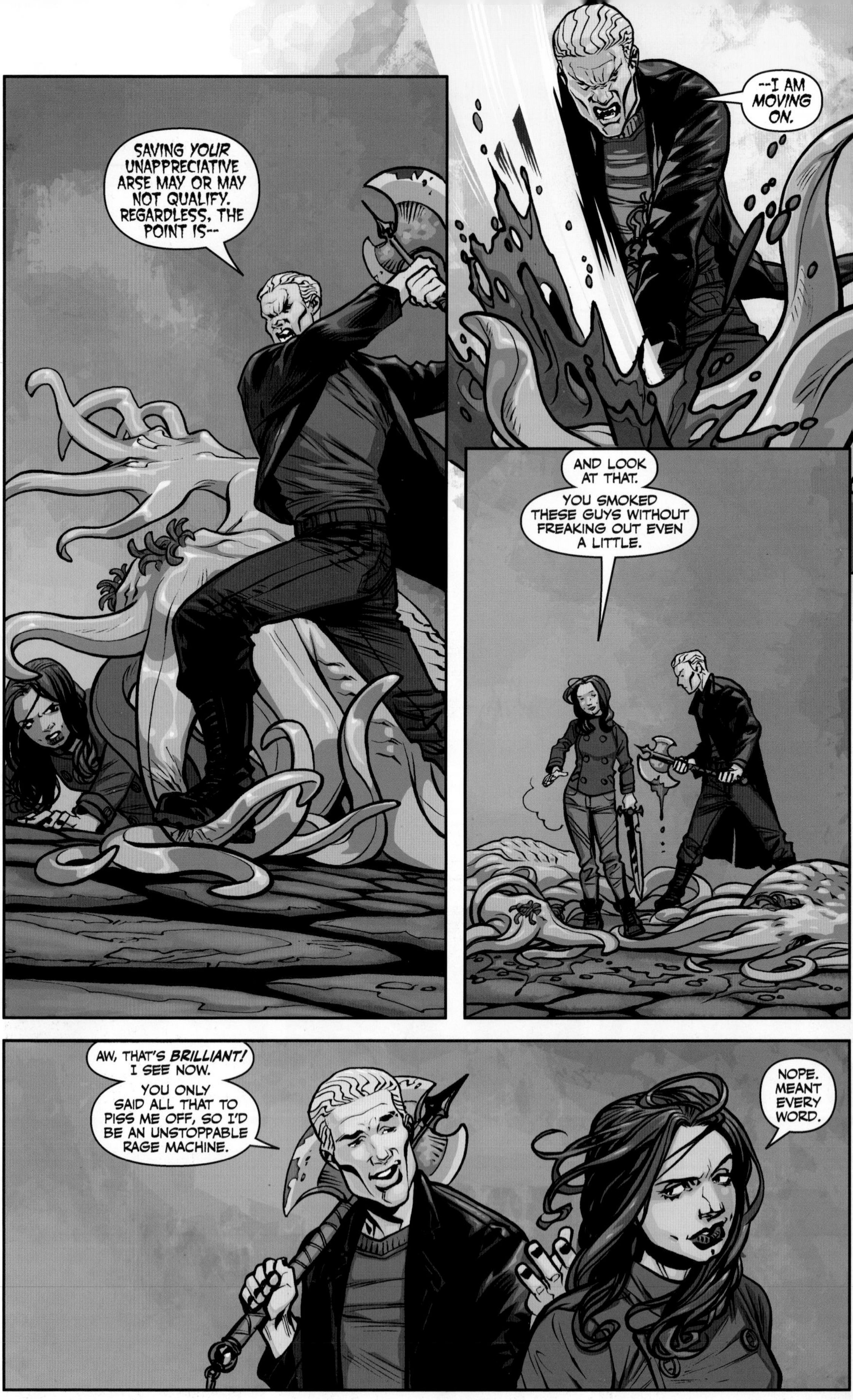
SAVING *YOUR* UNAPPRECIATIVE ARSE MAY OR MAY NOT QUALIFY. REGARDLESS, THE POINT IS--
--I AM *MOVING* ON.
AND LOOK AT THAT.
YOU SMOKED THESE GUYS WITHOUT FREAKING OUT EVEN A LITTLE.
AW, THAT'S ***BRILLIANT!*** I SEE NOW.
YOU ONLY SAID ALL THAT TO PISS ME OFF, SO I'D BE AN UNSTOPPABLE RAGE MACHINE.
NOPE. MEANT EVERY WORD.

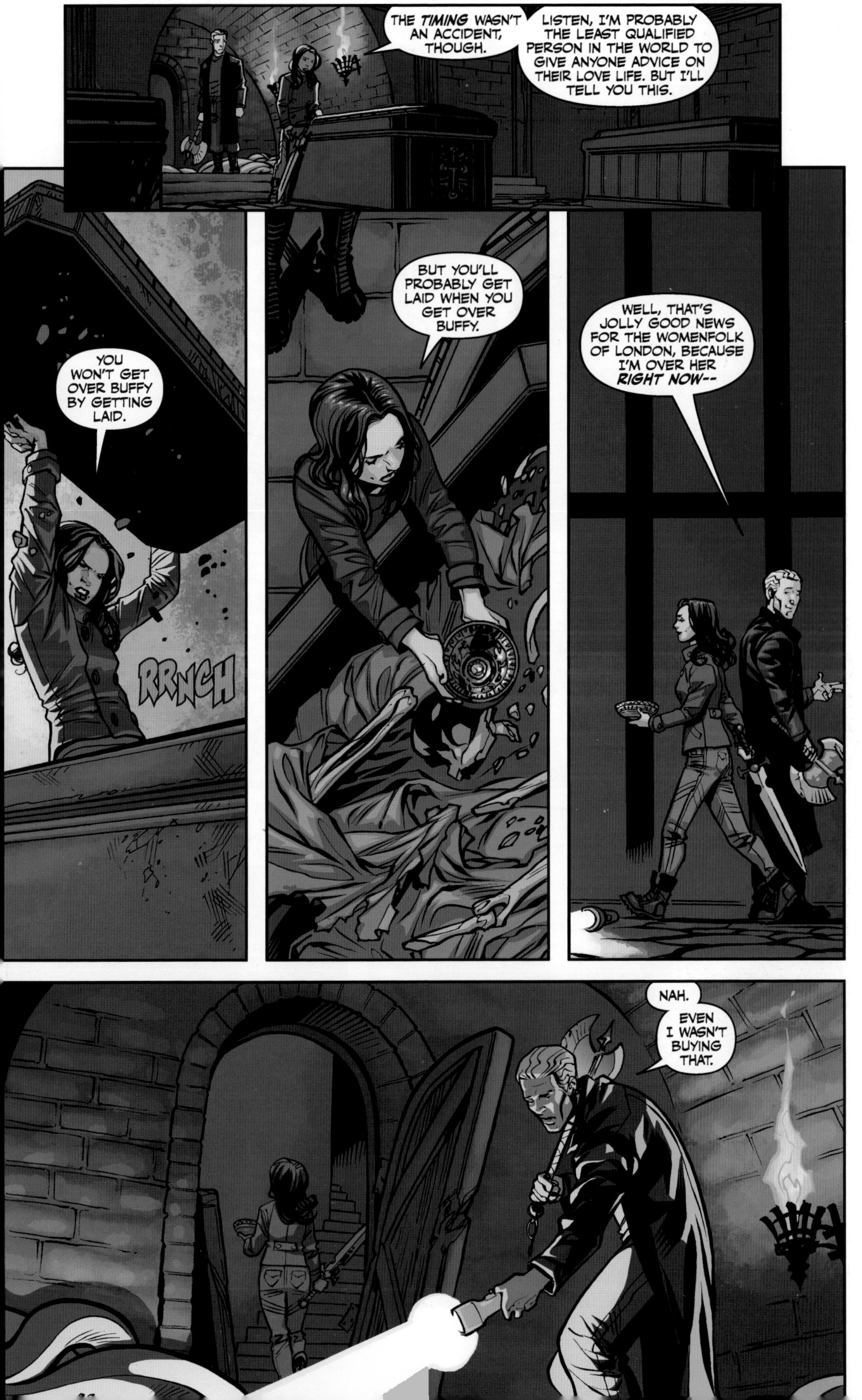
THE TIMING WASN'T AN ACCIDENT, THOUGH.
LISTEN, I'M PROBABLY THE LEAST QUALIFIED PERSON IN THE WORLD TO GIVE ANYONE ADVICE ON THEIR LOVE LIFE. BUT I'LL TELL YOU THIS.
YOU WON'T GET OVER BUFFY BY GETTING LAID.
RRNCH
BUT YOU'LL PROBABLY GET LAID WHEN YOU GET OVER BUFFY.
WELL, THAT'S JOLLY GOOD NEWS FOR THE WOMENFOLK OF LONDON, BECAUSE I'M OVER HER RIGHT NOW--
NAH.
EVEN I WASN'T BUYING THAT.

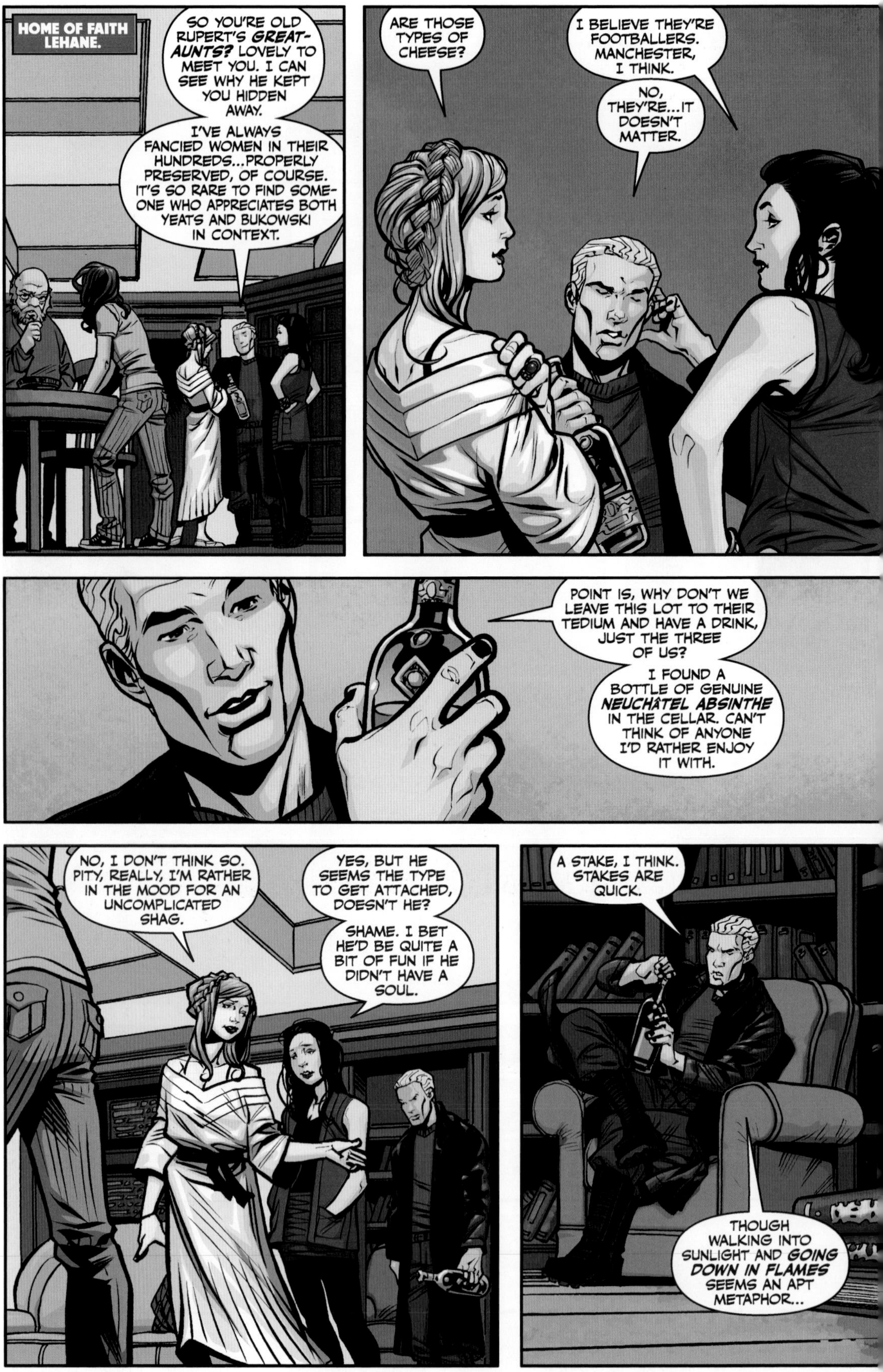
HOME OF FAITH LEHANE.
SO YOU'RE OLD RUPERT'S GREAT-AUNTS? LOVELY TO MEET YOU. I CAN SEE WHY HE KEPT YOU HIDDEN AWAY.
I'VE ALWAYS FANCIED WOMEN IN THEIR HUNDREDS...PROPERLY PRESERVED, OF COURSE. IT'S SO RARE TO FIND SOME-ONE WHO APPRECIATES BOTH YEATS AND BUKOWSKI IN CONTEXT.
ARE THOSE TYPES OF CHEESE?
I BELIEVE THEY'RE FOOTBALLERS. MANCHESTER, I THINK.
NO, THEY'RE...IT DOESN'T MATTER.
POINT IS, WHY DON'T WE LEAVE THIS LOT TO THEIR TEDIUM AND HAVE A DRINK, JUST THE THREE OF US?
I FOUND A BOTTLE OF GENUINE NEUCHÂTEL ABSINTHE IN THE CELLAR. CAN'T THINK OF ANYONE I'D RATHER ENJOY IT WITH.
NO, I DON'T THINK SO. PITY, REALLY, I'M RATHER IN THE MOOD FOR AN UNCOMPLICATED SHAG.
YES, BUT HE SEEMS THE TYPE TO GET ATTACHED, DOESN'T HE?
SHAME. I BET HE'D BE QUITE A BIT OF FUN IF HE DIDN'T HAVE A SOUL.
A STAKE, I THINK. STAKES ARE QUICK.
THOUGH WALKING INTO SUNLIGHT AND GOING DOWN IN FLAMES SEEMS AN APT METAPHOR...

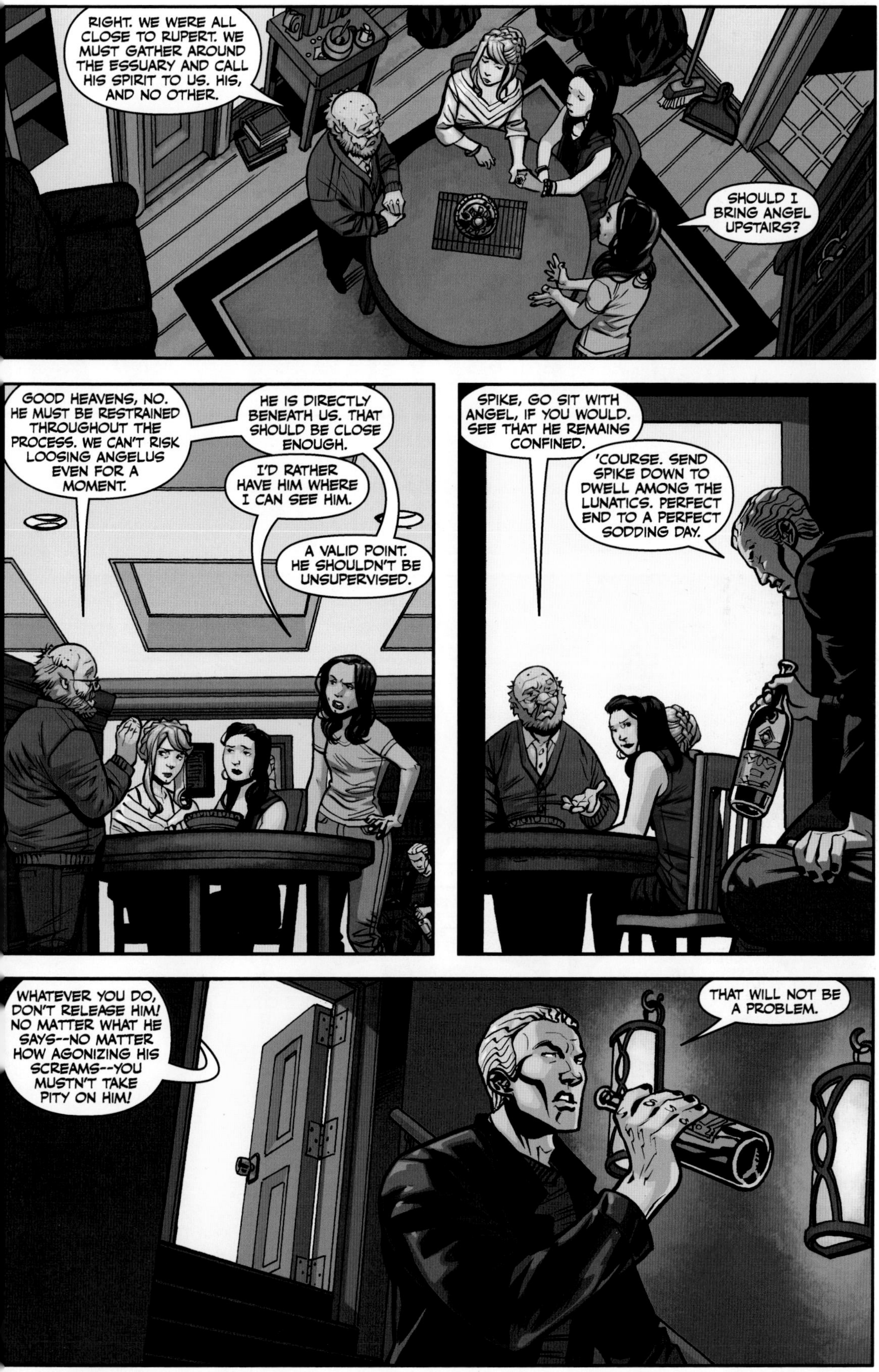
RIGHT. WE WERE ALL CLOSE TO RUPERT. WE MUST GATHER AROUND THE ESSUARY AND CALL HIS SPIRIT TO US. HIS, AND NO OTHER.
SHOULD I BRING ANGEL UPSTAIRS?
GOOD HEAVENS, NO. HE MUST BE RESTRAINED THROUGHOUT THE PROCESS. WE CAN'T RISK LOOSING ANGELUS EVEN FOR A MOMENT.
HE IS DIRECTLY BENEATH US. THAT SHOULD BE CLOSE ENOUGH.
I'D RATHER HAVE HIM WHERE I CAN SEE HIM.
A VALID POINT. HE SHOULDN'T BE UNSUPERVISED.
SPIKE, GO SIT WITH ANGEL, IF YOU WOULD. SEE THAT HE REMAINS CONFINED.
'COURSE. SEND SPIKE DOWN TO DWELL AMONG THE LUNATICS. PERFECT END TO A PERFECT SODDING DAY.
WHATEVER YOU DO, DON'T RELEASE HIM! NO MATTER WHAT HE SAYS--NO MATTER HOW AGONIZING HIS SCREAMS--YOU MUSTN'T TAKE PITY ON HIM!
THAT WILL NOT BE A PROBLEM.

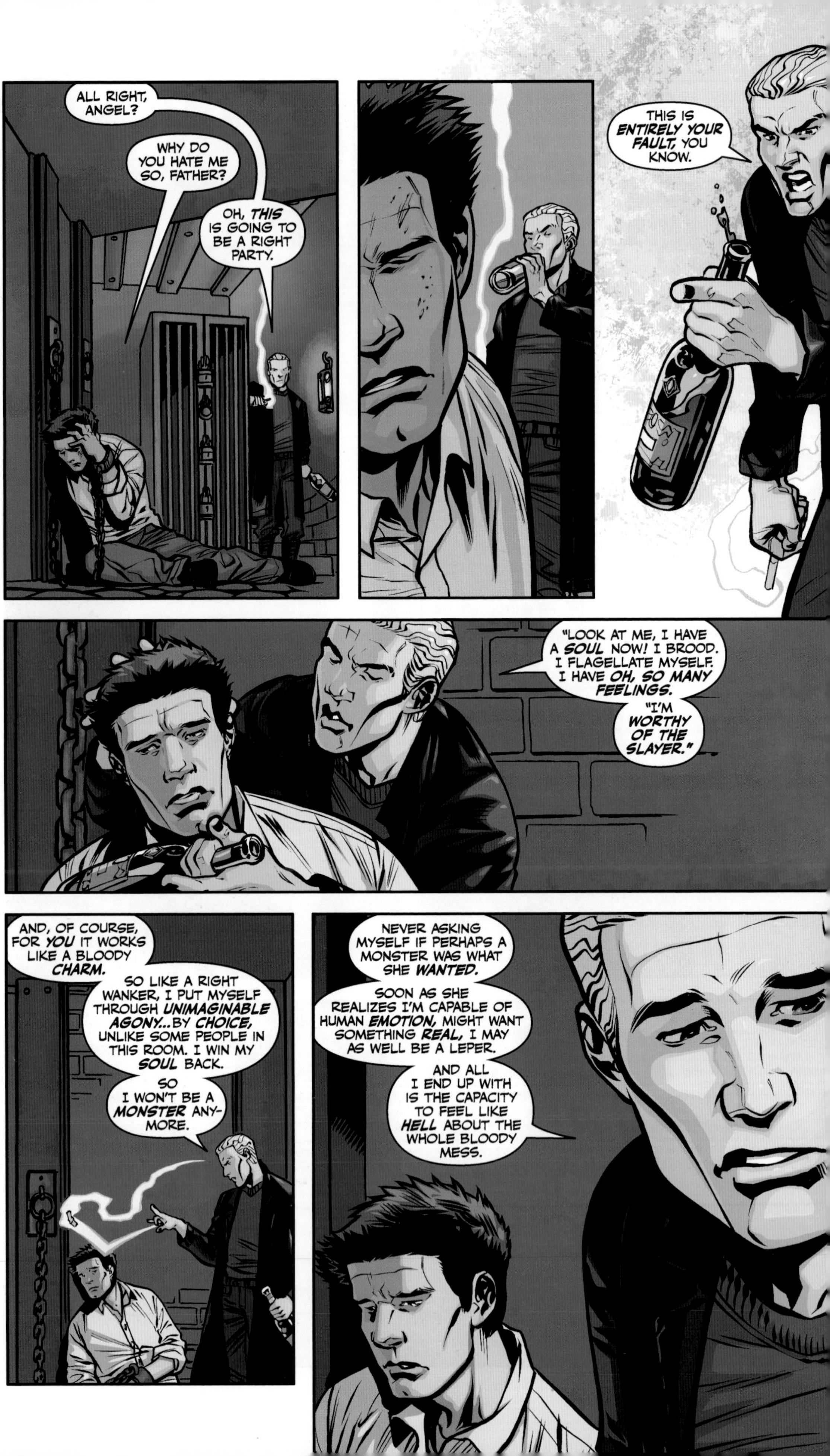
ALL RIGHT, ANGEL?
WHY DO YOU HATE ME SO, FATHER?
OH, THIS IS GOING TO BE A RIGHT PARTY.
THIS IS ENTIRELY YOUR FAULT, YOU KNOW.
"LOOK AT ME, I HAVE A SOUL NOW! I BROOD. I FLAGELLATE MYSELF. I HAVE OH, SO MANY FEELINGS.
"I'M WORTHY OF THE SLAYER."
AND, OF COURSE, FOR YOU IT WORKS LIKE A BLOODY CHARM.
SO LIKE A RIGHT WANKER, I PUT MYSELF THROUGH UNIMAGINABLE AGONY...BY CHOICE, UNLIKE SOME PEOPLE IN THIS ROOM. I WIN MY SOUL BACK.
SO I WON'T BE A MONSTER ANY-MORE.
NEVER ASKING MYSELF IF PERHAPS A MONSTER WAS WHAT SHE WANTED.
SOON AS SHE REALIZES I'M CAPABLE OF HUMAN EMOTION, MIGHT WANT SOMETHING REAL, I MAY AS WELL BE A LEPER.
AND ALL I END UP WITH IS THE CAPACITY TO FEEL LIKE HELL ABOUT THE WHOLE BLOODY MESS.

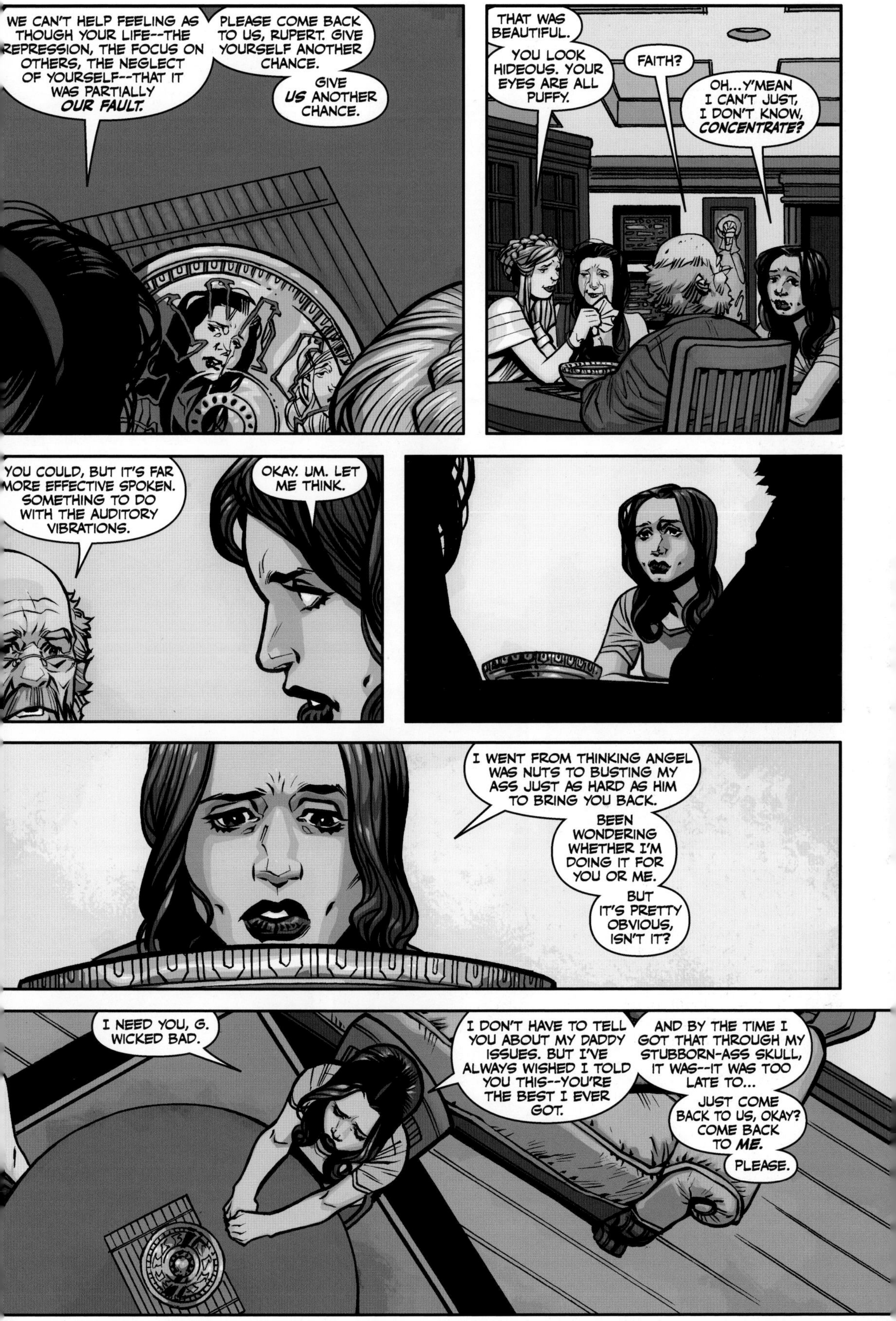
WE CAN'T HELP FEELING AS THOUGH YOUR LIFE--THE REPRESSION, THE FOCUS ON OTHERS, THE NEGLECT OF YOURSELF--THAT IT WAS PARTIALLY *OUR FAULT.*
PLEASE COME BACK TO US, RUPERT. GIVE YOURSELF ANOTHER CHANCE.
GIVE *US* ANOTHER CHANCE.
THAT WAS BEAUTIFUL.
YOU LOOK HIDEOUS. YOUR EYES ARE ALL PUFFY.
FAITH?
OH...Y'MEAN I CAN'T JUST, I DON'T KNOW, *CONCENTRATE?*
YOU COULD, BUT IT'S FAR MORE EFFECTIVE SPOKEN. SOMETHING TO DO WITH THE AUDITORY VIBRATIONS.
OKAY. UM. LET ME THINK.
I WENT FROM THINKING ANGEL WAS NUTS TO BUSTING MY ASS JUST AS HARD AS HIM TO BRING YOU BACK.
BEEN WONDERING WHETHER I'M DOING IT FOR YOU OR ME.
BUT IT'S PRETTY OBVIOUS, ISN'T IT?
I NEED YOU, G. WICKED BAD.
I DON'T HAVE TO TELL YOU ABOUT MY DADDY ISSUES. BUT I'VE ALWAYS WISHED I TOLD YOU THIS--YOU'RE THE BEST I EVER GOT.
AND BY THE TIME I GOT THAT THROUGH MY STUBBORN-ASS SKULL, IT WAS--IT WAS TOO LATE TO...
JUST COME BACK TO US, OKAY? COME BACK TO *ME.*
PLEASE.

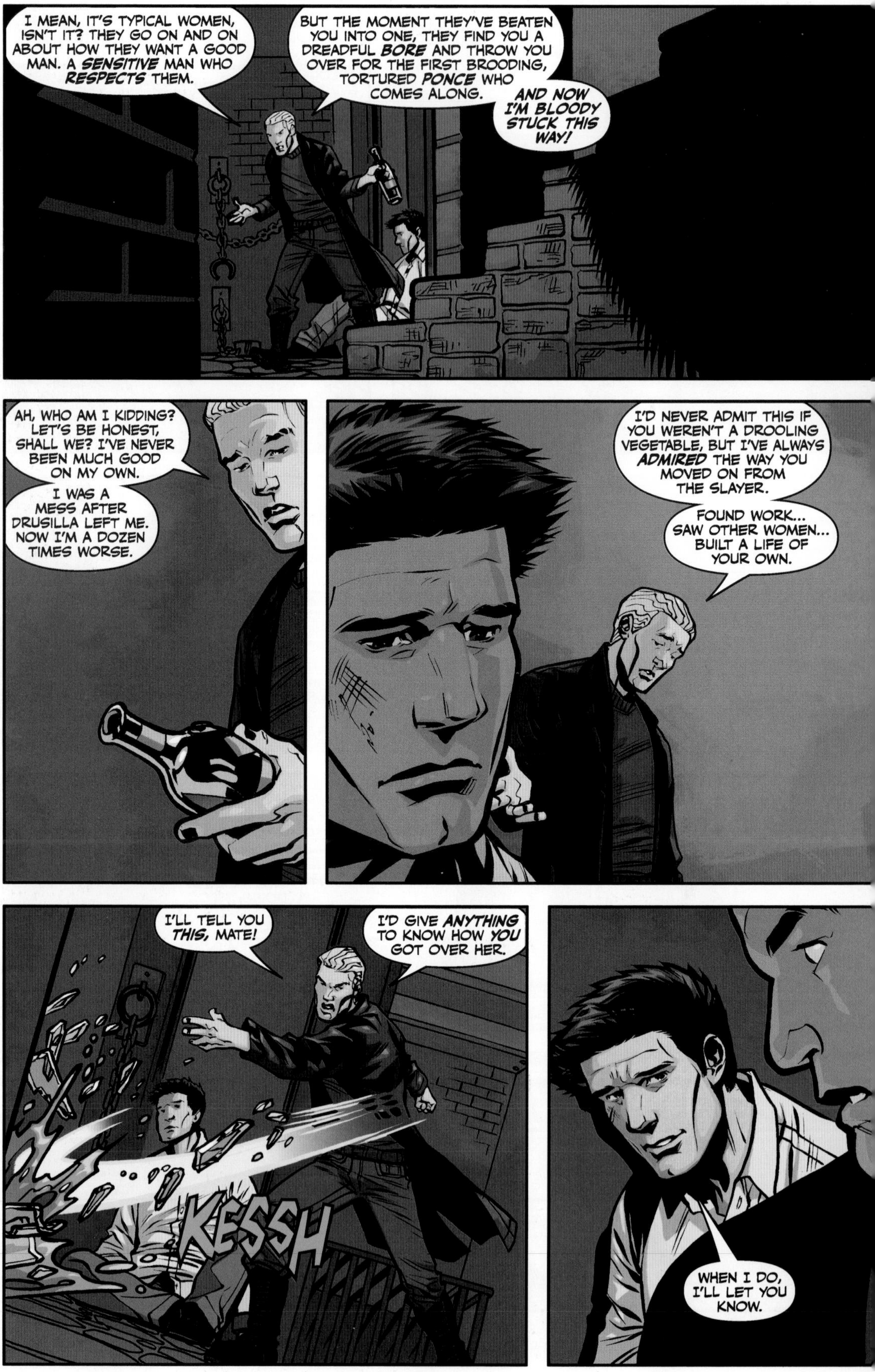
I MEAN, IT'S TYPICAL WOMEN, ISN'T IT? THEY GO ON AND ON ABOUT HOW THEY WANT A GOOD MAN. A *SENSITIVE* MAN WHO *RESPECTS* THEM.
BUT THE MOMENT THEY'VE BEATEN YOU INTO ONE, THEY FIND YOU A DREADFUL *BORE* AND THROW YOU OVER FOR THE FIRST BROODING, TORTURED *PONCE* WHO COMES ALONG.
AND NOW I'M BLOODY STUCK THIS WAY!
AH, WHO AM I KIDDING? LET'S BE HONEST, SHALL WE? I'VE NEVER BEEN MUCH GOOD ON MY OWN.
I WAS A MESS AFTER DRUSILLA LEFT ME. NOW I'M A DOZEN TIMES WORSE.
I'D NEVER ADMIT THIS IF YOU WEREN'T A DROOLING VEGETABLE, BUT I'VE ALWAYS *ADMIRED* THE WAY YOU MOVED ON FROM THE SLAYER.
FOUND WORK... SAW OTHER WOMEN... BUILT A LIFE OF YOUR OWN.
I'LL TELL YOU *THIS,* MATE!
I'D GIVE *ANYTHING* TO KNOW HOW *YOU* GOT OVER HER.
KESSH
WHEN I DO, I'LL LET YOU KNOW.

YOU-- DOES THIS MEAN--

YEAH. GILES'S SOUL WAS DRAWN OUT.

THEN I--THEN YOU--

THEN MY BRILLIANT PLAN *WORKED*!

PULLED YOU OUT OF THE VOID, DIDN'T I? KEPT YOU HERE WITH ALL THAT BOLLOCKS ABOUT THE SLAYER SO YOU DIDN'T ABSCOND WITH OLD RUPERT AND LEAVE US TO DEAL WITH ANGELUS.

UH-HUH.

NO NEED TO THANK ME. OF COURSE, IT'D BE THE DECENT THING TO DO...BUT I KNOW BETTER THAN TO EXPECT MANNERS FROM AN IRISHMAN.

OH. COULD'VE DONE THAT ANY-TIME, COULD YOU?

SPEND ENOUGH TIME WITH HOUDINI, YOU PICK THINGS UP. HELPS IF YOU DON'T MIND BREAKING YOUR THUMBS.

THANKS FOR KEEPING AN EYE ON ME. I NEVER WOULD'VE FORGIVEN MYSELF IF I HURT THEM.

YES, CAN'T HAVE YOU RIDDLED WITH *GUILT*, CAN WE...

DID YOU JUST *TEXT* ME? WHAT'S THIS, THEN?

ME THANKING YOU. NOT THE KIND OF THING I'D NORMALLY DO, BUT WITH SOME PEOPLE, "NORMAL" DOESN'T APPLY.

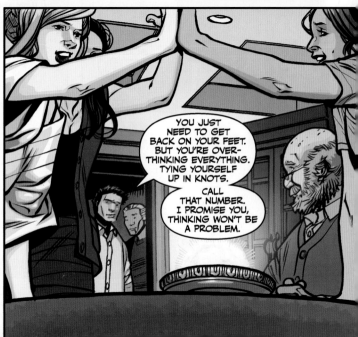

YOU JUST NEED TO GET BACK ON YOUR FEET. BUT YOU'RE OVER-THINKING EVERYTHING. TYING YOURSELF UP IN KNOTS.

CALL THAT NUMBER. I PROMISE YOU, THINKING WON'T BE A PROBLEM.

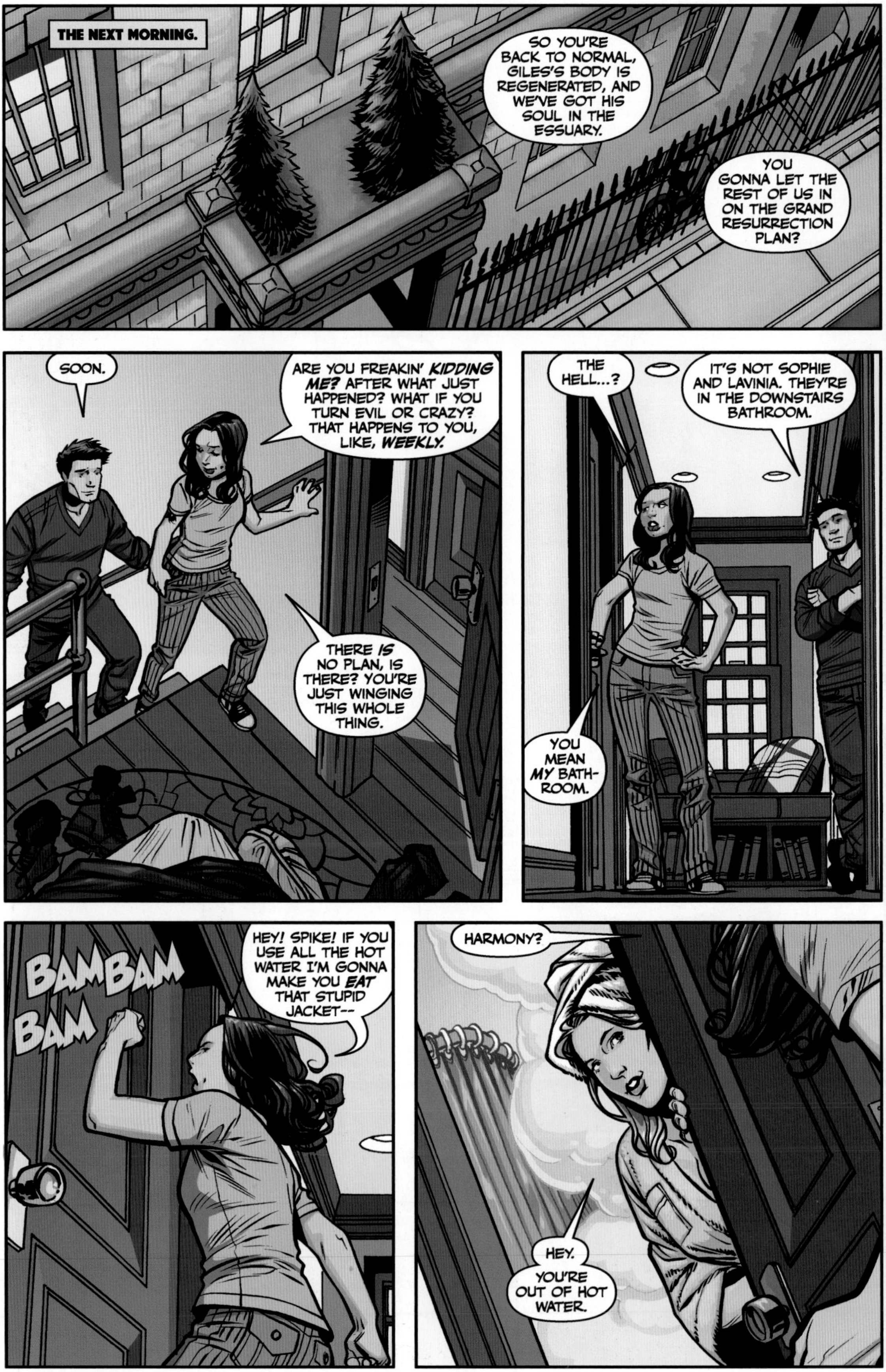
THE NEXT MORNING.
SO YOU'RE BACK TO NORMAL, GILES'S BODY IS REGENERATED, AND WE'VE GOT HIS SOUL IN THE ESSUARY.
YOU GONNA LET THE REST OF US IN ON THE GRAND RESURRECTION PLAN?
SOON.
ARE YOU FREAKIN' KIDDING ME? AFTER WHAT JUST HAPPENED? WHAT IF YOU TURN EVIL OR CRAZY? THAT HAPPENS TO YOU, LIKE, WEEKLY.
THERE IS NO PLAN, IS THERE? YOU'RE JUST WINGING THIS WHOLE THING.
THE HELL...?
IT'S NOT SOPHIE AND LAVINIA. THEY'RE IN THE DOWNSTAIRS BATHROOM.
YOU MEAN MY BATHROOM.
BAMBAM BAM
HEY! SPIKE! IF YOU USE ALL THE HOT WATER I'M GONNA MAKE YOU EAT THAT STUPID JACKET--
HARMONY?
HEY. YOU'RE OUT OF HOT WATER.

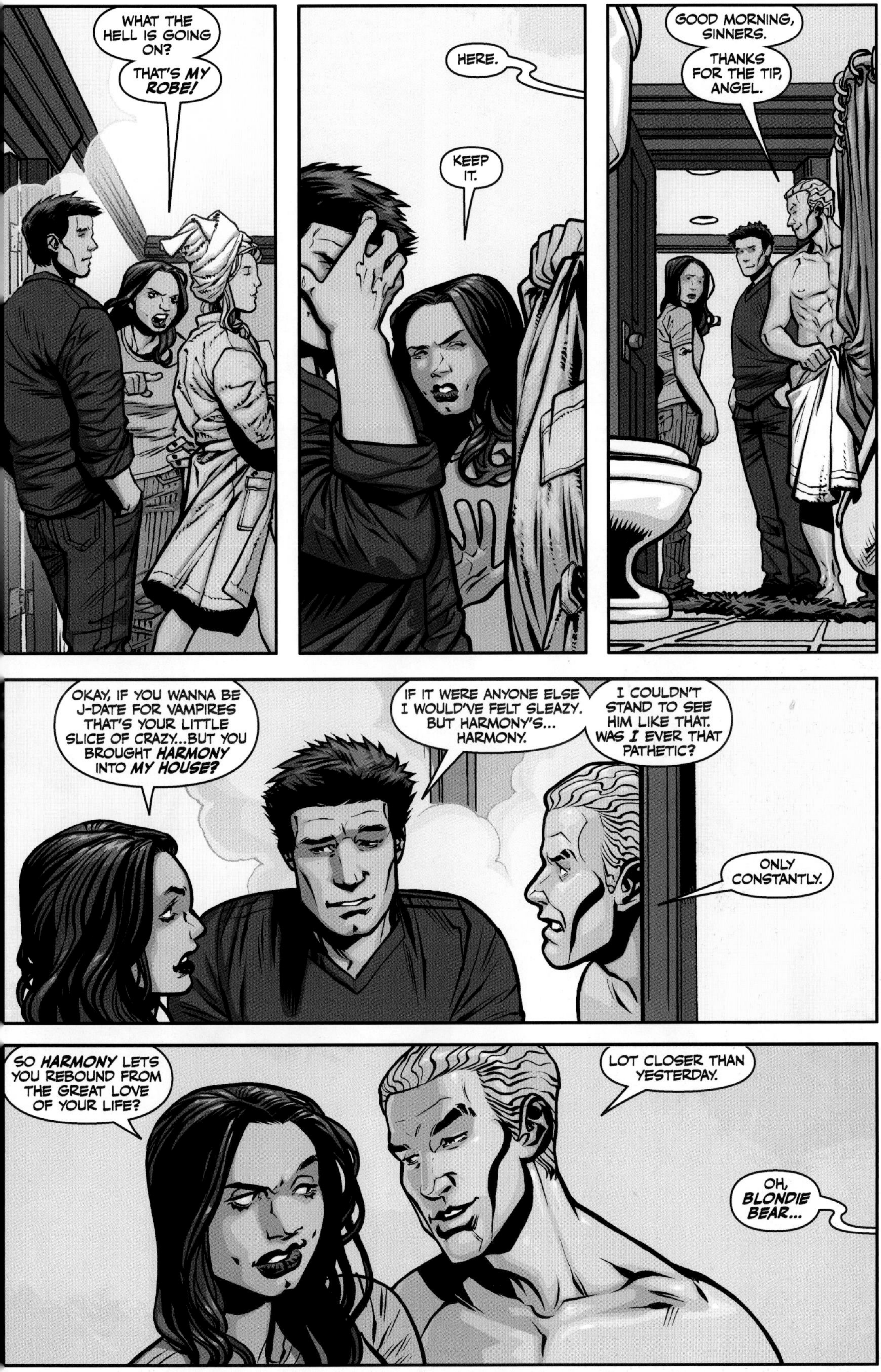
WHAT THE HELL IS GOING ON?
THAT'S MY ROBE!
HERE.
KEEP IT.
GOOD MORNING, SINNERS.
THANKS FOR THE TIP, ANGEL.
OKAY, IF YOU WANNA BE J-DATE FOR VAMPIRES THAT'S YOUR LITTLE SLICE OF CRAZY...BUT YOU BROUGHT HARMONY INTO MY HOUSE?
IF IT WERE ANYONE ELSE I WOULD'VE FELT SLEAZY. BUT HARMONY'S... HARMONY.
I COULDN'T STAND TO SEE HIM LIKE THAT. WAS I EVER THAT PATHETIC?
ONLY CONSTANTLY.
SO HARMONY LETS YOU REBOUND FROM THE GREAT LOVE OF YOUR LIFE?
LOT CLOSER THAN YESTERDAY.
OH, BLONDIE BEAR...

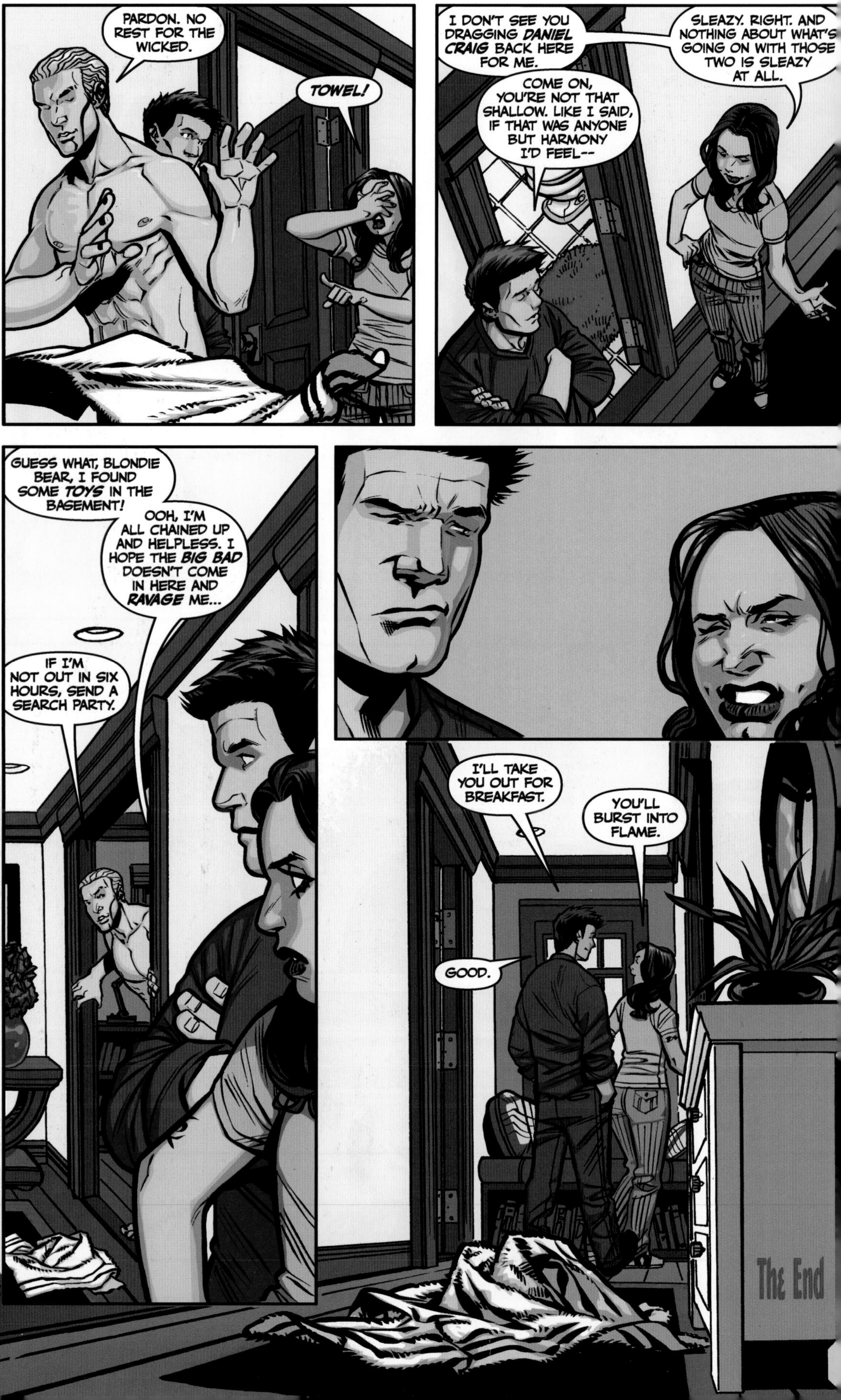
PARDON. NO REST FOR THE WICKED.
TOWEL!
I DON'T SEE YOU DRAGGING DANIEL CRAIG BACK HERE FOR ME.
SLEAZY. RIGHT. AND NOTHING ABOUT WHAT'S GOING ON WITH THOSE TWO IS SLEAZY AT ALL.
COME ON, YOU'RE NOT THAT SHALLOW. LIKE I SAID, IF THAT WAS ANYONE BUT HARMONY I'D FEEL--
GUESS WHAT, BLONDIE BEAR, I FOUND SOME TOYS IN THE BASEMENT!
OOH, I'M ALL CHAINED UP AND HELPLESS. I HOPE THE BIG BAD DOESN'T COME IN HERE AND RAVAGE ME...
IF I'M NOT OUT IN SIX HOURS, SEND A SEARCH PARTY.
I'LL TAKE YOU OUT FOR BREAKFAST.
YOU'LL BURST INTO FLAME.
GOOD.
The End

ANGEL & FAITH COVER GALLERY AND SKETCHBOOK

WITH NOTES FROM

REBEKAH ISAACS

While searching for the Crown of Coils, Angel and Faith encounter these regenerating mutant cave lizards. Since many adventurers had tried and failed before to retrieve the crown, the lizards are covered in bubbled-over scabs from their many regrown limbs and healed wounds. The crown itself was designed on the fly to save time, which usually works out well for smaller props with less "screen time." But for demons and monsters that are seen over many panels and from different angles, neglecting to do a separate design sketch can lead to major headaches.

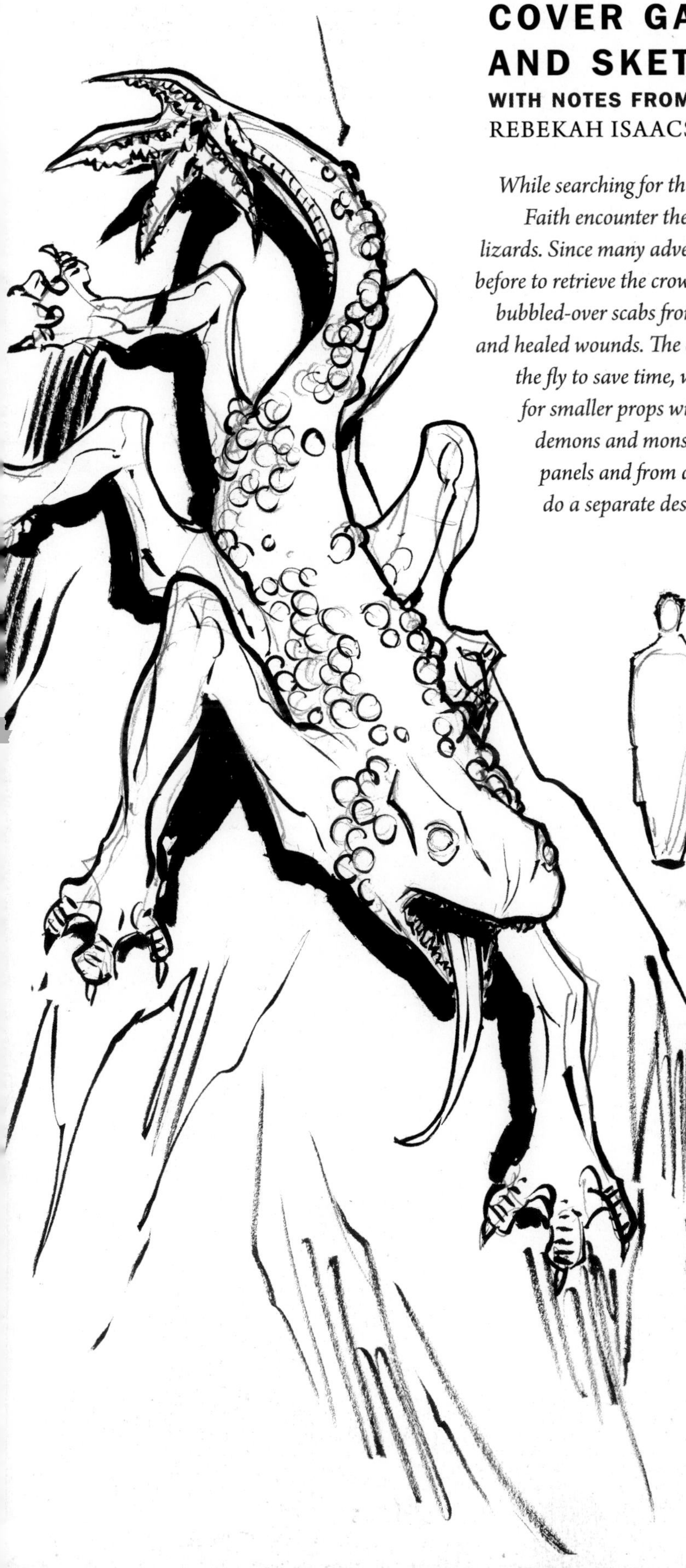

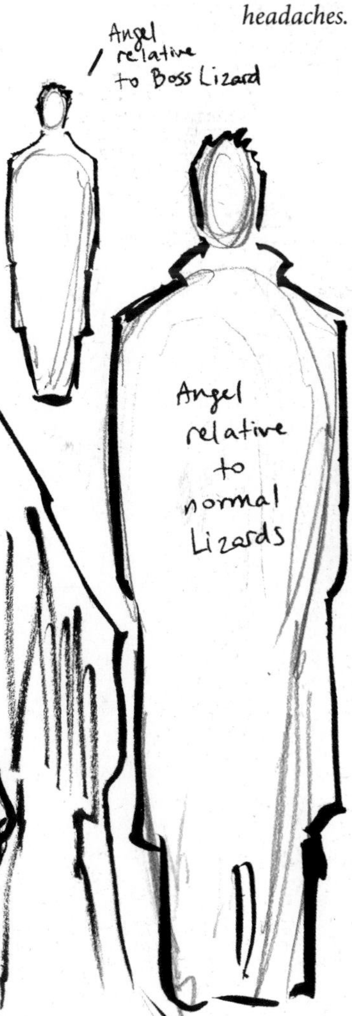
Angel relative to Boss Lizard
Angel relative to normal Lizards

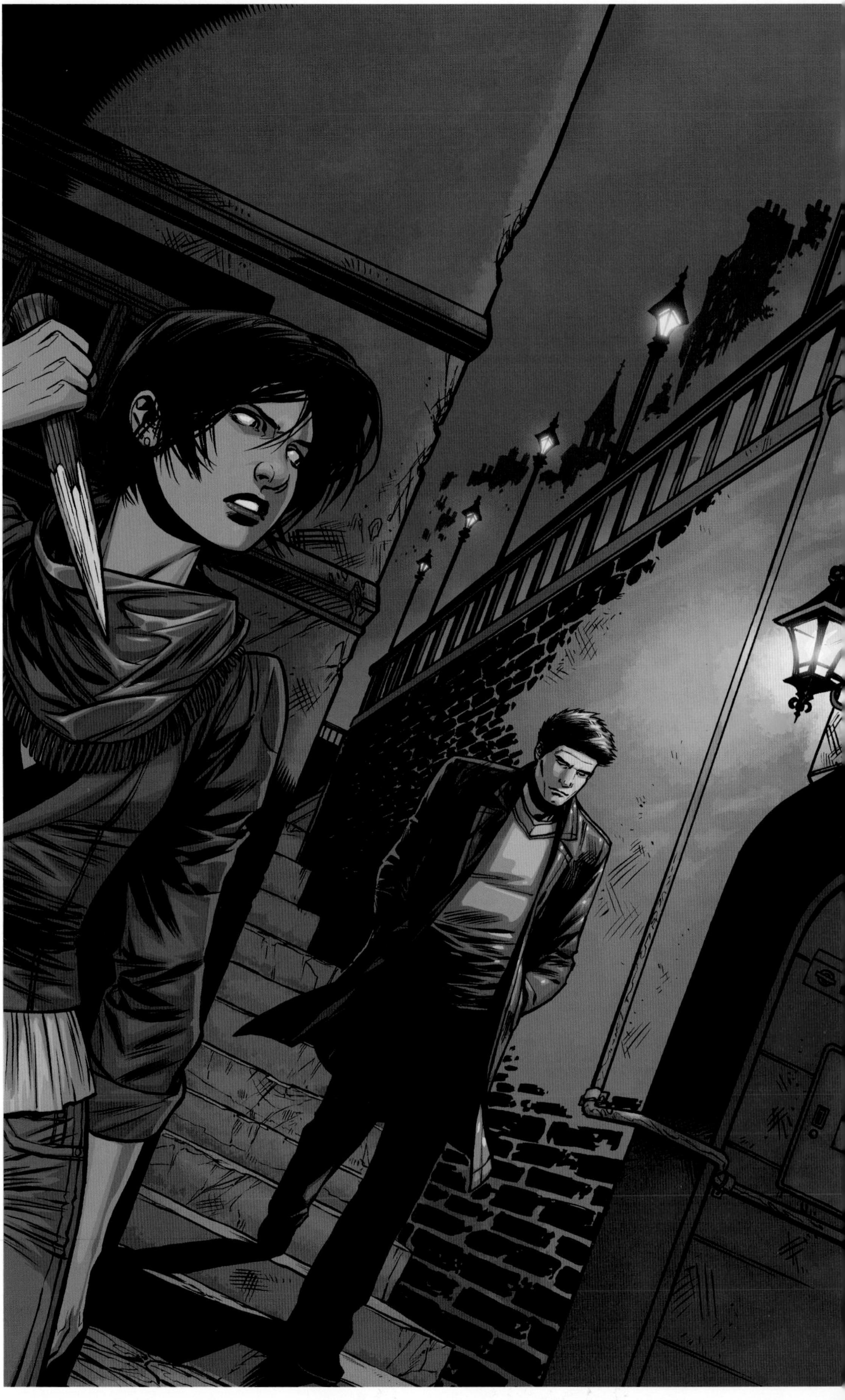

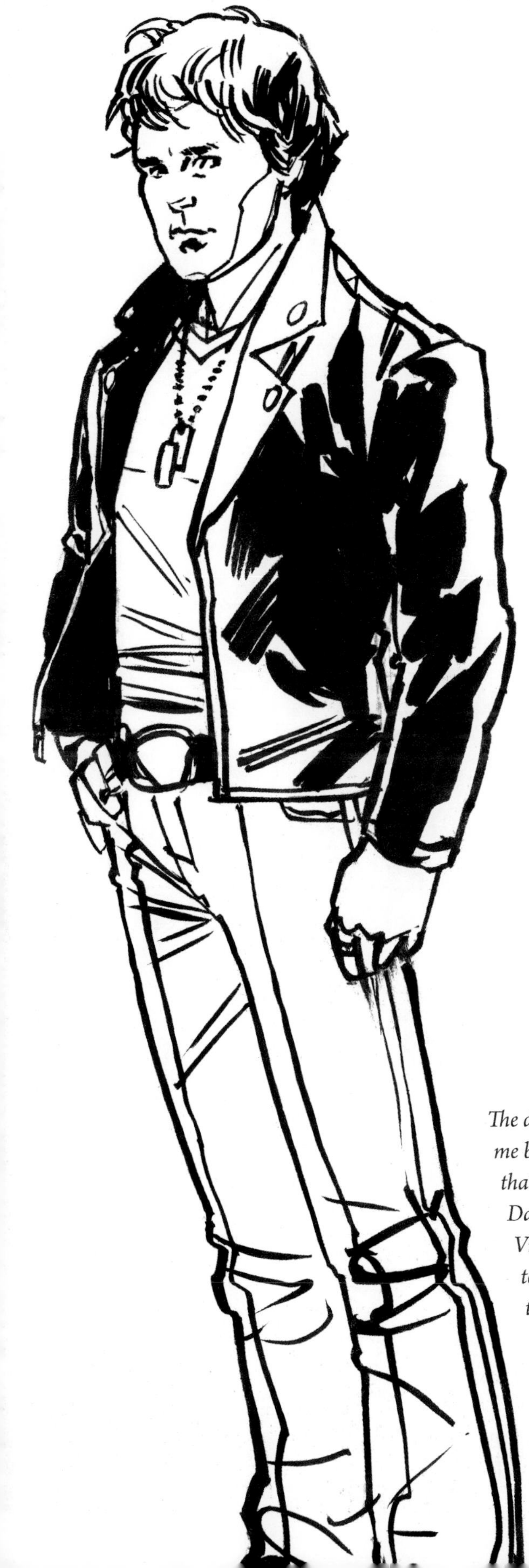

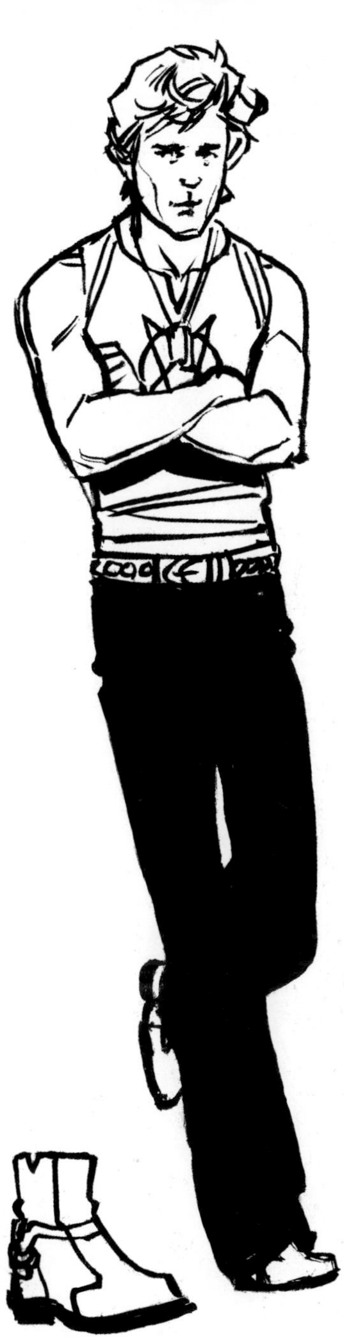

The design for Ripper was basically gift-wrapped for me by the Buffy *TV series. Although I recently read that the photo we see of young rocker Giles in "The Dark Age" was actually a doctored image of Sid Vicious, it's absolutely perfect. From there I just got to imagine various grotty and ripped-up outfits that fit his punk aesthetic, with a dash of psychedelic rock to hint at his interest in black magic.*

Opposite: *Variant cover to* Angel & Faith *#16, with colors by Dan Jackson.*

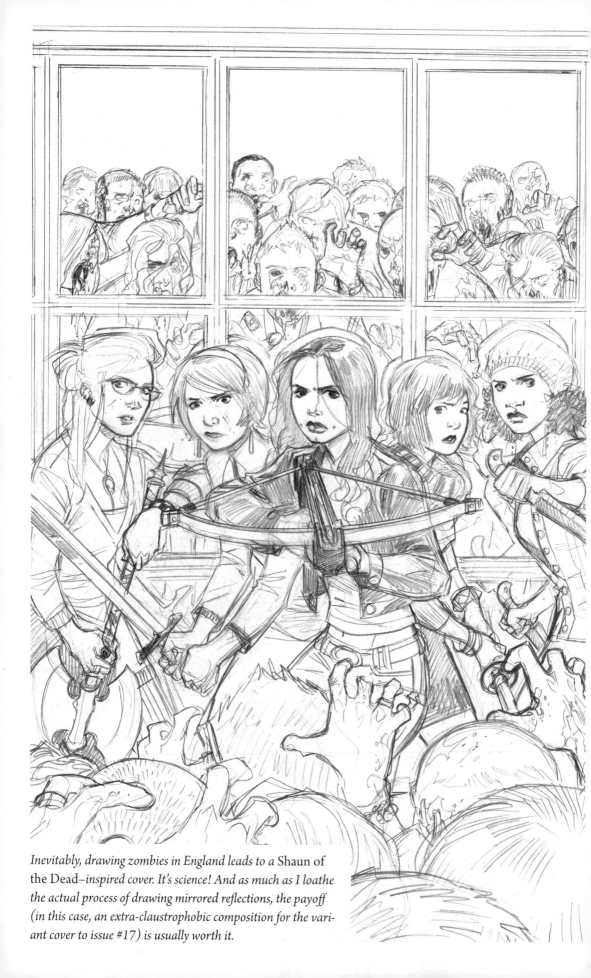

Inevitably, drawing zombies in England leads to a Shaun of the Dead–inspired cover. It's science! And as much as I loathe the actual process of drawing mirrored reflections, the payoff (in this case, an extra-claustrophobic composition for the variant cover to issue #17) is usually worth it.

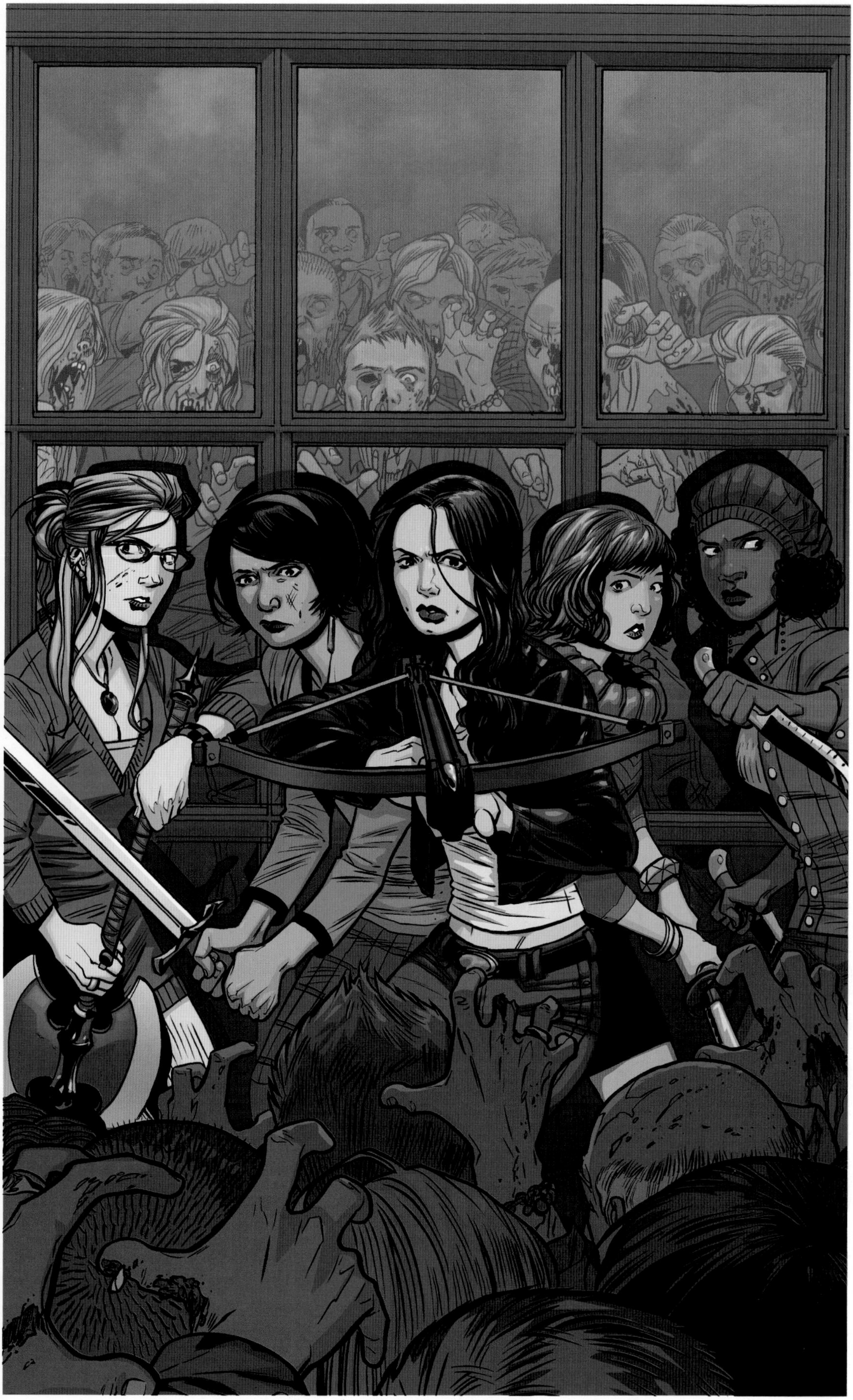

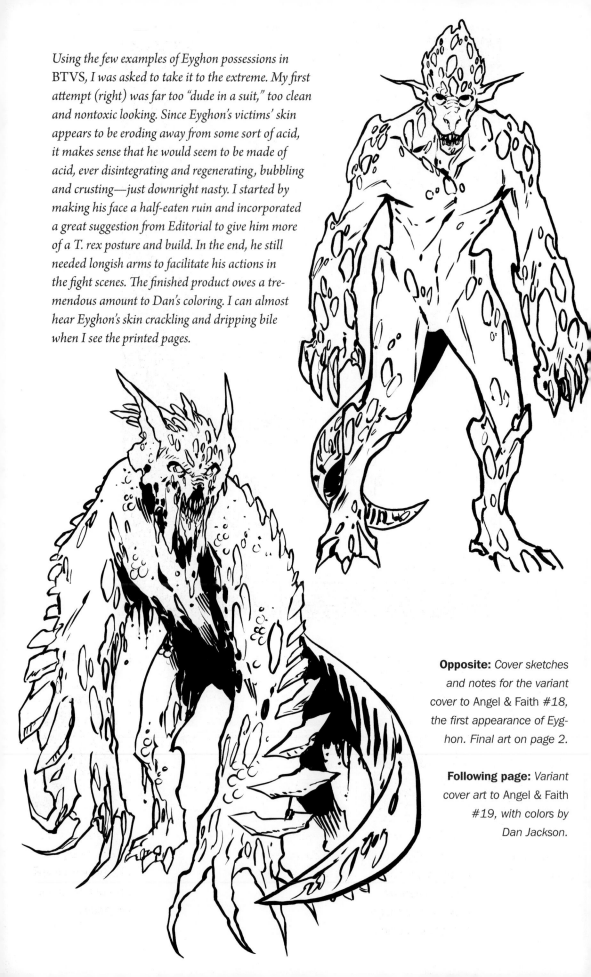

Using the few examples of Eyghon possessions in BTVS, I was asked to take it to the extreme. My first attempt (right) was far too "dude in a suit," too clean and nontoxic looking. Since Eyghon's victims' skin appears to be eroding away from some sort of acid, it makes sense that he would seem to be made of acid, ever disintegrating and regenerating, bubbling and crusting—just downright nasty. I started by making his face a half-eaten ruin and incorporated a great suggestion from Editorial to give him more of a T. rex posture and build. In the end, he still needed longish arms to facilitate his actions in the fight scenes. The finished product owes a tremendous amount to Dan's coloring. I can almost hear Eyghon's skin crackling and dripping bile when I see the printed pages.

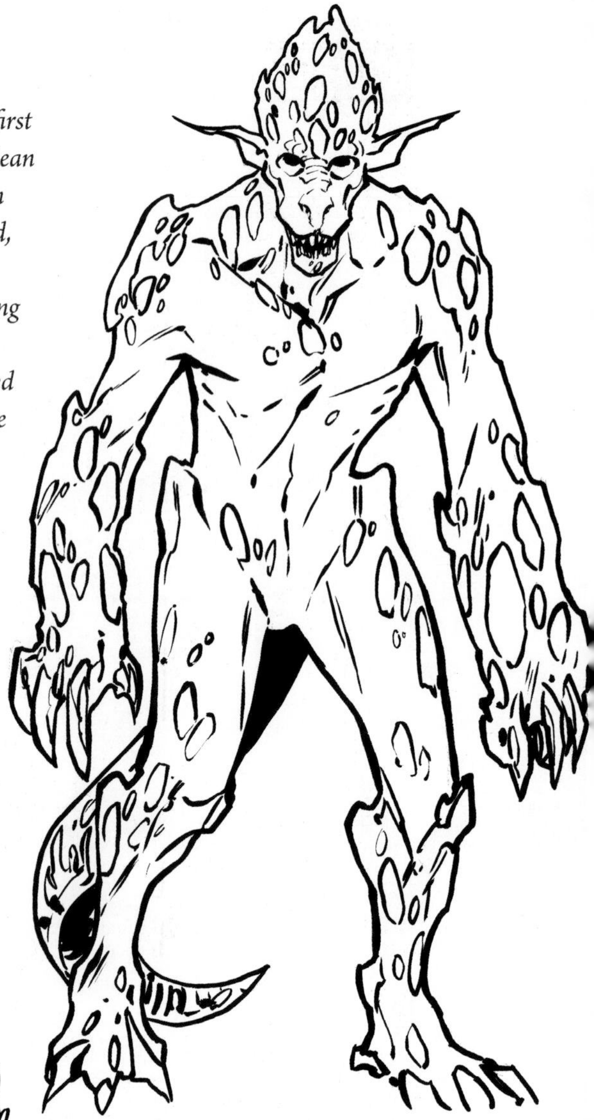

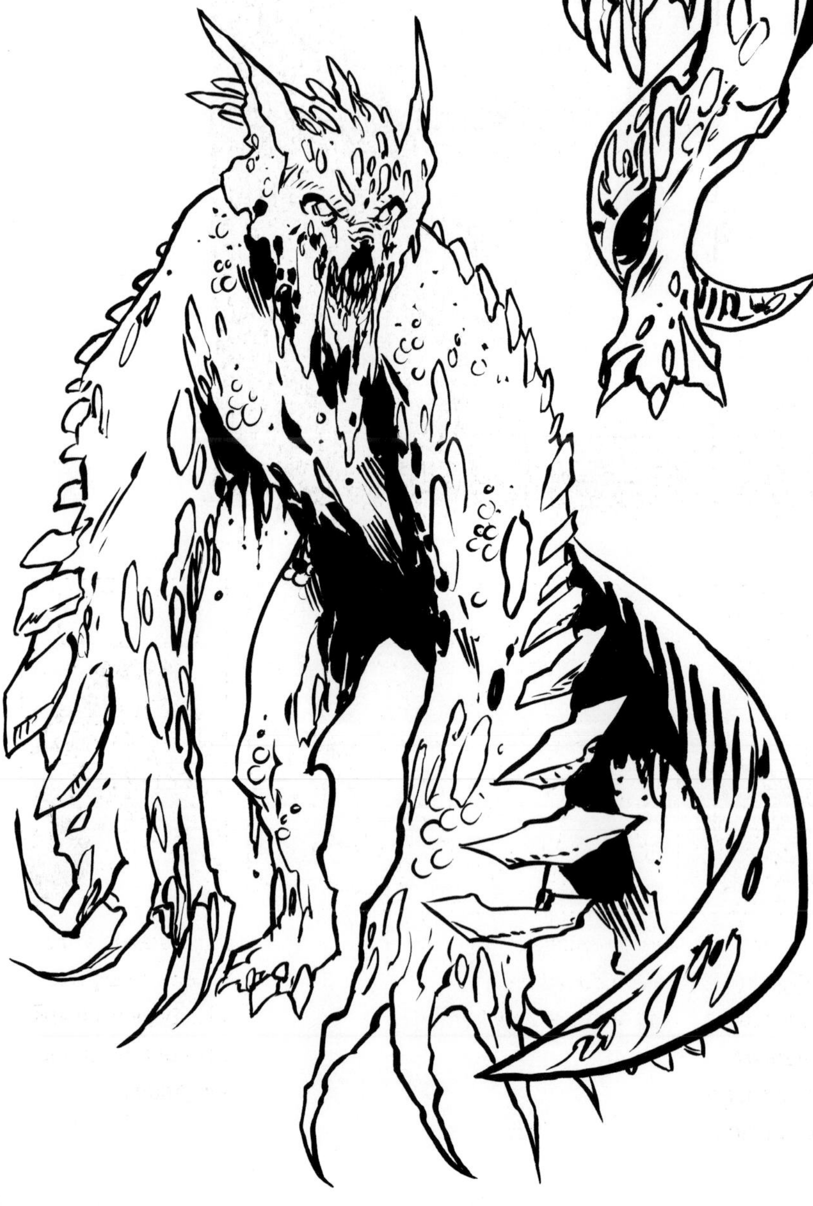

Opposite: *Cover sketches and notes for the variant cover to* Angel & Faith *#18, the first appearance of Eyghon. Final art on page 2.*

Following page: *Variant cover art to* Angel & Faith *#19, with colors by* Dan Jackson.

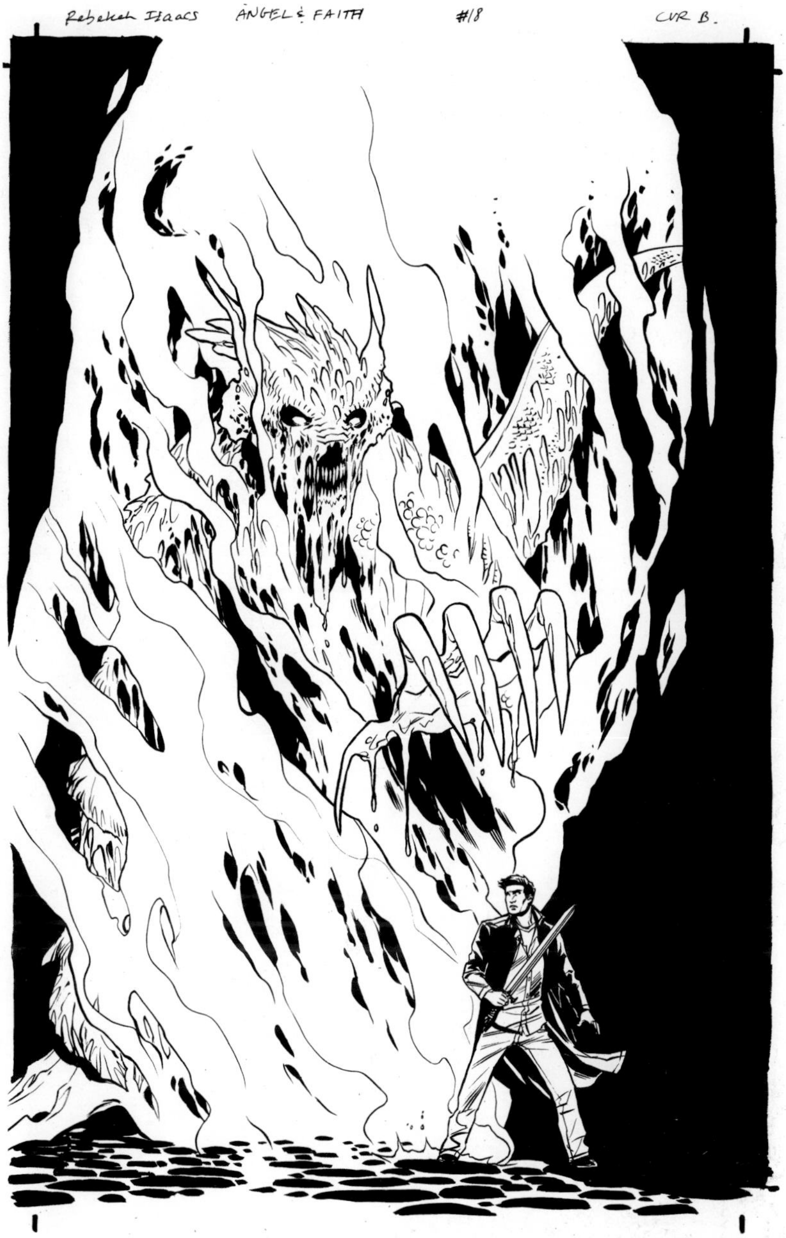
Rebekah Isaacs ANGEL & FAITH #18 CVR B.

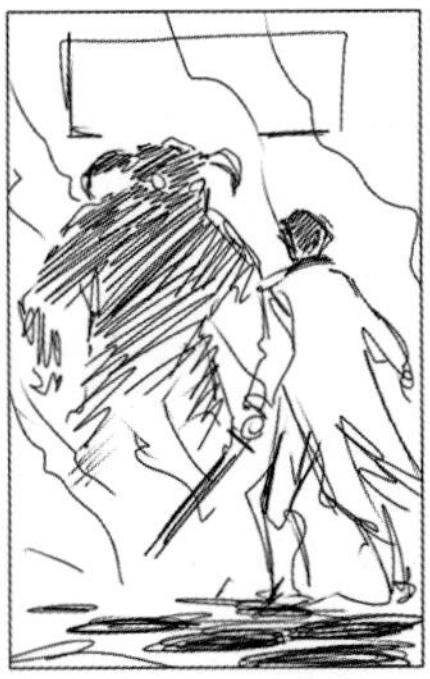

Eyghon emerges from the smoke rising from lava.

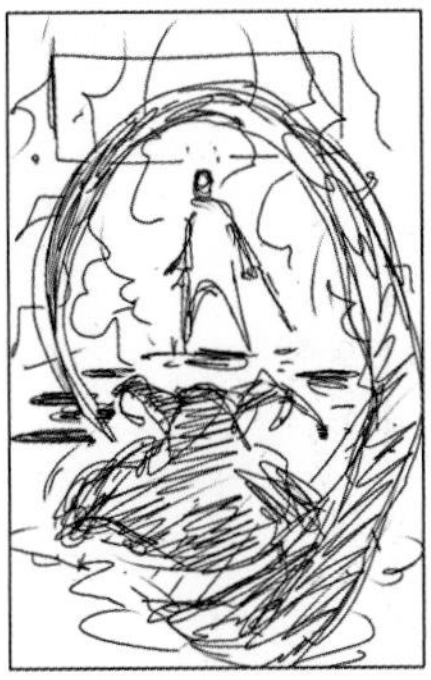

Kind of an Aliens homage: Eyghon rising from the lava itself, tail framing Angel, who is squaring off against him.

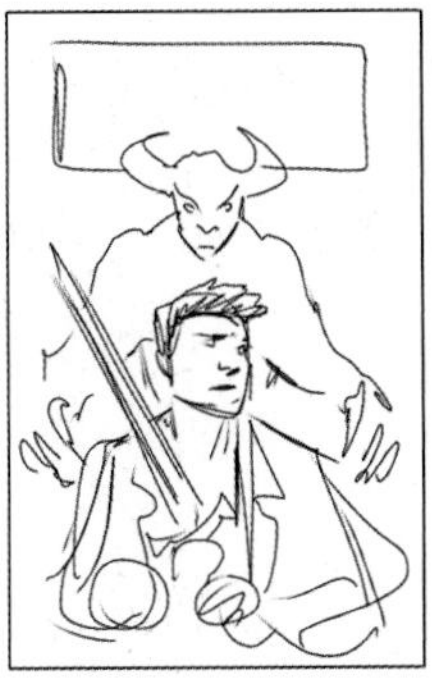

Eyghon emerges from shadows behind unaware Angel.

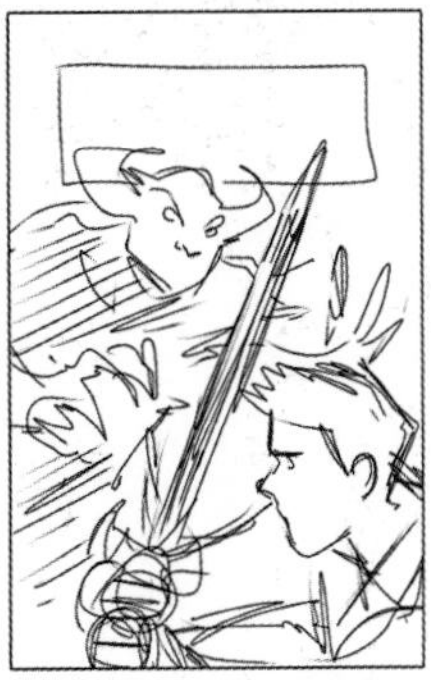

Fight!

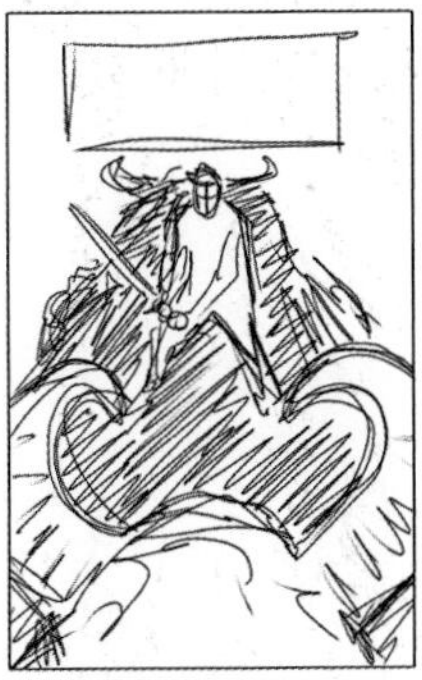

Angel stands in the shadow of Eyghon, with Eyghon's horns/ back of head in the foreground.

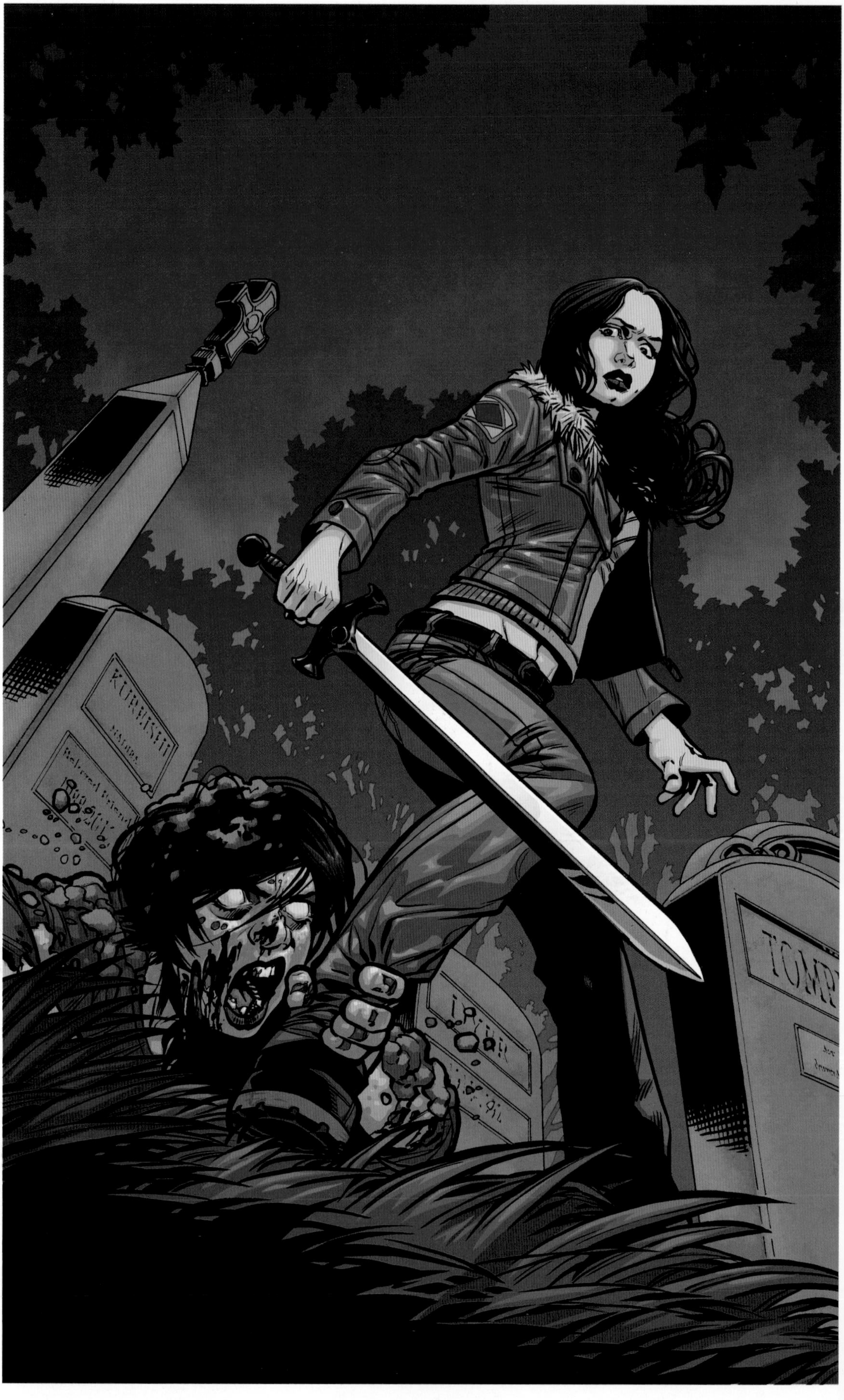

Spike was particularly fun to translate onto the page because of his incredibly delineated features. C'mon, those cheekbones! It's like brushes were invented just to ink them. At left is the initial likeness test that was made for Mr. Marsters's approval.

The Enders were inspired by Mind Flayers from Dungeons & Dragons, at an excellent suggestion from Christos. I took the gist of the upper body, replaced the eyes with more tentacles (missing eyes = instant creepy!), and made it less humanoid and more wriggly.

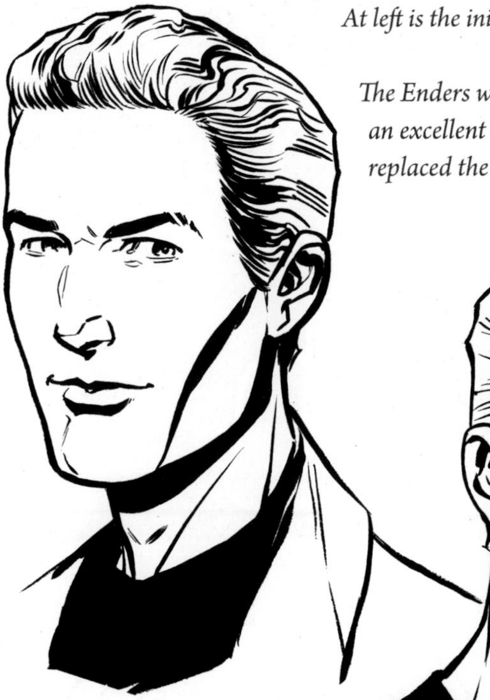

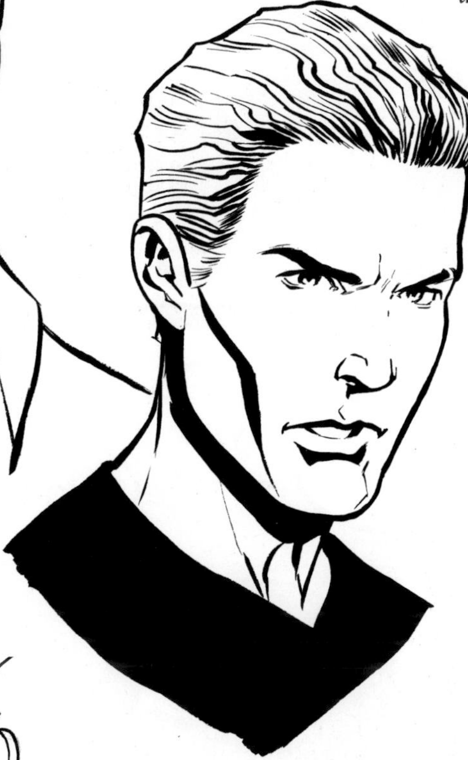

Following page: *Variant cover art to* Angel & Faith *#20, with colors by Dan Jackson.*

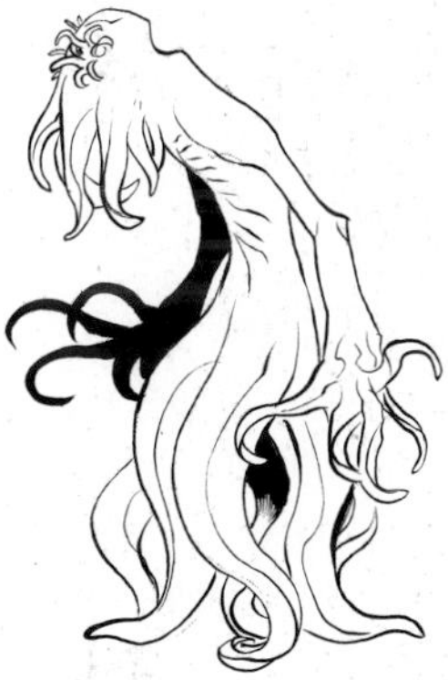

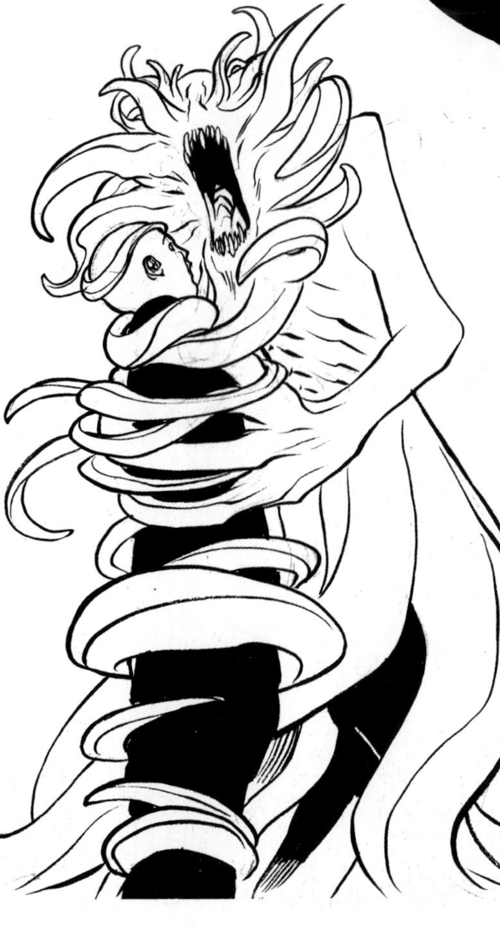

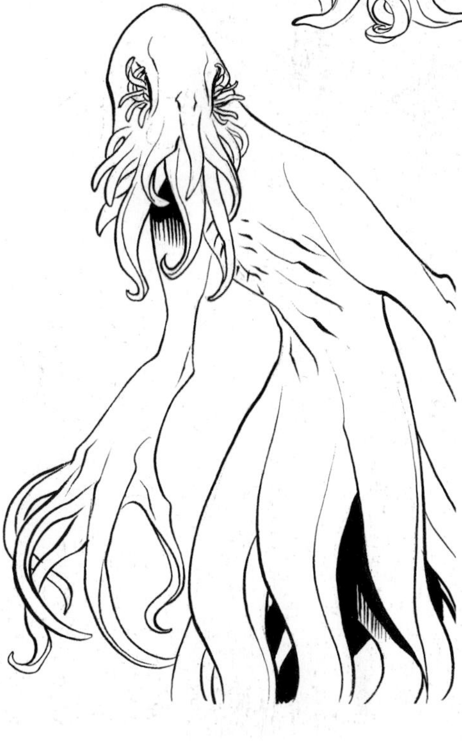

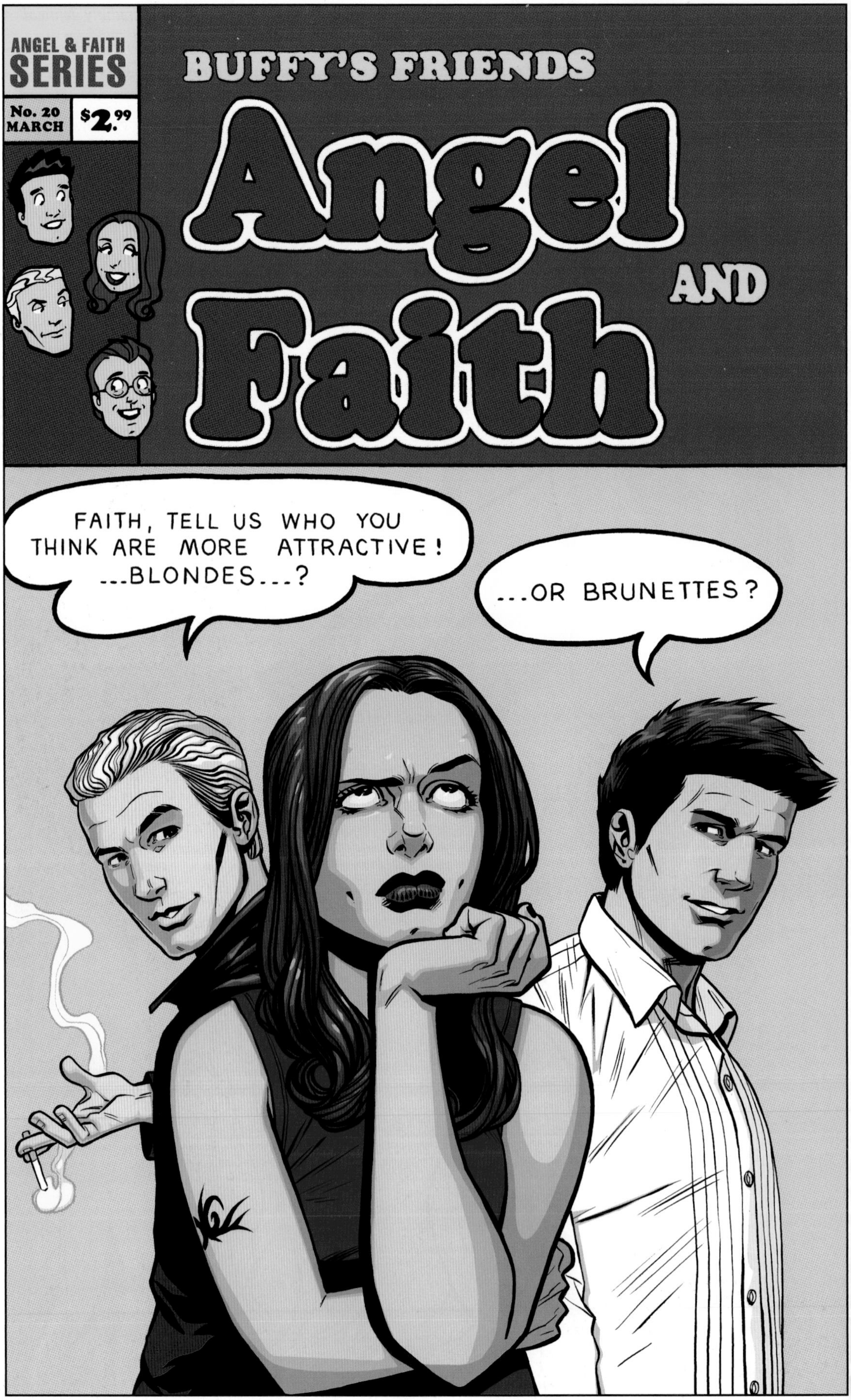
ANGEL & FAITH SERIES
No. 20 MARCH
$2.99
BUFFY'S FRIENDS
Angel AND Faith
FAITH, TELL US WHO YOU THINK ARE MORE ATTRACTIVE! ...BLONDES...?
...OR BRUNETTES?

FROM JOSS WHEDON

BUFFY THE VAMPIRE SLAYER SEASON 8

VOLUME 1: THE LONG WAY HOME
Joss Whedon and Georges Jeanty
ISBN 978-1-59307-822-5 | $15.99

VOLUME 2: NO FUTURE FOR YOU
Brian K. Vaughan, Georges Jeanty, and Joss Whedon
ISBN 978-1-59307-963-5 | $15.99

VOLUME 3: WOLVES AT THE GATE
Drew Goddard, Georges Jeanty, and Joss Whedon
ISBN 978-1-59582-165-2 | $15.99

VOLUME 4: TIME OF YOUR LIFE
Joss Whedon, Jeph Loeb, Georges Jeanty, and others
ISBN 978-1-59582-310-6 | $15.99

VOLUME 5: PREDATORS AND PREY
Joss Whedon, Jane Espenson, Georges Jeanty, Cliff Richards, and others
ISBN 978-1-59582-342-7 | $15.99

VOLUME 6: RETREAT
Joss Whedon, Jane Espenson, Georges Jeanty, Karl Moline, and others
ISBN 978-1-59582-415-8 | $15.99

VOLUME 7: TWILIGHT
Joss Whedon, Brad Meltzer, and Georges Jeanty
ISBN 978-1-59582-558-2 | $16.99

VOLUME 8: LAST GLEAMING
Joss Whedon, Scott Allie, and Georges Jeanty
ISBN 978-1-59582-610-7 | $16.99

BUFFY THE VAMPIRE SLAYER SEASON 8 LIBRARY EDITION

VOLUME 1
ISBN 978-1-59582-888-0 | $29.99

VOLUME 2
ISBN 978-1-59582-935-1 | $29.99

VOLUME 3
ISBN 978-1-59582-978-8 | $29.99

VOLUME 4
ISBN 978-1-61655-127-8 | $29.99

BUFFY THE VAMPIRE SLAYER SEASON 9

VOLUME 1: FREEFALL
Joss Whedon, Andrew Chambliss, Georges Jeanty, and others
ISBN 978-1-59582-922-1 | $17.99

VOLUME 2: ON YOUR OWN
Andrew Chambliss, Scott Allie, Georges Jeanty, and others
ISBN 978-1-59582-990-0 | $17.99

VOLUME 3: GUARDED
Joss Whedon, Jane Espenson, Drew Z. Greenberg, Georges Jeanty, and others
ISBN 978-1-61655-099-8 | $17.99

ANGEL & FAITH

VOLUME 1: LIVE THROUGH THIS
Christos Gage, Rebekah Isaacs, and Phil Noto
ISBN 978-1-59582-887-3 | $17.99

VOLUME 2: DADDY ISSUES
Christos Gage, Rebekah Isaacs, and Chris Samnee
ISBN 978-1-59582-960-3 | $17.99

VOLUME 3: FAMILY REUNION
Christos Gage, Rebekah Isaacs, Lee Garbett, and David Lapham
ISBN 978-1-61655-079-0 | $17.99

SPIKE

VOLUME 1: A DARK PLACE
ISBN 978-1-61655-109-4 | $17.99

WILLOW

VOLUME 1: WONDERLAND
ISBN 978-1-61655-145-2 | $17.99

DARK HORSE BOOKS

AVAILABLE AT YOUR LOCAL COMICS SHOP OR BOOKSTORE!
To find a comics shop in your area, call 1-888-266-4226. For more information or to order direct:
On the web: DarkHorse.com • E-mail: mailorder@darkhorse.com • Phone: 1-800-862-0052 Mon.–Fri. 9 AM to 5 PM Pacific Time

Buffy the Vampire Slayer™ & © 1998, 2013 Twentieth Century Fox Film Corporation. All rights reserved. (BL 5051)

ALSO FROM JOSS WHEDON

BUFFY THE VAMPIRE SLAYER OMNIBUS
VOLUME 1
ISBN 978-1-59307-784-6 | $24.99
VOLUME 2
ISBN 978-1-59307-826-3 | $24.99
VOLUME 3
ISBN 978-1-59307-885-0 | $24.99
VOLUME 4
ISBN 978-1-59307-968-0 | $24.99
VOLUME 5
ISBN 978-1-59582-225-3 | $24.99
VOLUME 6
ISBN 978-1-59582-242-0 | $24.99
VOLUME 7
ISBN 978-1-59582-331-1 | $24.99

BUFFY THE VAMPIRE SLAYER: PANEL TO PANEL
ISBN 978-1-59307-836-2 | $19.99

ANGEL OMNIBUS
Christopher Golden, Eric Powell, and others
ISBN 978-1-59582-706-7 | $24.99

TALES OF THE SLAYERS
Joss Whedon, Amber Benson, Gene Colan, P. Craig Russell, Tim Sale, and others
ISBN 978-1-56971-605-2 | $14.99

TALES OF THE VAMPIRES
Joss Whedon, Brett Matthews, Cameron Stewart, and others
ISBN 978-1-56971-749-3 | $15.99

BUFFY THE VAMPIRE SLAYER: TALES HARDCOVER
ISBN 978-1-59582-644-2 | $29.99

FRAY: FUTURE SLAYER
Joss Whedon and Karl Moline
ISBN 978-1-56971-751-6 | $19.99

SERENITY VOLUME 1: THOSE LEFT BEHIND SECOND EDITION HARDCOVER
Joss Whedon, Brett Matthews, and Will Conrad
ISBN 978-1-59582-914-6 | $17.99

SERENITY VOLUME 2: BETTER DAYS AND OTHER STORIES HARDCOVER
Joss Whedon, Patton Oswalt, Zack Whedon, Patric Reynolds, and others
ISBN 978-1-59582-739-5 | $19.99

SERENITY VOLUME 3: THE SHEPHERD'S TALE HARDCOVER
Joss Whedon, Zack Whedon, and Chris Samnee
ISBN 978-1-59582-561-2 | $14.99

DR. HORRIBLE AND OTHER HORRIBLE STORIES
Joss Whedon, Zack Whedon, Joëlle Jones, and others
ISBN 978-1-59582-577-3 | $9.99

DOLLHOUSE VOLUME 1: EPITAPHS
Andrew Chambliss, Jed Whedon, Maurissa Tancharoen, and Cliff Richards
ISBN 978-1-59582-863-7 | $18.99

AVAILABLE AT YOUR LOCAL COMICS SHOP OR BOOKSTORE!
To find a comics shop in your area, call 1-888-266-4226.
For more information or to order direct visit DarkHorse.com or call 1-800-862-0052 Mon.–Fri. 9 AM to 5 PM Pacific Time.

7

Firefly ™ and Serenity: Firefly Class 03-K64™ & © Twentieth Century Fox Film Corporation. Dr. Horrible © Timescience Bloodclub. Dollhouse ™ & © Twentieth Century Fox Film Corporation. Buffy the Vampire Slayer™ & © Twentieth Century Fox Film Corporation. © Joss Whedon. All rights reserved. (BL 5035)

DARK HORSE BOOKS

DarkHorse.com